true love
Like Fire That Cannot Be Quenched

true love
Like Fire That
Cannot Be Quenched
LACEY NICHOLE GODFREY

ISBN-13: 9798674556954

Table of Contents

1

Heart's Desire

You may be familiar with the phrase, *"Follow your heart."* Whenever making a decision, often the advice one receives is, *"Just follow your heart. Go where your heart leads you. Do whatever your heart tells you to do."* Have you ever followed your heart and wound up somewhere you didn't want to be? Sometimes following our heart can lead us into a big tangled mess.

Rather than tell you the details of a specific journey in my life, I'm going to share the emotions that I felt as I went through it. All of us go through trials in life, and we can't always relate to the exact circumstances of one another, but often we can relate to the mental and emotional trauma of an experience.

Strolling through this particular journey in my life, I found myself in darkness, trapped in a pit of despair. Had I known where my prior decisions were leading me, I could have done something about it along the way. I guess I thought that things would just work themselves out eventually, so I pressed on. After putting years of strong effort and dedication into this journey, I realized I was in over my head. I couldn't just climb out of the pit and walk away because every decision I made not only affected my own life, but it would greatly impact the lives of those around me. I am a wife and a mother. It wasn't worth shaking up their lives in order to be happy. Instead of tearing my home apart and dragging my family down with me, I took the affliction on myself. The sad part is, no one knew I was deeply hurting. No one knew of my shame and disappointment. I looked like success on the outside, but the truth is, I was a wreck!

"Oh, stop feeling sorry for yourself! There are so many people in this world with much worse situations than yours," I would say to myself. Yes, that was true, but it still didn't fix anything. It was just a band-aid I used to cover the wounds. *"You got yourself into this. Now you have to deal with it. It's no one's fault accept yours. Be thankful for what you have and make the best of it,"* I thought. So I did just that.

If my heart was a garden, you could say that the soil of my heart was full of weeds. Weeds can be pulled as they come, but if you don't get the roots, they are going to shoot back up and spread as soon as they are watered. Every time my feelings were hurt, tears of sorrow would nourish the roots of brokenness, causing raw emotions to rise back up. With a raging storm going on in my heart, there was no way I could keep up with the weeds any longer. They were being watered way too often. Weeds had spread thickly and even grew fruit; bitter, poisonous fruit. I did my best to smother the weeds by covering them up with self-encouragement; *"You can do this. Don't be so selfish. Toughen up. You have to hold it together."*

Disguised as an angel of light, the evil one that we know as the *accuser* or *deceiver* continued knocking on the door of my heart. In the midst of my troubles, I didn't realize who I was letting in, but I welcomed him. Thoughts of the "good ol' days" began to creep in. Instead of taking those thoughts captive and throwing them out, I entertained them. *"I wish things were like they used to be. If I could go back and do it all over again, I would change so many things. I would be happier if..."* I continued to daydream day after day after day. I thought to myself, *"If I can appear happy on the outside and be miserable on the inside, I might as well dream."* Right?

I took a bite of that forbidden fruit and began to dream. It's amazing how one little poisonous thought spread and consumed my life. It was a slow fade, but I began to imagine what it would be like if I had chosen a different route. I thought surely there was more to life than what I had, but, after all, I did choose it. I wondered what I would be doing had I done *this* differently and *that* differently. As I wished my life away, I felt I had robbed myself of what God had in mind for me. I missed it. I was preparing myself to settle for a mediocre life. You know, the kind where you just get through each day.

Leading from one thing to another, I had soon escaped reality in my mind and was living in the fantasy of my imagination. What could it hurt? After all, it was just pretend. It was only a nice thought. I knew it probably wasn't right, but it made me happy! I found joy in my heart. The taste was delicious, but what I didn't know was, it was destroying me.

Day after day, pleasing little thoughts would trickle in. Night after night, the wonderful scenes in my dreams would keep me sound asleep. The pictures and thoughts that ran through my head became tattoos on my mind. Even when I didn't want to see them, they were there on repeat, playing over and over on the screen of my mind. The thoughts were like a drug, and I was the addict. When my feelings got hurt and depression started to creep in, the fantasy in my mind helped me cope with the reality of my emotions. Strangely, it gave me a sense of hope. Without the "drug", life was dull and depressing, so I continued to dream about what I didn't have and thought about how nice it would be to actually have it.

At times I just couldn't wait to go to sleep because when I was dreaming it felt real. I was happy, and I wanted to stay there. The thoughts and dreams became more and more profound. They brought joy and excitement, but when I looked around and saw what reality was, I felt extremely... empty.

Finally, I had enough of daydreaming and fantasizing and began considering ways to make it *real*. I wanted so badly to get out of the mess that I had made and start over. If only I could wipe everything out and start fresh! I wanted to quit! I wanted to give up on what I had and start something new. I wasn't sure how much longer I could stand the torture of my crazy emotions. I was weary from darkness and depression. I felt detached to life in every way. I was faking happy to everyone. I wasn't a good wife. I wasn't even a good mother any longer. I felt useless. I felt like a failure, defeated in every way. I was tired of wasting time and being caught up in my imagination. Reality was sucking the joy right out of me leaving me withered, cold, and lifeless. What good was I? I was flat out sick of being miserable and pretending that nothing was wrong, and my greatest enemy was *my own mind!*

I could see a key in arms reach that I could use to unlock the chains I was in and run free! But if I used that key to chase after my dreams and follow my heart and my own selfish desires, I would crush my family. What now? Pretend to be happy for their sake, or break their hearts for my own sake?

"The heart is deceitful above all things, and desperately wicked: who can know it?" (Jeremiah 17:9 KJV) Boy, isn't that the truth! I wasn't so sure I wanted to *"follow my heart"* anymore. Especially after reading that! Who wants to follow anything that could be deceitful and wicked? *"Guard your heart above all else, for it determines the course of your life."* (Proverbs 4:23)

I was blinded with confusion and stuck in the wilderness, locked in chains down in a pit of despair. I was left in darkness, not knowing which way to go. It was either *"stay here"* or *"go"*, and I wasn't quite sure which would be better. For my sake, my heart said, *"GO. RUN!"*, but for the sake of the lives attached to mine, I thought, *"I better stay here...or should I?"*

As I stood there in darkness trying to decipher what was to the left and consider what was to the right, I knew it was too big for me to figure out on my own, and I wasn't quite sure that I trusted myself. I was so worn out. My heart was restless trying to figure out what was right and what was wrong. I had worn a veil over the emotions of my heart for so long trying to disguise what was behind it. Eventually, the brokenness, pain, loneliness, bitterness, and confusion of my shattered heart began to bleed through for all to see. Those ugly things that consumed me and filled my mind day and night were becoming more and more difficult to hide. There was a brutal war taking place within me, leaving me wounded, weak, and completely exhausted. I found myself standing at a crossroads, a point at which a crucial decision must be made that would have far reaching consequences. I knew that if I did not choose a different direction, I would sink in the pit. My problem was *"which direction do I take?"*

"Your own ears will hear him. Right behind you a voice will say, 'This is the way you should go,' whether to the right or to the left." (Isaiah 30:21) *"Okay, Lord. I'm listening."*

"For the desires of the flesh are against the spirit, and the desires of the spirit are against the flesh, for these are opposed to each other, to keep you from doing the things you want to do." (Galatians 5:17 ESV) Yes! That is what was happening to me! I was tired of losing the battle against myself. I could not stay where I was any longer. I didn't even know what to pray for anymore. I just knew there had to be a change. This was my prayer, *"Lord, I know you hear me. I know you understand how I feel. You know what I want but have Your way. God, may Your will be done. Nothing more. Nothing less. In Jesus' name I pray, Amen."* As I fell to my knees in tears of desperation, begging the Lord for help, I was given a glimpse of hope: *"Take delight in the LORD, and he will give you your heart's desires."* (Psalm 37:4) What a delightful promise! He will give me my heart's desires!

Have you ever found your heart in a similar condition? Are you restless? Are you tired of losing the battle? Maybe you are tired of chasing satisfaction, tired of living only a mediocre life. Is life dull or perhaps you are unhappy about a situation and wanting change? It is possible that you may say the desires of your heart are unreachable, and you're settling for second best, or third, or fourth, or something that can't even be ranked. If you are searching for joy, seeking satisfaction, trying to find something to fill the void in your heart, or just looking for that spark to light the fire in your soul, I invite you to come along with me on an adventure that will lead you to the desires of your heart.

2

The Craving

We are all born with a deep craving inside us for something. I believe we all crave the same thing, but we satisfy it in different ways. Every one of us are born with the need to be loved. Babies crave the touch of their mother that fills them with a sense of security. They grow into toddlers, longing for the attention of their momma and daddy. Toddlers grow into young children who want more than anything to be loved and accepted by their parents and others. Children grow into young adults who begin to discover a desire for close friendships with people they can trust. Eventually they experience an attraction to the opposite sex. We live our entire lives driven by this thing called love, and we find it in relationships. Sure, there are other things that bring us happiness, like nature, our homes, music, animals, vehicles, hobbies, jobs, and materialistic gains, but even those things can't *keep* us satisfied if we don't have someone to share them with. Eventually, we all need someone to talk to, someone to connect with.

In the beginning, God created Adam and placed him in a perfect world. He had a stress-free life. No worries. No pain. No bad. The world he lived in was fantastic! He was given authority over *all* that God created. Adam had it made! But, even then, God said *"It is not good that man should be alone; I will make him a helper comparable to him."* (Genesis 2:18 NKJV) Adam had everything in the world to make him happy, but he had no one to share it with! So, *"Out of the ground the Lord God formed every beast of the field and every bird of the air, and brought them to Adam to see what he would call them. And whatever Adam called each living creature, that was its name. So Adam gave names to all cattle, to the birds of the air, and to every beast of the field. But for Adam there was not found a helper comparable to him."* (Genesis 2:19-20 NKJV) God tried bringing the animals to Adam to keep him company, but he still had no one to relate to. *"So the Lord God caused the man to fall into a deep sleep. While the man slept, the Lord God took out one of the man's ribs and closed up the opening. Then the Lord God made a woman from the rib, and he brought her to the man. 'At last!' the man exclaimed. 'This one is bone from my bone, and flesh from my flesh! She will be called "woman," because she was taken from "man."'"* (Genesis 2:21-23)

Can you hear the excitement?! At last! From that Scripture, I hear God's heart expressing, *"It is not my intention that you be disconnected, isolated, or alone."* Something was missing in Adam's "perfect world."

The world isn't perfect anymore, but at the end of the day, the one thing that we all desire, whether we want to admit it or not, is love. We spend our lives searching for authentic relationships. We put our highest hopes into these relationships wanting them to be solid and lasting. Single men and women search to find their perfect love, chasing after someone to fill a desire that only another human being can fill. Married men crave the love of their wives, desiring to have that physical touch and affirmation that says to him, *"You are my man, and I want you."* Married women long for the deep emotional connection with their husbands; a connection that says to the woman, *"I know you, and my eyes are only for you. I want to know you more."* Widows ache for their lost loved ones. Men who have lost their wives may feel empty and incomplete. Love is a part of our lives.

Relationships can also very easily disappoint when one isn't receiving the attention they need. When we disappoint each other, we begin to search for happiness wherever it can be found. Lack of love causes divorce. Families get torn apart. Children rebel when they don't feel loved. Lack of love causes confusion, depression, and anxiety. Emptiness. Loneliness. Fear. Hearts turn cold and hard. When a heart lacks love, it becomes broken and shattered. Emotionally and spiritually speaking, a heart without love is a heart that is dying. Some turn to drugs or alcohol to find a *feeling* that pleases. Some turn to sex to fill that desire of needing to be wanted, or it can solely be sought for the feeling, seeking pleasure. Some turn to money looking for happiness in material things. Some put their heart and soul into their job, for it fills the desire to be important, needed, to be somebody. Some seek fame and fortune. Behind all the many cravings, there is a deep purpose. Sometimes we don't even realize why we do the things we do. We just do it. Maybe because we are simply *following our hearts.* We do whatever makes us feel good, even if it is actually destroying us. Ultimately, there is one thing we all crave. It is part of our innermost being. It is a part of us that we cannot escape from. There is nothing we can do to turn off the ever so deep longing that is hardwired into us. The thing that we all crave is called True Love, a love like fire that cannot be quenched.

On this journey, we will uncover the amazing True Love that we all crave. It is a love that satisfies the soul and fills the hole in our hearts. It is a love that we were born to know. We are created and designed to contain it. True Love is what allows us to thrive. Without it, we are incomplete.

The Scriptures in the Bible are full of treasures to uncover. Sometimes we overlook or miss them because we have to dig beneath the surface to see the whole treasure. *"For the word of God is living and active, sharper than any two-edged sword, piercing to the division of soul and of spirit, of joints and of marrow, and discerning the thoughts and intentions of the heart."* (Hebrews 4:12 ESV) We are going to journey together through the land of the living word to find this so-called "True Love."

Before we move forward, let's be sure we understand a few things. Scripture tells us that God cannot lie. *"God is not a man, that He should lie, nor a son of man, that He should repent. Has He said, and will He not do? Or has He spoken, and will He not make it good?"* (Numbers 23:19 NKJV) *"So God has given both his promise and his oath. These two things are unchangeable because it is impossible for God to lie. Therefore, we who have fled to him for refuge can have great confidence as we hold to the hope that lies before us."* (Hebrews 6:18) *"All scripture is given by inspiration of God, and is profitable for doctrine, for reproof, for correction, for instruction in righteousness."* (2 Timothy 3:17 KJV)

God is completely true, and all Scripture is given by inspiration of God, the One who is completely true. We can trust His word and trust that He is faithful to His promises. There are some wild things that we can read about in the Bible, including multiple stories that seem too good to be true, too crazy to be true, or just flat out impossible! Part of having faith means that if I am going to believe one part of the Bible, I have to believe in the whole thing. Otherwise, there is nothing promising about it.

Speaking of promises, what was that promise that we read earlier? *"Take delight in the Lord and He will give you your heart's desires."* (Psalm 37:4)

When I read, *"He WILL give you your heart's desires,"* I saw some light break through the darkness that I was in. I knew there was some hope because God does not lie! So I cried out to the Lord and said, *"God You know my heart's desire, and I trust that You will give it to me because Your word says so."*

I was holding on to that promise. I wasn't sure how God was going to prove it to me, or when He would do something, but I was determined to believe that He would because of the fact that it is written in His word and because I believe His word is completely true. I held that verse so close to my heart. I was holding on to it as if it were the last shred of hope that I had. If I didn't have that, I had nothing but hopelessness. Defeat. Misery.

Soon, it occurred to me that I was so focused on the second part of that verse that I totally overlooked the first part. It says He will give you the desires of your heart *when* you take delight *in Him*. What does it mean to take delight in something or someone? Here are some other ways to say delight: to admire, to adore, to appreciate, to be sweet on, to care for, to be gratified by, to be keen on, to cherish, to derive pleasure from, to be pleased by, to get a kick out of, to hold dear, to love, to rejoice in, to take satisfaction in, or to take an interest in. Delighting in the Lord is more than just believing in Him and deeper than knowing He is Jesus Christ, the Son of God. Delighting in Him is more than saying a simple prayer and taking a Bible study; more than knowledge and reading words written in a book. According to the definition, to take delight in the Lord is more than following a list of rules and acknowledging that He exists. Don't get me wrong! Those things are good for us, but what God is wanting here is for someone to admire, cherish, and appreciate Him. He wants to be loved and to be enjoyed. He wants us to get a kick out of life! I discovered that He wanted me to take complete interest in Him, love Him, and be pleased by *Him*. I realized if I wanted the desires of my heart, I better start taking interest in God and start appreciating Him.

Do you want the desires of your heart? Well then, let's delight in Him! What are we waiting for? Oh yeah, *how* and *where* do we begin?

There is a multitude of ways to begin this journey. There is not merely one correct answer, but throughout this book, I am going to share with you the path that I took that led me to the desires of my heart by delighting in the Lord.

Soon after I began to pray, asking the Lord to give me the desires of my heart and to teach me how to delight in Him, He drew me to my amazing mentor who walked beside me and suggested that I read Psalm 119, eight verses a day, until I reached the end. Immediately, I could relate to the psalmist that wrote it because his life was up and down just like mine. He didn't have it all figured out, but he was trying. His life was not perfect, and he was seeking satisfaction just like I was. From this point on, we will walk together through the trails of Psalm 119, eight verses at a time, relating our lives to the life of the psalmist and discover together what the living word, the Bible, says to us and find out who God is. Let's get started!

[1] Joyful are people of integrity,
who follow the instructions of the Lord.
[2] Joyful are those who obey his laws
and search for him with all their hearts.
[3] They do not compromise with evil,
and they walk only in his paths.
[4] You have charged us
to keep your commandments carefully.
[5] Oh, that my actions would consistently
reflect your decrees!
[6] Then I will not be ashamed
when I compare my life with your commands.
[7] As I learn your righteous regulations,
I will thank you by living as I should!
[8] I will obey your decrees.
Please don't give up on me!

Psalm 119:1–8

3

Joyful

I am so thankful the writer of this psalm shared his true feelings. *"Please don't give up on me!"* Do you ever feel like you just can't get ahead? I kept going around and around the same mountain, and I was tired of the same old thing.

Joyful?! I would like to be full of joy, wouldn't you? The psalm starts by telling us what it takes to be joyful: *"Joyful are people of integrity."* What does it mean to be a person of integrity? Other ways to say *integrity* are blameless, perfect, undefiled, and complete. Ouch! Well, I can forget that one! I am far from blameless or perfect. How about you?

Remember the Scriptures we read before, that say that God cannot lie, all Scripture is inspired by God, and that His word is unchangeable? Well, then let's go to His word about this matter. How does He see you and me?

"But now God has shown us a way to be made right with him without keeping the requirements of the law, as was promised in the writings of Moses and the prophets long ago. We are made right with God by placing our faith in Jesus Christ. And this is true for ***everyone who believes, no matter who we are.*** *For everyone has sinned; we all fall short of God's glorious standard. Yet God, in his grace,* ***freely makes us right*** *in his sight. He did this through Christ Jesus when he freed us from the penalty for our sins. For God presented Jesus as the sacrifice for sin. People are made right with God when they* ***believe*** *that Jesus sacrificed his life, shedding his blood. This sacrifice shows that God was being fair when he held back and did not punish those who sinned in times past, for he was looking ahead and including them in what he would do in this present time. God did this to*

demonstrate his righteousness, for he himself is fair and just, and he makes sinners right in his sight when they believe in Jesus." (Romans 3:21-26, emphasis added)

Wow! Go back and read that again slowly as many times as you need to right now so that you can really uncover the many treasures lying right there in front of you and receive them as yours.

Anything that contradicts the word of God is a lie. If you believe in Jesus, believe God's word is true, belong to Him by accepting Jesus as your Savior, and you believe that He sacrificed His life by shedding His blood, then you are 100% righteous in God's eyes. His word says so! Go back and read it again if you need to.

Jesus paid for every sin once and for all when He gave His life up on the cross. We just read above that no matter who you are, when you believe that Jesus came to this earth and died on the cross as the *ULTIMATE* sacrifice to pay for *ALL* sins, past, present, and future, then you are made right in the eyes of God. When you place faith in Jesus as your Savior, absolutely nothing can take away that salvation because no matter what you do, God looks on you and sees you as righteous. Is that a tough truth to receive? If you are like me, I sure don't see myself as righteous, nor do I feel like it, but God says that I *am* because I believe in Jesus Christ and what He did for me.

We have an enemy who *hates* for us to discover truths like this. *"Be strong in the Lord and in his mighty power. Put on all of God's armor so that you will be able to stand firm against all strategies of the devil. For we are not fighting against flesh-and-blood enemies, but against evil rulers and authorities of the unseen world, against mighty powers in this dark world, and against evil spirits in the heavenly places."* (Ephesians 6:10-12) Satan will bring up accusations and condemnation about your past. He will bring up things you did long ago or something you did yesterday, and he will hold that over your head trying to keep you from believing in the way that God sees you. Satan does not want you drawing close to God.

Even though God sees you as holy and righteous, when you and I do things that do not line up with the righteousness of God, we put a wedge between us and our relationship with Him.

God's eyesight doesn't change. He always sees us the same because of the sacrifice that Jesus made for us. We are the ones that distance ourselves from Him by choosing to act and think in ways that do not align with the way that He sees us, causing us to feel unworthy and undeserving of the grace that He has shown us. We may turn our face from Him and refuse to believe that we could ever be righteous. This results in a mindset that believes we must actually follow all of the rules in order to be accepted, which snowballs into constant failure and hopelessness. This kind of lifestyle goes on stuck under heaps of shame and disgrace.

On the other end of the spectrum, there are those who abuse the truth that we are righteous in the eyes of God because of Jesus and choose to live their lives however they wish because no matter what, God looks at them as holy. Jesus already paid for all sins, so why not just do whatever I want, and He will forgive me afterwards, right? The problem with that is any person living that way will never be satisfied, will constantly find themselves in trouble, and will miss out on the promises that God provides for them. When we are sinning, we are not delighting in the Lord, therefore our hearts will be aching for something more.

If a man and woman are married, the man sees the woman as his wife. She *is* his wife. Now if she decides to treat him with disrespect by saying degrading things to him because she wants things her way, he will feel hurt by those words, but it does not change the fact that she is his wife. If she begins to lie to him in order to get by with things that he may not like, he will feel dishonored, but it doesn't change the fact that she is his wife. The wife may go and cheat on her husband, and, although that is a very wrong act, it doesn't change the fact that she is his wife. The wife may want all of the benefits that a marriage provides, but if she doesn't honor and respect her husband with gentleness, faithfulness, and honesty, she isn't going to have the relationship with her husband that she desires to have even though she is his wife.

The point is, to those who have placed faith in Jesus, nothing changes the fact that we are righteous in the eyes of God, but the way we choose to act, affects the *benefits* we receive and the closeness of our relationship that we have with God.

Just in case those Scriptures we read in Romans about how God sees us were not enough to have you convinced that you are righteous in the eyes of God, let's take a moment to ponder some more of His word. *"The old system under the law of Moses was only a shadow, a dim preview of the good things to come, not the good things themselves. The sacrifices under that system were repeated again and again, year after year, but they were never able to provide perfect cleansing for those who came to worship. If they could have provided perfect cleansing, the sacrifices would have stopped, for the worshipers would have been purified once for all time, and their feelings of guilt would have disappeared.*

But instead, those sacrifices actually reminded them of their sins year after year. For it is not possible for the blood of bulls and goats to take away sins. That is why, when Christ came into the world, he said to God,

"You did not want animal sacrifices or sin offerings. But you have given me a body to offer. You were not pleased with burnt offerings or other offerings for sin. Then I said, 'Look, I have come to do your will, O God—as is written about me in the Scriptures.'"

First, Christ said, "You did not want animal sacrifices or sin offerings or burnt offerings or other offerings for sin, nor were you pleased with them" (though they are required by the law of Moses). Then he said, "Look, I have come to do your will." He cancels the first covenant in order to put the second into effect. ***For God's will was for us to be made holy by the sacrifice of the body of Jesus Christ, once for all time****.*

Under the old covenant, the priest stands and ministers before the altar day after day, offering the same sacrifices again and again, which can never take away sins. But our High Priest offered himself to God as a ***single*** *sacrifice for sins,* ***good for all time.*** *Then he sat down in the place of honor at God's right hand. There he waits until his enemies are humbled and made a footstool under his feet.* ***For by that one offering he forever made perfect those who are being made holy.***

And the Holy Spirit also testifies that this is so. For he says, "This is the ***new covenant*** *I will make with my people on that day says the Lord: I will put my laws in their hearts, and I will write them on their minds." Then he says, "I will never again remember their sins and lawless deeds."*

And when sins have been forgiven, there is no need to offer any more sacrifices. And so, dear brothers and sisters, we can boldly enter heaven's Most Holy Place because of the blood of Jesus. By his death Jesus opened a new and life-giving way through the curtain into the Most Holy Place. And since we have a great High Priest who rules over God's house, ***let us go right into the presence of God with sincere hearts fully trusting him.*** *For our guilty consciences have been sprinkled with Christ's blood to make us clean, and our bodies have been washed with pure water.*

Let us hold tightly without wavering to the hope we affirm, for ***God can be trusted to keep his promise****. Let us think of ways to motivate one another to acts of love and good works. And let us not neglect our meeting together, as some people do, but encourage one another, especially now that the day of his return is drawing near."* (Hebrews 10:1-25, emphasis added)

Go back and note how many times it explains in those verses the reason for Jesus' sacrifice. God's will is for us to be made holy by the sacrifice of Jesus once and for all time! That was His whole point. It was His desire to allow Jesus to die so that we can be perfect and holy and forgiven forever. To top it all off, He would remember our sin no more! Jesus is the ultimate sacrifice once for all time. If you have accepted Jesus Christ as your Savior and you believe in Him with all your heart, then your sins have been cleansed by *His* blood because of *His* mercy and *His* grace. Why? Because He loves you that much! That right there is one reason to *delight* in the Lord! If that isn't a reason to be joyful, I don't know what is! We can start delighting in Him right now because of this one GREAT truth and promise.

The sixth chapter of Ephesians tells us to put on every piece of God's armor so that we can resist the devil in times of evil and stand firm. One of those pieces of armor that we are to put on is the breastplate of righteousness. Remember that we are completely righteous in God's eyes when we believe in Jesus. It almost feels wrong to even say that we are righteous, but if we don't put on that breastplate of righteousness that he FREELY gives us, Satan can knock us down. Don't go to war without it. As undeserving as we are of His righteousness that is freely given to us, God says it is true. It is not by our good deeds, but by the blood of Jesus Christ that we are made right in the eyes of God. It may be given to us freely, but it was paid for by the blood of Jesus. Don't let Satan tell you otherwise!

Seeing righteousness as a breastplate, a piece of God's Armor, shows me that righteousness is for our protection. Just like parents want their children to make wise choices for their own good, God wants us to make wise decisions for our own good. He doesn't demand for us to do what He says just because He is God so that He can pridefully look at us and say, *"Look at them. They look so good. They are so perfect. My children are flawless because they work so hard to do as I demand."* No. For the same reason parents give guidelines to their children, God gives us guidelines for our protection. We must choose to put on the breastplate of righteousness that God has given us and follow His instructions for our protection. God is not after *perfection*. He is all about *protection*. Apparently, He already sees perfection when He looks at us through His eyes. He deeply desires for His children to be safe.

Now let's look at the next seven verses from the first section of Psalm
119. [2]*Joyful are those who obey his laws and search for him with all their*
hearts. [3]*They do not compromise with evil, and they walk only in his*
paths.[4]*You have charged us to keep your commandments carefully.*[5]*Oh,*
that my actions would consistently reflect your decrees![6]*Then I will not be*
ashamed when I compare my life with your commands.[7]*As I learn your*
righteous regulations, I will thank you by living as I should! [8]*I will obey your*
decrees. Please don't give up on me!

You see, following the instructions of the Lord and obeying God brings us joy because it provides safety for us. It doesn't mean that if we mess up, we lose our righteousness. God has given you righteousness as a breastplate. It belongs to you, and it is always available to you. Sometimes we choose not to wear it, and when we choose not to, we put ourselves in danger, and we lose joy.

God knows we are not perfect in our own strength, but He still chooses to see us as holy. That is why He sent Jesus to take care of sin for us. Now we can say along with the psalmist, *"Please don't give up on me!"* and we can rest assured that He will never give up on us.

Before reading on, spend some time here talking with the Lord and thanking Him for the free gift of righteousness that *He* paid for. Free for us, but it cost Him His life. Hide that truth in your heart. Make it your breastplate and be joyful because you are blessed! *"For everyone has sinned; we all fall short of God's glorious standard. Yet God, in his grace, freely makes us right in his sight."* (Romans 3:23-24a)

Now that is ***True Love!*** Because of it, you can be Joyful.

9 How can a young person stay pure?
By obeying your word.
10 I have tried hard to find you—
don't let me wander from your commands.
11 I have hidden your word in my heart,
that I might not sin against you.
12 I praise you, O Lord;
teach me your decrees.
13 I have recited aloud
all the regulations you have given us.
14 I have rejoiced in your laws
as much as in riches.
15 I will study your commandments
and reflect on your ways.
16 I will delight in your decrees
and not forget your word.

Psalm 119:9–16

4

HOW

The psalmist asks a question and then answers his own question. "*How can a young person stay pure?*" The answer is, "*By obeying God's word.*" Let's review some of Hebrews 10. *"The old system under the law of Moses was only a shadow, a dim preview of the good things to come, not the good things themselves. The sacrifices under that system were repeated again and again, year after year, but they were never able to provide perfect cleansing for those who came to worship... Then he [Jesus] said, "Look, I have come to do your will." He cancels the first covenant in order to put the second into effect."* (Hebrews 10:1,9, emphasis added)

If we want to do what God instructs us to do, we need to know what the second covenant is because if any of us read the Old Testament and try to follow all of the laws, the regulations, the rules, and the demands, we will never succeed. What is the second covenant?

This is what God says about Jesus: *"Thus says God, the Lord, who created the heavens and stretched them out, who spread out the earth and what comes from it, who gives breath to the people on it and spirit to those who walk in it: "I am the Lord; I have called you [Jesus] in righteousness; I will take You by the hand and keep You; I will give <u>You as a covenant</u> for the people, a light for the nations."* (Isaiah 42:5-6 ESV, emphasis added)

Jesus *is* the second covenant. You may be wondering how a person can *be* a covenant. A covenant is a law or an agreement between two or more people. Jesus is the agreement. God agrees that the blood of Jesus Christ makes us right with Him. Scripture describes Jesus as a mediator. A mediator is a person who attempts to make people involved in a conflict come to an agreement, a go-between. Before Jesus came and conquered death and sin for us, we were people involved in a conflict. Our sin caused us to be far from God which is why we needed a mediator to help us. Jesus Himself became the agreement which reconciled us with God. He made peace between us and God. He is the covenant that restores our relationship and allows us to become friends of God.

"But there was an oath regarding Jesus. For God said to him, 'The Lord has taken an oath and will not break his vow: "You are a priest forever."' Because of this oath, Jesus is the one who guarantees this better covenant with God. There were many priests under the old system, for death prevented them from remaining in office. But because Jesus lives forever, his priesthood lasts forever. Therefore, he is able, once and forever, to save those who come to God through him. ***He lives forever to intercede with God on their behalf.*** *He is the kind of high priest we need because he is holy and blameless, unstained by sin. He has been set apart from sinners and has been given the highest place of honor in heaven. Unlike those other high priests, he does not need to offer sacrifices every day. They did this for their own sins first and then for the sins of the people. But Jesus did this once for all when he offered* ***himself*** *as the sacrifice for the people's sins. The law appointed high priests who were limited by human weakness. But after the law was given, God appointed his Son with an oath, and his Son has been made the perfect High Priest forever."* (Hebrews 7:21-28, emphasis added)

"But now Jesus, our High Priest, has been given a ministry that is far superior to the old priesthood, <u>for he is the one who mediates for us a far better covenant with God, based on better promises.</u> If the first covenant had been faultless, there would have been no need for a second covenant to replace it. But when God found fault with the people, he said:

'The day is coming, says the Lord, when I will make a new covenant with the people of Israel and Judah. This covenant will not be like the one I made with their ancestors when I took them by the hand and led them out of the land of Egypt. They did not remain faithful to my covenant, so I turned my back on them, says the Lord. But this is the <u>new covenant</u> I will make with the people of Israel on that day, says the Lord: <u>I will put my laws in their minds, and I will write them on their hearts.</u> I will be their God, and they will be my people. And they will not need to teach their neighbors, nor will they need to teach their relatives, saying, "You should know the Lord." for everyone, from the least to the greatest, will know me already. And I will forgive their wickedness, and I will never again remember their sins.' When God speaks of a 'new' covenant, it means he has made the first one obsolete. It is now out of date and will soon disappear." (Hebrews 8:6-13, emphasis added)

Wow! Isn't that cool! The Bible is so full of amazing treasures. What we just read clearly states that God cancelled out the old covenant and made a new one! If Jesus is the new covenant, then He is the One that we need to be seeking. Remember the psalmist asked, *"How can a young person stay pure?"* and the answer was *"By obeying God's word."* He went on to explain what he did to obey.

10 *I have tried hard to find you—*
don't let me wander from your commands.
11 *I have hidden your word in my heart,*
that I might not sin against you.
12 *I praise you, O Lord;*
teach me your decrees.
13 *I have recited aloud*
all the regulations you have given us.
14 *I have rejoiced in your laws*
as much as in riches.
15 *I will study your commandments*
and reflect on your ways.
16 *I will delight in your decrees*
and not forget your word.
(Psalm 119:10-16)

We need to take into consideration that the psalmist who wrote that was living in the days before Jesus was living in the flesh on the earth. He was following all the old regulations and commands. We have the privilege to explore and learn what the new covenant is. This is exciting because I often wanted to find ways to better myself and my life. When the solution to doing so became a list of instructions to follow and goals to meet, I would get overwhelmed to easily and exhausted from striving to get things right. Praise Jesus, there is another way!

"Jesus replied, 'The most important commandment is this: "Listen, O Israel! The Lord our God is the one and only Lord. And you must love the Lord your God with all your heart, all your soul, all your mind, and all your strength." The second is equally important: "Love your neighbor as yourself." No other commandment is greater than these.'" (Mark 12:29-31)

"All the Law and the Prophets hang on these two commandments." (Matthew 22:40) Instead of giving us a list of laws and rules to follow, this New Covenant of ours instructs that His greatest commandment is to *love* Him. That doesn't sound too bad, does it? He wants us to love Him. We can do that. Right?!

Not only does He want us to love Him, but to love Him with *all* our heart, with *all* our soul, *all* our mind, and *all* our strength. Every time I heard that command and allowed it to run through my mind, part of me was relieved because it wasn't a long list of rules and regulations that He wanted me to follow. Instead, He just wanted my love. But as I seriously pondered it, my heart nearly broke because I knew I wasn't loving Him the way that He desired. He wants True Love. He wants *all* my heart. To be quite honest my heart was divided. There were things that my heart desired more than Him. He wants all my soul. I like to think of a soul as one's will, and emotions. I can tell you that my will and emotions were consumed by seeking satisfaction in other ways than by Him. He wants all my mind. I don't know about you, but I didn't leave much room for Jesus in my mind. If I thought about Him, it was because I was asking Him for help or busy telling Him what I needed. I tried to remember to pray throughout the day, but it was just a quick heartless prayer and then my mind went right back to the demands of the day: *"What are we going to eat for dinner? I need to pay that bill. He really made me mad today. I am a mess. Speaking of mess, the house is a wreck! I need to spend time with so and so, but I just don't have time. I should have done my devotions today, but I'll do it tonight. I'm really tired. I'll try again tomorrow. I was mean to my child because there's just too much going on. I've really done it now!"* and so on and so on! As much as I wanted Jesus to be part of my every thought, the truth was, He wasn't. He wants all my strength. I was trying to give Him my all, and I wanted to, but I'll admit, I wasn't giving Him my best. I could have done better. I knew that God was supposed to be my number one priority, above all else. I liked to say He was top priority, but, honestly, I was not giving Him that position in my life. I wanted so badly for God to be number one in my life. I wanted to love Him with all my heart. I wanted to love Him with all my soul, and my mind, and with all my strength. I wanted to be obedient to His greatest command. I really did! I just didn't know how. *"How do I love you like that, Lord?"*

As I meditated on His command, I thought about what it was like to love a person like that. Then I realized that Jesus desires to have an intimate relationship with me! The meaning of intimate is closely acquainted, familiar, or personal. Think of a person you love dearly, whether it be your spouse, your child, your mom or dad, a grandparent, or a friend. Every relationship that is dear to you starts by spending time together. You live your life with them. A huge part of that relationship is communication, spending time getting to know each other, and doing things for each other simply because you love them and enjoy their presence. We don't have close, intimate relationships with people we only know the name of. In order to love Jesus with all of my heart, soul, mind, and strength, I needed to *really* know Him.

Listen to what Paul says about this. *"Yes, everything else is worthless when compared with the <u>infinite value of knowing</u> Christ Jesus my Lord. For* *his sake I have discarded everything else, counting it all as garbage, so that I could gain Christ and become one with him. I no longer count on my own righteousness through obeying the law; rather, I become righteous through faith in Christ. For God's way of making us right with himself depends on faith. I want* *<u>to know</u>* *Christ* *<u>and experience</u>* *the mighty power that raised him from the dead."* (Philippians 3:8-10, emphasis added)

Again, Scripture speaks of how the law does not make us righteous. Paul reminds us that we become righteous through faith in Christ. We are made right with God by faith. Paul says everything else is worthless compared to the value of *knowing* Jesus. God wants us to know and to *experience* Him. God says, *"I want you to show love, not offer sacrifices. I want you to know me more than I want burnt offerings."* (Hosea 6:6)

Clearly, God wants to have a relationship with us, and Paul prayed, *"We ask God to give you complete knowledge of his will and to give you spiritual wisdom and understanding. Then the way you live will always honor and please the Lord, and your lives will produce every kind of good fruit. All the while,* ***you will grow as you learn to know God better and better.*** (Colossians 1:9-10, emphasis added)

Those verses tell us that the result of understanding God's will is living in ways that please the Lord! He makes it sound like it is a natural response. What I receive from the verses above is that as I seek to know God better and better, I will grow and desire to do things that please Him. It does not say that as you force yourself to be a good person and follow all the rules, then you will understand. Instead, it's just the opposite. As we seek to know the character of God, then we will naturally live the way we were created to live. The Creator of the universe wants to be closer to you. He already knows you completely because He is your Maker. Now He wants you to know Him.

I want to conclude this chapter by meditating on how we can stay on a right path. Allow the truths we have learned today to settle into your heart, soul, and mind as we learn to understand this New Covenant, Jesus. Maybe you can read the psalm again and allow it to become your own words after hearing the words of Jesus again.

"Jesus replied, 'You must love the Lord your God with all your heart, all your soul, and all your mind.' This is the first and greatest commandment. A second is equally important: 'Love your neighbor as yourself.' The entire law and all the demands of the prophets are based on these two commandments." (Matthew 22:37-40)

"How can a young person stay pure? By obeying your word. I have tried hard to find you—don't let me wander from your commands. I have hidden your word in my heart, that I might not sin against you. I praise you, O Lord; teach me your decrees. I have recited aloud all the regulations you have

given us. I have rejoiced in your laws as much as in riches. I will study your commandments and reflect on your ways. I will delight in your decrees and not forget your word." (Psalm 119:9-16)

If His decrees are love, then we can delight in loving Him. Admire Jesus today for being the New Covenant and consider asking Him how He has interceded for you personally.

17 Be good to your servant,
that I may live and obey your word.
18 Open my eyes to see
the wonderful truths in your instructions.
19 I am only a foreigner in the land.
Don't hide your commands from me!
20 I am always overwhelmed
with a desire for your regulations.
21 You rebuke the arrogant;
those who wander from your commands are cursed.
22 Don't let them scorn and insult me,
for I have obeyed your laws.
23 Even princes sit and speak against me,
but I will meditate on your decrees.
24 Your laws please me;
they give me wise advice.

Psalm 119:17–24

5

OPEN MY EYES

Let's ask God to open our eyes to see the wonderful truths in His instructions. The instructions that I am referring to are those that He says are most important: *To love Him with all our heart, soul, mind, and strength.* In order to truly love someone that much, we must know them well. We can't just force ourselves to give someone all of our love. Not true love anyways. First, we learn about them. Second, we have to like what we learn!

Think of that person you know or the pet that you have a heart connection with. Your love for them is inseparable because you have spent much time bonding and building a relationship with them. Things may come against you or between you, but there is always a special place in your heart for them. Nothing can take away the love you have for each other. That is the kind of relationship that God wants with you and for you. We have to get to know Him so that we can relate to Him.

God is so complex, and there are some things that we may never understand until the day that we meet Him face to face in Heaven. I believe He leaves it that way on purpose. I heard someone say it this way, *"If we could figure God out completely, then we wouldn't need Him to be our God."* He is all powerful, all mighty, unconditionally loving Creator of all things. Who could understand all His ways? Although, the character of God does not have to be a mystery. His word is full of His personality. It reveals His heart and who He is in so many ways.

You have probably heard at some point in your life that God is three in one, meaning that He is God, Jesus, and the Holy Spirit. It can be a bit confusing, which can make it hard to relate to Him. When someone is confusing to us, it is extremely hard to draw close to them. That is why I would like to start right here. One way we can grasp the concept of God, Jesus, and the Holy Spirit being one is to look at how God made us.

"So God created human beings in his own image. In the image of God, he created them; male and female he created them." (Genesis 1:27) We have a body, a soul, and a spirit. If we are created in the image of God, then He, too, has a body, a soul, and a spirit. Here are a couple of Scriptures that talk about body, soul, and spirit.

"For the word of God is alive and powerful. It is sharper than the sharpest two-edged sword, cutting between ***soul*** *and* ***spirit****, between* ***joint and marrow*** [body]. *It exposes our innermost thoughts and desires."* (Hebrews 4:12, emphasis added)

"Now may the God of peace make you holy in every way, and may your whole ***spirit*** *and* ***soul*** *and* ***body*** *be kept blameless until our Lord Jesus Christ comes again."* (1 Thessalonians 5:23, emphasis added)

Let's examine each part. Our soul can be referred to as our mind, our will, and our emotions. My soul makes up my personality. We all have our own personalities. We may be considered meek, out-going, humorous, serious, spontaneous, honest, or respectful. There are so many different characteristics that make up the personalities of each of us. We all have our own mind, our own motives, our own emotions, and we all make our own choices. If I could take my soul away from myself, I would be only a body with a conscience, but no personality. I would look like me on the outside but would not be completely me without my soul. Everyone's soul is unique, making *you* who *you* are.

I see God as the Soul. God is the personality of the three parts of Him. He is righteous, He is holy, He is love, He is mercy, He is grace, He is powerful. Those are some of the characteristics that make up the personality of God. *"Righteousness and justice are the foundation of thy throne: Lovingkindness and truth go before thy face."* (Psalm 89:14 ASV) God is often identified by His foundation; Righteous and Just. While it is true that He is a Righteous and Holy God, it so often is the very thing that keeps people from drawing close to the Lord because they feel unworthy or undeserving of His love. If one believes they can never be good enough for God, the result is a constant feeling of judgement. It is so important that we do not miss the other characteristics of God. While righteousness and justice are the foundations of His throne, what is it that goes before God's face? *Lovingkindness, truth,* other versions say *mercy, faithfulness, unfailing love, and grace.* God is seated on justice and righteousness. He is all Good. There is no bad in Him. Therefore, justice and righteousness are very vital pieces of His being. The second part of that verse explains how He handles things, and that is with love and grace.

How do you see God? Do you see Him as a big old man with a long gray beard holding a rod in His hand ready to strike you every time you mess up? Let me ask you, is that lovingkindness or merciful or graceful? No. Do you see God as a joy kill with a strict set of rules to follow, and it is His way or no way? Is there truth in that or faithfulness, or unfailing love, mercy, or grace? No. Do you see God as an impersonal God just doing as He pleases somewhere up in outer space sitting properly on His throne judging the world? Once again, that description is not loving or kind or merciful, or true.

I have wondered about the characteristics of God that are displayed in the Old Testament. Many stories speak of God destroying nations and turning away from people. If I only skimmed through the first parts of the Bible, I might get the impression that God is one angry, violent man! After being brave enough to read through the stories as a whole, His intentions and His heart are very clear. God is righteous, and He is just. When God wiped out groups of people, they were people that had no good intention in them. They were completely and totally evil. The reason God brought destruction was for our protection. If He allowed wickedness to continue, the whole world would suffer greatly because of it.

We see it in the days of Noah. *"And GOD saw that the wickedness of man was great in the earth, and that every imagination of the thoughts of his heart was only evil continually."* (Genesis 6:5 KJV) *"So the Lord was sorry he had ever made them and put them on the earth. It broke his heart. And the Lord said, 'I will wipe this human race I have created from the face of the earth. Yes, and I will destroy every living thing—all the people, the large animals, the small animals that scurry along the ground, and even the birds of the sky. I am sorry I ever made them.' But Noah found favor with the Lord. This is the account of Noah and his family. Noah was a righteous man, the only blameless person living on earth at the time, and he walked in close fellowship with God. Noah was the father of three sons: Shem, Ham, and Japheth.*

Now God saw that the earth had become corrupt and was filled with violence. God observed all this corruption in the world, for everyone on earth was corrupt. So God said to Noah, 'I have decided to destroy all living creatures, for they have filled the earth with violence. Yes, I will wipe them all out along with the earth!' (Genesis 6:6-13)

"'Look! I am about to cover the earth with a flood that will destroy every living thing that breathes. Everything on earth will die. But I will confirm my covenant with you. So enter the boat—you and your wife and your sons and their wives.'" (Genesis 6:17-18)

"So Noah did everything exactly as God had commanded him." (Genesis 6:22)

"When everything was ready, the Lord said to Noah, 'Go into the boat with all your family, for among all the people of the earth, I can see that you alone are righteous.'" (Genesis 7:1)

It may seem like God is cruel, but look at His reasoning. In verse 11, it says God saw that the earth was *filled* with violence. Then it tells us that He observed all the corruption. He didn't just make a rash decision. He looked it over, thought it out, then He made the decision to destroy all living creatures, for they had filled the earth with violence. Violence is a strong word. It doesn't mean that the people were making a few unwise decisions here and there. The definition of violence is *behavior involving physical force intended to hurt, damage, or kill someone or something; strength of emotion or an unpleasant or destructive natural force.* Violence. Ugly. Scary. *"And GOD saw that the wickedness of man was great in the earth, and that every imagination of the thoughts of his heart was only evil continually."* (Genesis 6:5 KJV) Even their thoughts were constantly and only evil.

We can see how it affected God in verse 6. It broke His heart. God wasn't just an angry beast who had decided to destroy the earth over some small nonsense. The whole world was being swallowed up with wickedness, evil, violence! I am thankful that He did something about it. How often do we examine the behavior of someone who is acting wrong and come to the conclusion that some sort of punishment needs to take place? Think of someone you consider to be violent, evil, wicked in all their ways. What about the ones who kill Christians just because they are believers in Jesus Christ? Does something need to be done or should they be able to continue in their wicked ways and be left alone?

It broke God's heart to see what was happening. What was going on in the world wasn't His intention, but it was the choice of the people. He was sorry, and His heart had been crushed. But notice what God noticed: Noah. He noticed Noah. He found a righteous man, and what did God do? He came up with an escape plan for Noah and his family. God had Noah build an enormous boat, big enough for him and his family and two of each animal and then some! I don't know how long it took Noah to build that ship, but I would have to guess that it took a long while!

Can you see the patience of God? He could have acted out in anger and destroyed everyone instantly, but He saw Noah, and He allowed Noah to play a part in His story. God waited for Noah to be ready. He put up with the violence that much longer for the sake of Noah and his family. I don't see an angry beast. I see a heartbroken, patient God, who loves Noah so much that He came up with a plan to rescue him from an evil world.

Here is another example in the Old Testament, the story of Sodom and Gomorrah: *"So the Lord told Abraham, 'I have heard a great outcry from Sodom and Gomorrah, because their sin is so flagrant. I am going down to see if their actions are as wicked as I have heard. If not, I want to know.'*

The other men turned and headed toward Sodom, but the Lord remained with Abraham. Abraham approached him and said, 'Will you sweep away both the righteous and the wicked? Suppose you find fifty righteous people living there in the city—will you still sweep it away and not spare it for their sakes? Surely you wouldn't do such a thing, destroying the righteous along with the wicked. Why, you would be treating the righteous and the wicked exactly the same! Surely you wouldn't do that! Should not the Judge of all the earth do what is right?'

And the Lord replied, 'If I find fifty righteous people in Sodom, I will spare the entire city for their sake.'

Then Abraham spoke again. 'Since I have begun, let me speak further to my Lord, even though I am but dust and ashes. Suppose there are only forty-five righteous people rather than fifty? Will you destroy the whole city for lack of five?' And the Lord said, 'I will not destroy it if I find forty-five righteous people there.'

Then Abraham pressed his request further. 'Suppose there are only forty?' And the Lord replied, 'I will not destroy it for the sake of the forty.'

'Please don't be angry, my Lord,' Abraham pleaded. 'Let me speak—suppose only thirty righteous people are found?' And the Lord replied, 'I will not destroy it if I find thirty.'

Then Abraham said, 'Since I have dared to speak to the Lord, let me continue—suppose there are only twenty?'

And the Lord replied, 'Then I will not destroy it for the sake of the twenty.'

Finally, Abraham said, 'Lord, please don't be angry with me if I speak one more time. Suppose only ten are found there?' And the Lord replied, 'Then I will not destroy it for the sake of the ten.'" (Genesis 18:20-32)

"That evening the two angels came to the entrance of the city of Sodom. Lot was sitting there, and when he saw them, he stood up to meet them. Then he welcomed them and bowed with his face to the ground. 'My lords,' he said, 'come to my home to wash your feet, and be my guests for the night. You may then get up early in the morning and be on your way again.'

'Oh no,' they replied. 'We'll just spend the night out here in the city square.'

But Lot insisted, so at last they went home with him. Lot prepared a feast for them, complete with fresh bread made without yeast, and they ate. But before they retired for the night, all the men of Sodom, young and old, came from all over the city and surrounded the house. They shouted to Lot, 'Where are the men who came to spend the night with you? Bring them out to us so we can have sex with them!'

So Lot stepped outside to talk to them, shutting the door behind him. 'Please, my brothers,' he begged, 'don't do such a wicked thing. Look, I have two virgin daughters. Let me bring them out to you, and you can do with them as you wish. But please, leave these men alone, for they are my guests and are under my protection.'

'Stand back!' they shouted. 'This fellow came to town as an outsider, and now he's acting like our judge! We'll treat you far worse than those other men!' And they lunged toward Lot to break down the door.

But the two angels reached out, pulled Lot into the house, and bolted the door. Then they blinded all the men, young and old, who were at the door of the house, so they gave up trying to get inside.

Meanwhile, the angels questioned Lot. 'Do you have any other relatives here in the city?' they asked. 'Get them out of this place—your sons-in-law, sons, daughters, or anyone else. For we are about to destroy this city completely. The outcry against this place is so great it has reached the Lord, and he has sent us to destroy it.'

So Lot rushed out to tell his daughters' fiancés, 'Quick, get out of the city! The Lord is about to destroy it.' But the young men thought he was only joking.

At dawn the next morning the angels became insistent. 'Hurry,' they said to Lot. 'Take your wife and your two daughters who are here. Get out right now, or you will be swept away in the destruction of the city!'

When Lot still hesitated, the angels seized his hand and the hands of his wife and two daughters and rushed them to safety outside the city, for the Lord was merciful. When they were safely out of the city, one of the angels ordered, 'Run for your lives! And don't look back or stop anywhere in the valley! Escape to the mountains, or you will be swept away!'

'Oh no, my lord!' Lot begged. 'You have been so gracious to me and saved my life, and you have shown such great kindness. But I cannot go to the mountains. Disaster would catch up to me there, and I would soon die. See, there is a small village nearby. Please let me go there instead; don't you see how small it is? Then my life will be saved.'

'All right,' the angel said, 'I will grant your request. I will not destroy the little village. But hurry! Escape to it, for I can do nothing until you arrive there.' (This explains why that village was known as Zoar, which means 'little place.')

Lot reached the village just as the sun was rising over the horizon. Then the Lord rained down fire and burning sulfur from the sky on Sodom and Gomorrah. He utterly destroyed them, along with the other cities and villages of the plain, wiping out all the people and every bit of vegetation. But Lot's wife looked back as she was following behind him, and she turned into a pillar of salt.

Abraham got up early that morning and hurried out to the place where he had stood in the Lord's presence. He looked out across the plain toward Sodom and Gomorrah and watched as columns of smoke rose from the cities like smoke from a furnace.

But God had listened to Abraham's request and kept Lot safe, removing him from the disaster that engulfed the cities on the plain." (Genesis 19:1-29)

What a horrible place to be in! Two men enter the town, and all the men, young and old, from the city surround the home they are in so they can call them out and rape them! Then Lot offered to send out his two virgin daughters just to keep those men safe! There seems to be nothing right about any of that. Thankfully, those two men were angels, and I believe they would have kept the girls safe, regardless. Apparently, the men of the city had no interest in girls. Oh my! Something needed to be done in that place! Don't you think? Thank goodness that there weren't ten righteous people in that city because God would have spared the whole city for their sake! I can't imagine living in a place like that!

God made sure that the people, who hadn't turned completely wicked, had a chance to escape. He sent two angels to rescue the good. Not only did the angels go into the town and rescue Lot and his family that went with him, but the angels insisted that they leave and basically forced them out of the city to save their lives. They could have said, *"You missed your chance,"* but the angels literally grabbed Lot and his wife and daughters by the hands and pulled them out of the city.

God is merciful, and He is completely good. Therefore, He cannot put up with evil wicked ways forever because He is also righteous and just. When He destroys the wicked, it is because there is no good in them by their own choice, and He takes their lives for the protection of those who still have some good in their hearts. He is patient, He is kind, and when He gets angry, He has every right to be angry. He only does what is right. Even if we can't completely understand His ways, we can trust in the fact that He can see the whole story, and He will do what is best. Nothing goes unseen. At the right time, God will destroy that which is completely and totally evil, all the while, protecting that which is good. *"The Lord isn't really being slow about his promise, as some people think. No, he is being patient for your sake. He does not want anyone to be destroyed, but wants everyone to repent."* (2 Peter 3:9)

The story of Esther paints another picture of God's patience and kindness. There was an evil man named Haman, who had plotted to kill the entire race of the Jews, and the good Lord turned the tables and empowered the Jews to defend themselves and kill anyone who tried to attack them. No one could stand against the Jews. The wicked were defeated and the lives that were spared were those who had good intentions.

It might seem as if God gave His people the right to be murderers. How can that make them any better? They are just as guilty, right? If someone were planning to come in and kill my entire family, I would hope that God wouldn't say, *"Now you can't murder anyone so you'll just have to run for your lives and hope you don't get caught."* No! It is self-defense. Murder is what the enemy was going to do. Murder is intentionally and forcefully taking the life of another because of hatred. Self-defense is preventing that from happening. I am thankful that God empowered them to protect themselves.

When we read and hear of the stories about God ordering armies to go and wipe out vast numbers of people, we have to remember the other side of the story. If God didn't do something, violence would have taken over. Evil people were going to kill innocent people. There's no telling what kind of wicked schemes they had going on in their minds, but it was nothing good. Imagine what the world would look like today, had God not done anything back then. It's bad enough today! Multiply that hundreds of times, and you and I would wish we didn't exist!

If one only skims through the Old Testament without thoroughly reading the whole story, unpleasant verses will be found, especially through the books of the prophets, that talk about the wrath of God; verses that state that He will destroy cities, stories of God instructing people to go to war and kill armies of men, verses that say God turned His back on people and so on. If you pick and choose verses here and there, God could look very harsh and unlikeable. It is important to read the *entire* story. The whole story reveals the true intentions of God's heart. You will discover that there were very wicked, evil, violent, and hateful people. In some cases, parents were burning their own children as sacrifices to other gods; gods made by human hands. The land was filled with murderers, adulterers, and liars. Not only were they completely evil, but they had been told *repeatedly* that they *could* turn from their wicked ways and give their hearts to God. They refused! God didn't give them a day to turn from there wicked ways, and He didn't give them a week, or a month, or several months for that matter. He gave them *several* years! Year, after year, after year, God was patient. He endured the nonsense as long as He could, hoping that they would turn back to Him. God's wrath is what protects you and me. *"The Lord is slow to anger and filled with unfailing love, forgiving every kind of sin and rebellion. But he does not excuse the guilty."* (Numbers 14:18a) God is not going to sit back and make excuses for wrongdoing.

If you struggle with understanding the ways of God in the Old Testament, I challenge you to get a chronological Bible and read through the Old Testament in order. If you do, ask the Holy Spirit to reveal the truth to you, and you will be amazed at what you find. The patience of God is phenomenal. God never wanted to destroy people, but because He is just and righteous and loving and faithful, He could not allow detestable acts of the people to continue. He did what was best. If He had allowed the violent and perverse acts to continue, eventually the entire world would be corrupted. Strangely, His decision to destroy cities and nations was an act of love. See for yourself. You will be stunned by our God's love.

"For Jerusalem will stumble, and Judah will fall, because they speak out against the Lord and refuse to obey him. They provoke him to his face. The very look on their faces gives them away. They display their sin like the people of Sodom and don't even try to hide it. They are doomed! They have brought destruction upon themselves. ***Tell the godly that all will be well for them.*** *They will enjoy the rich reward they have earned! But the wicked are doomed, for they will get exactly what they deserve.* (Isaiah 3:8-11, emphasis added)

"*Tell the godly that all will be well for them*," says verse 10. God is not going to reward wicked behavior. He is not going to honor a hard, defiant heart that deliberately turns away from Him and speaks against Him, but if that rebellious heart decides to repent and turn to Him, then He is gracious and fully forgiving.

In the story of Jonah, God shows us a beautiful example of His complete forgiveness. He sent Jonah to Nineveh, a place full of people who had turned away from God. Jonah's job was to go and tell them that God was going to destroy their city if they didn't turn back to Him. The people listened, and God forgave them and didn't destroy the land.

It breaks God's heart to see us do things that only hurt us. *The Lord observed the extent of human wickedness on the earth, and he saw that everything they thought or imagined was consistently and totally evil. So the Lord was sorry he had ever made them and put them on the earth. It broke his heart.* (Genesis 6:5-6) He was sorry He made man because their hearts were completely evil, and it hurt Him to see something He loved so much, hurt themselves, hurt others, and betray Him. From the beginning to the end, God chases after our hearts hoping that we will turn and see His heart and accept the love He has to offer us.

When we read in the Old Testament about the people of Israel and Judah and about the Jews, we need to understand that God's compassion toward those specific people, includes us. God's "children" are all who believe in Him. Jesus took care of that on the cross. *"Don't forget that you Gentiles used to be outsiders. You were called 'uncircumcised heathens' by the Jews, who were proud of their circumcision, even though it affected only their bodies and not their hearts. In those days you were living apart from Christ. You were excluded from citizenship among the people of Israel, and you did not know the covenant promises God had made to them. You lived in this world without God and without hope. But now you have been united with Christ Jesus. Once you were far away from God, but now you have been brought near to him through the blood of Christ.*

For Christ himself has brought peace to us. He united Jews and Gentiles into one people when, in his own body on the cross, he broke down law with its commandments and regulations. He made peace between Jews and Gentiles by creating in himself one new people from the two groups. Together as one body, Christ reconciled both groups to God by means of his death on the cross, and our hostility toward each other was put to death.

He brought this Good News of peace to you Gentiles who were far away from him, and peace to the Jews who were near. Now all of us can come to the Father through the same Holy Spirit because of what Christ has done for us." (Ephesians 2:11-18)

"And this is God's plan: Both Gentiles and Jews who believe the Good News share equally in the riches inherited by God's children. Both are part of the same body, and both enjoy the promise of blessings because they belong to Christ Jesus." (Ephesians 3:6)

"There is no longer Jew or Gentile, slave or free, male and female. For you are all one in Christ Jesus." (Galatians 3:28)

"In this new life, it doesn't matter if you are a Jew or a Gentile, circumcised or uncircumcised, barbaric, uncivilized, slave, or free. Christ is all that matters, and he lives in all of us." (Colossians 3:11)

So now, when you read about God speaking to a specific group of people back then, know that you are included in that today.

Let's examine the heart of God in the Scriptures. *"'When Israel was a child, I loved him, and I called my son out of Egypt. But the more I called to him, the farther he moved from me, offering sacrifices to the images of Baal and burning incense to idols. I myself taught Israel how to walk, leading him along by the hand. But he doesn't know or even care that it was I who took care of him. I led Israel along with my ropes of kindness and love. I lifted the yoke from his neck, and I myself stooped to feed him. But since my people refuse to return to me, they will return to Egypt and will be forced to serve Assyria. War will swirl through their cities; their enemies will crash through their gates. They will destroy them, trapping them in their own evil plans. For my people are determined to desert me. They call me the Most High, but they don't truly honor me. Oh, how can I give you up, Israel? How can I let you go? How can I destroy you like Admah or demolish you like Zeboiim? My heart is torn within me, and my compassion overflows. No, I will not unleash my fierce anger. I will not completely destroy Israel, for I am God and not a mere mortal. I am the Holy One living among you, and I will not come to destroy.'"* (Hosea 11:1-9)

Can you see God's heart? Can you hear the tone of voice He uses? God loves us. He loves all the people He created.

What would that message from God sound like if you personalized it? More than likely, you were not a slave in Egypt and are not worshipping Baal, I pray. But *our* Egypt could represent our personal struggles that we are dealing with now, and Baal could be whatever satisfaction we are trying to receive from the world today outside of God. If God were to speak those words directly to you and me, they could sound something like this:

"When you were a child, I loved you, and I called you out of the pit of despair. But the more I called to you, the farther you moved from me, chasing satisfaction and going whichever way the wind would blow. I myself taught you how to walk, leading you along by the hand. But you don't know or even care that it was I who took care of you. I led you along with my ropes of kindness and love. I lifted the yoke from your neck, and I myself stooped to feed you. But since you refuse to return to me, you will return to the darkness and will be forced to serve depression and fear. War will swirl through your mind; the evil one will knock down the gates to your heart. He will destroy you, trapping you in his own evil plans. For you are determined to desert me. You call me the Most High, but you don't truly honor me. Oh, how can I give you up? How can I let you go? How can I destroy you or demolish you? My heart is torn within me, and my compassion overflows. No, I will not unleash my fierce anger. I will not completely destroy you, for I am God and not a mere mortal. I am the Holy One living among you, and I will not come to destroy."

God does not want to hurt us. That's the last thing He has in mind. He just wants us to stop hurting ourselves. It breaks His heart to see us take paths that lead to our destruction. This is His heart's desire. *"'But then I will win her back once again. I will lead her into the desert and speak tenderly to her there. I will return her vineyards to her and transform the valley of trouble into a gateway of hope. She will give herself to me there, as she did long ago when she was young, when I freed her from her captivity in Egypt. When that day comes,' says the Lord, 'you will call me "my husband" instead of "my master." O Israel, I will wipe the many names of Baal from your lips, and you will never mention them again. On that day I will make a covenant with all the wild animals and the birds of the sky and the animals that scurry along the ground so they will not harm you. I will remove all weapons of war from the land, all swords and bows, so you can live unafraid, in peace and safety. I will make you my wife forever, showing you righteousness and justice, unfailing love and compassion. I will be faithful to you and make you mine, and you will finally know me as the Lord.'"*

God longs for us with such a deep compassion that He compares our relationship with Him to a marriage relationship. He longs for us to know Him and to love Him. He is not looking for people who follow rules and get it all right, thank goodness. If that were the case, He could have created us all without giving us a choice, making us to do whatever He programmed us to do. He gave you a choice because God isn't looking for perfection, He craves True Love. That is the soul of your God. The personality of God all stems from love. When God has every right to unleash His fierce anger and give up on us, love always crashes over Him, and love ultimately rules. The love God has for us keeps Him constantly in pursuit of us.

As this section comes to a close, ponder the words of the psalmist: *"17 Be good to your servant, that I may live and obey your word. 18 Open my eyes to see the wonderful truths in your instructions. 19 I am only a foreigner in the land. Don't hide your commands from me! 20 I am always overwhelmed with a desire for your regulations. 21 You rebuke the arrogant; those who wander from your commands are cursed. 22 Don't let them scorn and insult me, for I have obeyed your laws. 23 Even princes sit and speak against me, but I will meditate on your decrees. 24 Your laws please me; they give me wise advice."* (Psalm 119:17-24)

As we continue to seek what it means to follow Jesus's greatest commandment, *Love the Lord your God with all your heart, soul, mind, and strength*, let's ask the Lord, like the psalmist did, to open our eyes to see the wonderful truths of Who He is so that we can love Him with a true love that He desires. As we do this, we will also be able to say, *"Even though many may insult me or speak against me, I will meditate on Who You are. Your commandments please me, and You give me wise advice."*

[25] I lie in the dust;
revive me by your word.
[26] I told you my plans, and you answered.
Now teach me your decrees.
[27] Help me understand the meaning of your commandments,
and I will meditate on your wonderful deeds.
[28] I weep with sorrow;
encourage me by your word.
[29] Keep me from lying to myself;
give me the privilege of knowing your instructions.
[30] I have chosen to be faithful;
I have determined to live by your regulations.
[31] I cling to your laws.
Lord, don't let me be put to shame!
[32] I will pursue your commands,
for you expand my understanding.

Psalm 119:25–32

6

Help Me

By reading the writer's words, his struggle is evident. *"I'm lying in the dust weeping with sorrow. Keep me from lying to myself. Don't let me be shamed! Help me!"* He knows where his answers come from. He knows where to find new strength, encouragement, and greater understanding, and it's in God's word. Do you think the greatest commandment that Jesus stated in the New Testament was a new commandment? Could it be possible that the writer of Psalm 119 may have heard that commandment as well, even though his life was before Jesus came to live on the earth?

"Listen, O Israel! The Lord is our God, the Lord alone. And you must love the Lord your God with all your heart, all your soul, and all your strength." (Deuteronomy 6:4-5) That is Old Testament. *"And you must commit yourselves wholeheartedly to these commands that I am giving you today. Repeat them again and again to your children. Talk about them when you are at home and when you are on the road, when you are going to bed and when you are getting up. Tie them to your hands and wear them on your forehead as reminders. Write them on the doorposts of your house and on your gates."* (Deuteronomy 6:6-9)

The greatest commandment that Jesus came and spoke of was God's intention all along. There's nothing new about it. It is what God has wanted from the very beginning. If it is love that God craves, then let's continue on our journey of getting to know Him personally.

God is the Creator of relationships. He is the Designer of Love. The Bible is the Designers blueprint for relationships. *"For everything was created by Him, in heaven and on earth, the visible and invisible, whether thrones or dominions or rulers or authorities- all things have been created through Him and for Him."* (Colossians 1:16) Look at those last two words, *"for Him."* We are incomplete people without Him. *He* is the only thing that can completely make us whole because we were made *for* Him.

There is a story of a woman named Leah in the Bible. I love the way that God tended to her needs. The compassion God had for Leah is beautiful. Let's read her story.

"After Jacob had stayed with Laban for about a month, Laban said to him, 'You shouldn't work for me without pay just because we are relatives. Tell me how much your wages should be.'

Now Laban had two daughters. The older daughter was named Leah, and the younger one was Rachel. There was no sparkle in Leah's eyes, but Rachel had a beautiful figure and a lovely face. Since Jacob was in love with Rachel, he told her father, 'I'll work for you for seven years if you'll give me Rachel, your younger daughter, as my wife.'

'Agreed!' Laban replied. 'I'd rather give her to you than to anyone else. Stay and work with me.' So Jacob worked seven years to pay for Rachel. But his love for her was so strong that it seemed to him but a few days.

Finally, the time came for him to marry her. 'I have fulfilled my agreement,' Jacob said to Laban. 'Now give me my wife so I can sleep with her.'

So Laban invited everyone in the neighborhood and prepared a wedding feast. But that night, when it was dark, Laban took Leah to Jacob, and he slept with her. (Laban had given Leah a servant, Zilpah, to be her maid.)

But when Jacob woke up in the morning—it was Leah! 'What have you done to me?' Jacob raged at Laban. 'I worked seven years for Rachel! Why have you tricked me?'

'It's not our custom here to marry off a younger daughter ahead of the firstborn,' Laban replied. 'But wait until the bridal week is over; then we'll give you Rachel, too—provided you promise to work another seven years for me.'

So Jacob agreed to work seven more years. A week after Jacob had married Leah, Laban gave him Rachel, too. (Laban gave Rachel a servant, Bilhah, to be her maid.) So Jacob slept with Rachel, too, and he loved her much more than Leah. He then stayed and worked for Laban the additional seven years.

When the Lord saw that Leah was unloved, he enabled her to have children, but Rachel could not conceive. So Leah became pregnant and gave birth to a son. She named him Reuben, for she said, 'The Lord has noticed my misery, and now my husband will love me.'

She soon became pregnant again and gave birth to another son. She named him Simeon, for she said, 'The Lord heard that I was unloved and has given me another son.'

Then she became pregnant a third time and gave birth to another son. He was named Levi, for she said, 'Surely this time my husband will feel affection for me, since I have given him three sons!'

Once again Leah became pregnant and gave birth to another son. She named him Judah, for she said, 'Now I will praise the Lord!' And then she stopped having children." (Genesis 29:16-35)

That is a wild story! How in the world did Jacob not know he was sleeping with Leah instead of Rachel until the next morning? Marriage customs back then were a little, okay maybe a lot, different than what I am used to now. I imagine that Leah's face was covered and there was no electricity. Since it was night- time it would have been very dark. Leah and Rachel were sisters, therefore, they could have looked and sounded a lot alike. I'm only making guesses because I haven't taken the time to find out the customs of marriage during that time, but if you want to, it could be a very interesting study! Regardless of how it happened, the point is, it did happen.

What I want to focus on in this story is the heart of Leah. Can you imagine being married to someone who didn't chose you or even want you? Leah *longed* to be loved by her husband. God saw her broken heart and He had compassion on Leah and gave her a child. Leah was hoping that the child would cause her husband to love her. Having a child didn't change anything between Leah and Jacob because she said that the Lord saw that she was unloved and gave her another child. The second child still didn't bring her the love that she craved from her husband. God gave her a third son and Leah thought surely Jacob would love her after that. Did it work? No.

Leah was so focused on her marriage that she couldn't even see that it was the Lord who was tending to her needs and trying to offer her True Love. His love is unconditional. If having children had caused Jacob to love Leah, it would have been conditional love. *"I love you because you give me children."* That is conditional love, and often we humans work that way. *"I will love you if you do this for me."* Thankfully, that isn't the way that God loves. He loves us no matter what.

I believe Leah started realizing where True Love came from. She must have figured out that it wasn't a man that was going to complete her, and it wasn't children either. Yes, she loved her precious children, and I would say she loved Jacob as well, but her heart was still empty. Her heart was craving a kind of love that she couldn't seem to find until God opened her eyes and showed her that it was *Him* that noticed her. *God* knew her hearts desires and gave her what she wanted. *He* listened to her and heard her cries. *He* was the one pouring His love out to her, hoping that she would see *His* heart and accept it. *God* cared about Leah. He *saw* Leah. He *loved* Leah.

Notice how Leah's response changed after God had given her and Jacob their fourth child. *"This time I will praise the Lord,"* she said. And then she stopped having children. Leah found True Love. Finally, she realized that it was God that loved her perfectly. Yes, He also blesses us with the love of others and children, but no human is capable of completing us. God Himself is the only One who can complete us. If we could find complete satisfaction and fulfillment in each other, we would not need *Him*. We are created to have an eternal relationship and connection with God Almighty.

Ephesians 2:10 says we are God's masterpiece, His workmanship, His handiwork. God knew what He was doing when He made each one of us. Our hearts are designed to love Him and be loved by Him. If you feel like there is a hole in your heart that you just can't seem to fill, it's because it is a God sized space, and no one or no thing can fill it except for Him.

It is vital to our existence that we know our God because He is a big part of us and our well-being. Another way we can learn about God's character and personality is by looking at Jesus. After all, Jesus is God, which brings us to the second part of God's being; body.

We acknowledged that we are made up of a body, a soul, and a spirit, and we are made in the image of God. In the last chapter, we examined God as being the *"soul"* part of Him. God is the personality of the three parts of Him: God, Jesus, Holy Spirit. Now let's examine the body.

Our body is the most tangible part of us. It is the physical part that we can see and feel. We can feel our heart beat as it pumps blood through our body. We can feel our lungs expanding with every breath of oxygen we take. We eat food and drink water to nourish our bodies. If you were standing next to me, I could see you, and you could see me. Jesus is the body.

"In the beginning the Word already existed. The Word was with God, and the Word was God. (John 1:1) *He came into the very world he created, but the world didn't recognize him.* (John 1:10) *So the Word became human and made his home among us. He was full of unfailing love and faithfulness. And we have seen his glory, the glory of the Father's one and only Son."* (John 1:14)

Those Scriptures reveal to us that Jesus is God. It's hard to catch that because the Scripture doesn't actually say *Jesus* was God, it says the *Word* was God. How do we know that the Word is referring to Jesus? If you look back at John 1:14, you will notice that it says the Word became human. Well who became human and made His home among us? Yes, Jesus. John 1:10 says that He came into the very world He created. Who created the world? God. This proves that Jesus is God, because Jesus is the One who came into this world and dwelt among us. According to the Scriptures, Jesus is God, and He created the world. If we were to put Jesus' name in the place of *Word* in John 1:1, it would read like this: *"In the beginning Jesus already existed. Jesus was with God, and Jesus was God."*

Wow! Did you realize that Jesus was there when God created the earth? For the longest time, I never imagined Jesus existing until He was born as a baby on this earth! But the Scriptures tell us that Jesus already existed with God, and He is God! It can be a bit confusing trying to grasp the fact that Jesus and God are One, yet they are described as two. This is where understanding the body, soul, and spirit can bring clarity.

Like I described before, our soul is our personality, our character. Our soul makes each one of us uniquely us. Our body is the obvious part, the part of us that we can see. If I were able to separate my body from my soul and spirit, my body would only look like me, but it would have no personality and no purpose. I am not completely me without the three parts together. My body, soul, and spirit together define who I am.

God is God. He's the Creator. He's the One who speaks things into existence. God can do whatever He wants. He is the Boss. Everything we see only exists because there is a God with a wild imagination who chose to make His dreams come true. So, God, having a body, soul, and a spirit can separate His body, soul, and spirit and be in many places at one time. God's body, Jesus, who was with Him from the beginning, was formed in the womb of an ordinary woman to be born a baby just like you and me so that people could witness a physical, tangible God.

Even though Jesus was God, He still suffered physical pain because He took on the limitations of the flesh, which means He felt everything in His body like we do.

"You must have the same attitude that Christ Jesus had. Though he was God, he did not think of equality with God as something to cling to. Instead, he gave up his divine privileges; he took the humble position of a slave and was born as a human being. When he appeared in human form, he humbled himself in obedience to God and died a criminal's death on a cross." (Philippians 2:5-8)

Those verses reveal that Jesus is very humble. He could have been the most conceited, big headed person that ever walked the face of this earth because He is God. But no, He didn't even consider Himself equal to God. He could have come to this earth as a wealthy man. Instead, He took the position of a slave. It goes even further. He was an innocent man, the most innocent that one can find, yet He died a criminal's death. That is what kind of attitude God has. Soak that in! What a man!

"Because God's children are human beings--made of flesh and blood--the Son also became flesh and blood. For only as a human being could he die, and only by dying could he break the power of the devil, who had the power of death." (Hebrews 2:14)

"Therefore, it was necessary for him to be made in every respect like us, his brothers and sisters, so that he could be our merciful and faithful High Priest before God. Then he could offer a sacrifice that would take away the sins of the people." (Hebrews 2:17)

"Therefore, when Christ came into the world, he said: 'Sacrifice and offering you did not desire, but a body you prepared for me.'" (Hebrews 10:5)

The Scriptures are clear that Jesus is God in a fully human body. He felt everything we have felt and was tempted in every way we have been tempted. *"This High Priest of ours understands our weaknesses, for he faced all of the same testings we do, yet he did not sin."* (Hebrews 4:15) The God of the universe, the one who spoke creation into existence, the Almighty who lives in Heaven where there is no sin or destruction, chose to leave His perfect home and His peaceful life to be born as a baby and become one of us. He did it to experience and face the world and die a criminal's death, though He was perfect and innocent, all so that you and I could have everlasting life and a real relationship with Him. There is not a selfish bone in His body. If that isn't True Love, I don't know what is.

We can examine the character and heart of God through the life of Jesus from many accounts. While Jesus was in bodily form, fully human, He left evidence of Who God really is.

"Jesus went into the synagogue again and noticed a man with a deformed hand. Since it was the Sabbath, Jesus' enemies watched him closely. If he healed the man's hand, they planned to accuse him of working on the Sabbath. Jesus said to the man with the deformed hand, 'Come and stand in front of everyone.' Then he turned to his critics and asked, 'Does the law permit good deeds on the Sabbath, or is it a day for doing evil? Is this a day to save life or to destroy it?' But they wouldn't answer him. He looked around at them angrily and was deeply saddened by their hard hearts. Then he said to the man, 'Hold out your hand.' So the man held out his hand, and it was restored!" (Mark 3:1-5)

What made Jesus angry and upset was the hard, calloused hearts of the people. Instead of getting to know Jesus, they just wanted to catch Him in a "wrong" act and accuse Him of not following the law. They were so caught up in the law they were taught to follow and dismissed the importance of the wellbeing of the people. *"Does the law permit good deeds and saving lives on this day?"* Jesus asked. His words and actions showed them what was important. In this case, the man's healing was more important to Jesus than their man-made rules that said no one could do anything on the Sabbath.

"Jesus replied, 'You hypocrites! Isaiah was right when he prophesied about you, for he wrote, "These people honor me with their lips, but their hearts are far from me. Their worship is a farce, for they teach man-made ideas as commands from God." For you ignore God's law and substitute your own tradition.'" (Mark 7:6-8)

Jesus was upset and saddened because the hearts of the people were hardened and far from Him. How close is your heart to Him today? My prayer is that, as you ponder these Scriptures, God will become more real to you. Some things are a mystery, but He wants us to know Him. His word is full of truth. My hope is that you will begin to know God so well that He becomes the One that has that special place in your heart. If you will allow Him, He will capture your heart and satisfy your soul. He will give you your heart's desire as you delight in Him. *"And this hope will not lead to disappointment. For we know how dearly God loves us, because he has given us the Holy Spirit to fill our hearts with his love."* (Romans 5:5)

Speaking of the Holy Spirit, that is the third piece of God that we haven't discussed. We've covered God, being soul; His personality, His emotions, what makes Him who He is. We've covered Jesus, who represents the physical body of God. Now let's look at the Holy Spirit which is the Spirit of God.

Our spirit could also be referred to as our heart. Our spirits contain purpose, meaning, desires, love, *or*... hate, envy, contempt... It is what drives us to do what we do. As we read above, God has given us the Holy Spirit to fill our hearts with His *LOVE*. We connect with God through our spirit. While Jesus was here on earth, He was able to carry out the will of God through the Holy Spirit. Everything He did and said was what the Father told Him to do and say through the Holy Spirit.

"So Jesus explained, 'I tell you the truth, the Son can do nothing by himself. He does only what he sees the Father doing. Whatever the Father does, the Son also does. For the Father loves the Son and shows him everything he is doing.'" (John 5:19-20a)

"'I don't speak on my own authority. The Father who sent me has commanded me what to say and how to say it.'" (John 12:49)

"So Jesus told them, 'My message is not my own; it comes from God who sent me.'" (John 7:16)

"'I can do nothing on my own. I judge as God tells me. Therefore, my judgment is just, because I carry out the will of the one who sent me, not my own will.'" (John 5:30)

The Holy Spirit is the connection that communicated the desires of God to Jesus so that He could act it out in the flesh. We can also read about what the Holy Spirit does for us, knowing that if He does it for us, then He surely did the same for Jesus.

"But the person who is joined to the Lord is one spirit with him." (1 Corinthians 6:17)

"For his Spirit joins with our spirit to affirm that we are God's children." (Romans 8:16)

"The Spirit of God, who raised Jesus from the dead, lives in you. And just as God raised Christ Jesus from the dead, he will give life to your mortal bodies by this same Spirit living within you." (Romans 8:11)

"But it was to us that God revealed these things by his Spirit. For his Spirit searches out everything and shows us God's deep secrets. No one can know a person's thoughts except that person's own spirit, and no one can know God's thoughts except God's own Spirit. And we have received God's Spirit (not the world's spirit), so we can know the wonderful things God has freely given us.

When we tell you these things, we do not use words that come from human wisdom. Instead, we speak words given to us by the Spirit, using the Spirit's words to explain spiritual truths. But people who aren't spiritual can't receive these truths from God's Spirit. It all sounds foolish to them and they can't understand it, for only those who are spiritual can understand what the Spirit means. Those who are spiritual can evaluate all things, but they themselves cannot be evaluated by others. For, 'Who can know the Lord's thoughts? Who knows enough to teach him?' But we understand these things, for we have the mind of Christ." (1 Corinthians 2:10-16)

The Scriptures above tell us that God reveals things through His Spirit, shows us His deep secrets, gives us words to speak, and allows us to know the mind of Christ! Whoa! Now that is cool! If His Spirit reveals things to us, then He absolutely revealed things to Jesus through His Spirit as well.

When Jesus made those statements that we read from John: *"I cannot do anything on my own. I only say what the Father tells me. I only do what I see Him do,"* He was listening to the Holy Spirit. Jesus walked this earth and stayed in communion with God through the power of the Holy Spirit. The Spirit of God reveals His heart to us. The Holy Spirit tells us God's desires, His purpose, what drives Him.

"And this hope will not lead to disappointment. For we know how dearly God loves us, because he has given us the Holy Spirit to fill our hearts with his love." (Romans 5:5) Once again, it is *LOVE* that drives Him. We can see that through the actions of Jesus. We read an example earlier of Jesus healing the man's hand on the Sabbath. If Jesus only did what the Father

told Him to do, then that means on that day, He healed the man's hand because the Holy Spirit revealed to Him what God wanted done. Jesus displayed the love of God through the encouragement of the Holy Spirit. The three parts of God work fully in unison as One being.

It made a huge impact on my life as I began to see the Holy Spirit as God, the very *power* of God and the *love* of God. The Holy Spirit is not an impersonal made up force from a distant God, but instead He is the pure essence of God's power and love given to us freely.

I pray that looking at the three specific parts of God helps you to understand Him better. God: His Soul; personality, mind, will, and emotions. Jesus: His Body; The body that felt everything including the pull of the world to walk in His own way versus the way of the Father, the tangible, physical part of God. Holy Spirit: His Spirit; The connection that keeps the three parts bonded, the love that held them together, the guide that directed Him to walk on the right path, the voice that told Him what to say and how to say it, and the power that raised Him from the dead. All three parts make one whole. God + Jesus + Holy Spirit = One; just like body, soul, and spirit makes up one person. It helped me tremendously to look at those three parts of God and see that they are each part of Him. Without one of them, we would be missing a huge piece of God. God is able to separate those three parts of Himself so that He can be in many places at one time. Even though they are in different places, they still work together as one unit. It's truly amazing. This picture has allowed me to see God more clearly. Some of the confusion that I had was untangled when the Holy Spirit helped me to understand the trinity of God. Now I don't have to worry about who to present my prayers to when I pray. I can say God, Jesus, or Holy Spirit, and it doesn't matter which One I choose because they are all Him.

Here is a wonderful verse that sums up the way that the three pieces of God work in unison. *"May the grace of the Lord Jesus Christ, the love of God, and the fellowship of the Holy Spirit be with you all."* (2 Corinthians 13:14) Jesus came to show grace, God's purpose is to love, and the Holy Spirit brings fellowship.

So what does all of that have to do with the portion of the psalm at the beginning of this chapter?

25 *I lie in the dust;*
revive me by your word.
26 *I told you my plans, and you answered.*
Now teach me your decrees.
27 *Help me understand the meaning of your commandments,*
and I will meditate on your wonderful deeds.
28 *I weep with sorrow;*

encourage me by your word.
29 *Keep me from lying to myself;*
give me the privilege of knowing your instructions.
30 *I have chosen to be faithful;*
I have determined to live by your regulations.
31 *I cling to your laws.*
Lord, don't let me be put to shame!
32 *I will pursue your commands,*
for you expand my understanding.
(Psalm 119:25-32)

The psalmist was weeping, lying in the dust discouraged. I was right there with him. Maybe you are too. Maybe you feel like you can't fight any longer. Do your circumstances have you feeling hopeless? Do people see you and think everything is perfect, and the moment you get alone, you lose it? Maybe you're past that point and can't even hide it anymore. Sometimes the hurt is written all over our faces, and we couldn't hide it if we wanted to. Maybe life is not so bad right now, but somehow you feel empty. Regardless of the struggle, sometimes we just need to be revived.

The psalmist knew that even though he was lying in the dust, basking in sorrow, there was one place he could go. That one place was the word of God. He made a decision to be faithful and chose to cling to God's laws. He was determined to live by God's ways. If I were to put this portion of the psalm into my own words, it would sound something like this, *"Here I am Lord! A mess! I don't understand how to get out of this, but please keep me from lying to myself. I have told you what I want. I told you my plans, and you showed me the right direction. It's not the direction I would have chosen, but I want to be faithful to You. I need You to revive me by Your word. Encourage me! Don't let me be put to shame as I cling to your laws. Help me understand who You are. Help me want to want You the way that You desire. Please help me, Lord! I will continue to pursue You and trust that You will expand my understanding."*

We read today that Jesus is God. Jesus said that the greatest and most important commandment is to love the Lord our God with all our heart, soul, mind, and strength. We have to make that decision, as the psalmist did, to be faithful to His commands and be determined to live by them. In order to keep from lying to ourselves and drowning in our own misery, we must press forward and continue to learn about who Jesus is, who God is, and who the Holy Spirit is, so that we can love Him with all of our heart, all of our soul, all of our mind, and all of our strength. We can't love anyone that much without knowing and understanding them first. Our goal is to continue to pursue His commands, trusting that, somehow, He will revive us through His word and encourage us to keep fighting. *"Help us, Lord!"*

[33] Teach me your decrees, O Lord;
I will keep them to the end.
[34] Give me understanding and I will obey your instructions;
I will put them into practice with all my heart.
[35] Make me walk along the path of your commands,
for that is where my happiness is found.
[36] Give me an eagerness for your laws
rather than a love for money!
[37] Turn my eyes from worthless things,
and give me life through your word.
[38] Reassure me of your promise,
made to those who fear you.
[39] Help me abandon my shameful ways;
for your regulations are good.
[40] I long to obey your commandments!
Renew my life with your goodness.

Psalm 119:33–40

7

Make Me

The two words that jump out at me from the eight verses we just read are, *"Make me."* Why do you think the writer of this psalm would say to the Lord, *"Make me walk along the path of your commands."* Why would we say to anyone, "Please make me do this."? The answer is in the second half of the verse, *"for that is where my happiness is found."*

The writer knows that God's ways and paths are where his happiness is found, but sometimes the *"want to"* just isn't there. *"So the trouble is not with the law, for it is spiritual and good. The trouble is with me, for I am all too human, a slave to sin. I don't really understand myself, for I want to do what is right, but I don't do it. Instead, I do what I hate. But if I know that what I am doing is wrong, this shows that I agree that the law is good. So I am not the one doing wrong; it is sin living in me that does it. And I know that nothing good lives in me, that is, in my sinful nature. I want to do what is right, but I can't. I want to do what is good, but I don't. I don't want to do what is wrong, but I do it anyway. But if I do what I don't want to do, I am not really the one doing wrong; it is sin living in me that does it. I have discovered this principle of life—that when I want to do what is right, I inevitably do what is wrong. I love God's law with all my heart. But there is another power within me that is at war with my mind. This power makes me a slave to the sin that is still within me. Oh, what a miserable person I am! Who will free me from this life that is dominated by sin and death? Thank God! The answer is in Jesus Christ our Lord. So you see how it is: In my mind I really want to obey God's law, but because of my sinful nature I am a slave to sin."* (Romans 7:14-25)

Can you relate? I can't tell you how many times I did the opposite of what I knew I should do and ended up kicking myself for it later! That includes getting to know the Lord. That snooze button was my weakness. I found myself putting God off with the intention of getting to Him later. Later came and later went because sleep sounded so much better than reading my Bible. The days that I did set aside time for the Lord were much better days, and I knew that. Getting myself to practice it was another story. Even though I knew what was best, I still chose to ignore it.

If there are times when you flat out don't *want to* open your Bible and read, don't get upset with yourself and think you are a bad person for feeling that way. You are not alone. Those are times that we need to begin to ask the Lord for help. After all, we do have an enemy that absolutely hates it when we draw close to the Lord and walk in His ways. Satan doesn't want you to *"want to"* or to follow through with it because even *he* knows the benefits it will bring you.

It's no coincidence that I'm begging the Lord to *"make me"* write at this very moment as I stare at my son snuggled up on a comfy mattress at my feet. Oh, how nice it would be to just curl up in bed with him and take a good long nap! Sleep is tempting, but I know that this is what the Lord would have me do right now. I know that I will be happy if I just press on. I know He will fill my heart with joy if I walk in the path that He has laid before me this morning, *and* He will give me rest.

You see, sometimes we have to discipline ourselves to do what we know is right. It doesn't always come naturally, so when the *"want to"* isn't there, then we cry out, *"Make me!"*

I pulled out my first journal that I had started in 2013. That was about the time that I was reading Psalm 119. I turned to a page where I had written this, *"Lord, help me to want to spend the time with you that I need to spend with you. Help Lord!"* We need to be real with God and ask Him for help. He already knows everything about us, so just tell Him how you feel, and ask Him to help you. Our relationship with the Lord is a journey just like any other relationship is. If your relationship with Him right now is not as deep as you would like it to be, you might agree with the well-known saying, "I love Him, but I'm not *in love* with Him." If that is where you are, then just be patient. Ask for His desires and keep doing what you know is best.

You probably recognize these lyrics to an old song that say, *"I want you to want me. I need you to need me. I'd love you to love me. I'm beggin' you to beg me."* That just might be what God desires of you and I: *True Love*. He wants us to want Him. He needs us to need Him. He'd love for us to love Him. He's begging us to beg Him. Now that's a thought to ponder. I believe it's what we all long for, we just don't realize that complete satisfaction is truly found in Jesus Christ our Lord and Savior. So today, even if you don't understand how, can you say to Jesus, *"I want to want you. I need to need you. I'd love to love you with all my heart, all my soul, all my mind, and all my strength. I'm begging you to show me."* The more I continue to get to know Jesus, the more I *"want to"* continue to come back to Him.

The names of God have been a place of confusion for me, so I will share with you more ways the Lord helped clear that up for me. We read from the Bible that Jesus is God. If Jesus is God, then how can He be God's Son? I never questioned it before. I just believed it. I believed it because the Bible says so. I still believe it because I believe all Scripture is true and that God cannot lie. I discovered that when there are any places in the Bible that seem to contradict itself, then that means there is more to learn because His word is completely true. God knew that I had questions in my mind, and He desired to answer them for me, but He had to wait until I was ready to learn more about Him before I could understand. I still don't understand everything fully, but I am so grateful for the way the Lord has shown me things so that I can be comfortable with Him and closer to Him.

I used to worry about who I was supposed to pray to when I prayed. Should I say, *"Dear God, or Jesus, or Holy Spirit?"* Some people say *"Father."* Then He showed me that it didn't matter because He is all of the above. I *do* say, *"In Jesus Name"* at the end of my prayers, because Jesus is the reason why I can communicate and be best friends with God. Jesus also tells us in the Scriptures to pray in His name. He is our mediator.

Back to Jesus being the Son of God, I just shared with you the way that God showed me to see the Holy Spirit, Jesus, and God as One: by seeing each part as Spirit, Body, and Soul; three parts, but one being. So now we have Jesus is God's one and only Son. Hmmm. How are we going to grasp that?

"This is how Jesus the Messiah was born. His mother, Mary, was engaged to be married to Joseph. But before the marriage took place, while she was still a virgin, **she became pregnant through the power of the Holy Spirit.** *Joseph, to whom she was engaged, was a righteous man and did not want to disgrace her publicly, so he decided to break the engagement quietly.*

As he considered this, an angel of the Lord appeared to him in a dream. 'Joseph, son of David,' the angel said, 'do not be afraid to take Mary as your wife. **For the child within her was conceived by the Holy Spirit.** *And she will have a son, and you are to name him Jesus, for he will save his people from their sins.'*

All of this occurred to fulfill the Lord's message through his prophet:
'Look! The virgin will conceive a child!
She will give birth to a son,

and they will call him Immanuel,
which means "God is with us."'

When Joseph woke up, he did as the angel of the Lord commanded and took Mary as his wife. But he did not have sexual relations with her until her son was born. And Joseph named him Jesus." (Matthew 1:18-25, emphasis added)

Now let's read the passage in Luke. *"In the sixth month of Elizabeth's pregnancy, God sent the angel Gabriel to Nazareth, a village in Galilee, to a virgin named Mary. She was engaged to be married to a man named Joseph, a descendant of King David. Gabriel appeared to her and said, 'Greetings, favored woman! The Lord is with you!'*

Confused and disturbed, Mary tried to think what the angel could mean. 'Don't be afraid, Mary,' the angel told her, 'for you have found favor with God! You will conceive and give birth to a son, and you will name him Jesus. He will be very great and will be called the Son of the Most High. The Lord God will give him the throne of his ancestor David. And he will reign over Israel forever; his Kingdom will never end!'

Mary asked the angel, 'But how can this happen? I am a virgin.'

The angel replied, ***'The Holy Spirit will come upon you, and the power of the Most High will overshadow you. So the baby to be born will be holy, and he will be called the Son of God.*** *What's more, your relative Elizabeth has become pregnant in her old age! People used to say she was barren, but she has conceived a son and is now in her sixth month. For the word of God will never fail.'*

Mary responded, 'I am the Lord's servant. May everything you have said about me come true.' And then the angel left her." (Luke 1:26-38, emphasis added)

"Because God's children are human beings—made of flesh and blood—the Son also became flesh and blood. For only as a human being could he die, and only by dying could he break the power of the devil, who had the power of death." (Hebrews 2:14)

How does Hebrews 2:14 describe God's children? *Flesh and blood.* That would be you and me. What did Jesus become? *Flesh and blood.* When the angel came to Mary, a virgin, to tell her she would become pregnant, how did she become pregnant? *Through the power of the Holy Spirit.* Mary was fully human, and the Holy Spirit came upon her, the power of God overshadowed her, and she became pregnant. Who is the Father of the child in Mary's womb? *God.*

God made Adam out of the dust of the ground, and He made Eve from Adam's rib. Every child born from then on came from a woman's womb. The child in Mary's womb was the first and only child that had one parent fully human and one parent fully *God.* God had a baby. He named Him Jesus.

The way I am seeing it here, is that God put part of *Himself* inside of Mary's womb and intertwined *Himself* with human so that He could be born the same way that you and I were born. He put Himself completely in our shoes, and even became a baby. So that baby, being God, had to have a Father. Therefore, He was called "Son of God." He had to have a name, and that name was Jesus. Imagine God watching part of Himself be born as flesh and blood. I imagine it was somewhat like what we experience. In a sense, that's the way it works for us, too. A part of the man joins with a part of the woman, and a whole new life is created. It's like watching a part of you be born.

Yes, Jesus was fully God, but He was also in a fully human body which means He had to face everything that a human faces and endure all that a human body endures. You may be thinking, *"Duh!"* and that's okay. For the longest time, I just couldn't understand how Jesus was God, yet He was called the Son of God. Which one was He? God or God's Son? Well, He was both. He was God, but because He was born from a woman's womb, He was also flesh and blood; which is why He was called God's one and only *begotten* son. Every child that is born has a mother and a father. Jesus' Father was God. Fully human. Fully God. God is Boss! He can do anything. I don't have to understand it all. I just need to trust Him. After all, He had very good reasons for making Jesus His child.

"Only in this way could he set free all who have lived their lives as slaves to the fear of dying. We also know that the Son did not come to help angels; he came to help the descendants of Abraham. ***Therefore, it was necessary for him to be made in every respect like us, his brothers and sisters****, so that he could be our merciful and faithful High Priest before God. Then he could offer a sacrifice that would take away the sins of the people."* (Hebrews 2:15-17)

It is so amazing to discover all that God is to us! Jesus was made like us in every way. *We* are children of God, and *He* is the Son of God, so Jesus is our *Brother!* How many roles and names does God have?

"So now we can rejoice in our wonderful new relationship with God because our Lord Jesus Christ has made us ***friends of God****."* (Romans 5:11, emphasis added)

"Greater love hath no man than this, that a man lay down his life for ***his friends****."* (John 15:13 KJV, emphasis added)

"'No longer do I call you servants, for the servant does not know what his master is doing; but ***I have called you friends,*** *for all that I have heard from my Father I have made known to you.'"* (John 15:15 ESV, emphasis added)

"'But ***the Comforter,*** *which is the Holy Ghost, whom the Father will send in my name, he shall* ***teach you*** *all things, and bring all things to your remembrance, whatsoever I have said unto you.'"* (John 14:26 KJV, emphasis added)

"For a child is born to us, a son is given to us. The government will rest on his shoulders. And he will be called: ***Wonderful Counselor, Mighty God, Everlasting Father, Prince of Peace.****"* (Isaiah 9:6, emphasis added)

"So you have not received a spirit that makes you fearful slaves. Instead, you received God's Spirit when he ***adopted you as his own children.*** *Now we call him,* ***'Abba, Father.'"*** (Romans 8:15, emphasis added)

"The LORD is a ***warrior; Yahweh*** *is his name!"* (Exodus 15:3, emphasis added)

"That men may know that thou, whose name alone is ***JEHOVAH,*** *art the most high over all the earth."* (Psalm 83:18 KJV, emphasis added)

"For your ***Creator*** *will be your* ***husband;*** *the* ***Lord of Heaven's Armies*** *is his name! He is your* ***Redeemer,*** *the* ***Holy One*** *of Israel, the God of all the earth."* (Isaiah 54:5, emphasis added)

"'I, I am ***Yahweh,*** *and there is no other* ***Savior*** *but Me.'"* (Isaiah 43:11 HCSB, emphasis added)

Did you know that God has so many names and titles? And there are more! We can relate to that. Let's just use a mother as an example. She is called Mom by her children, and she will always be a mother. Her friends don't call her Mom. They call her by her name. Some friends have nicknames for her. Even though she is a mother, she can still be a wife, a sister, and a grandmother all at the same time. Some may say she is an encourager. She might be a teacher. She can have many names and several roles.

Most of my life I just called God, *"God."* One day it was brought to my attention that He has a name! There is nothing wrong with calling Him *God* because He is God, but I started thinking about how it would be if I was always called, *'Woman'* or *'Wife'*, or maybe even *'strong Woman'*, *'encouraging Woman'*, *'wonderful Wife'* or *'amazing Mom'*. Those are nice names, but I have a chosen name. When someone says *my name* or *my nickname* there's just something personal about it.

We are friends of God, and we can call Him by His name, *Jehovah.* Other names are *Yahweh* or *Yeshua* to name a few. I don't know if you are like me, but the first time I call someone by their name, it's a little bit awkward. The more I get to know them the more comfortable I get, and their name becomes written into the story of my life. I still call God, *'God'*, most of the time, but when I do call Him by His name, it makes the conversation so much more personal.

By looking at the many examples in the Scriptures we just read, we can see that God can fill our every need. If you are in need of a friend, you have One! Call Him Jesus, Jehovah, Yahweh. If you are in need of comfort, call on the Holy Spirit and He will be there. If you need a teacher, the Holy Spirit will fill you with wisdom and understanding. If you need counsel, He is a Wonderful Counselor. If you need some power and strength, He is God Almighty, a Warrior, Jehovah, the God of Angel Armies. Nothing can stand against Him. If you need a father, He is the Everlasting Father, the Perfect One, the One who chose you and loves you unconditionally. He never gives up on you. He calls you His own and wants you to be so close to Him that you feel comfortable calling Him Dad. Abba; Daddy. If you are looking for peace, He is the Prince of Peace who contains a peace that the world cannot give. If you need someone to understand you, He is your Maker. He knows every detail about you, and He cares. You are His masterpiece. He calls His people His bride, and says He is our husband; meaning that He desires to have a relationship with us like that of a godly marriage. Like a marriage that consists of a man and a woman working together with their whole hearts. With Him you can have a unique and special relationship that is worth fighting for and one that never comes to an end. If you are looking for a significant other, Jehovah has it covered! He's there with arms open wide, and He will never bring disappointment. He is Faithful and True. If you are lost, seeking forgiveness, in need of freedom and a fresh start, He is the Redeemer and the One and Only Savior. Yahweh is all we need. He covers all the bases. Wherever you are lacking, call on the One who can rescue you and fill your needs and desires.

Every single role that God plays for us requires a personal relationship. A true friend is one you can trust and one you enjoy being around. If Jehovah wants to be your friend, then He wants you to call Him and hang out with Him. He wants you to trust Him. He wants to make you laugh. He wants you to tell Him things that you wouldn't tell even those closest to you. He wants to be there in the middle of the night when you can't sleep because you're worried or scared or upset about something. He wants to be the shoulder you cry on, the One you lean on. Yahweh wants to go on adventures with you and be your True Friend.

When you need someone to comfort you, more than likely, you aren't going to go to someone you don't know very well. The Holy Spirit wants to be your Comforter. He wants to be the One that makes you feel safe, the One who warms your soul, and the One you run to whenever you need to be comforted. He wants you to know Him deeply.

A teacher or a counselor spends much time figuring out who you are and how you learn. They take the time to understand you well so that you can excel. Jesus is a Wonderful Counselor and Teacher. He is all knowing, and He wants to take you to new levels. Jesus wants to be the Healer of your heart and help you through the tough places. He wants to give you wisdom and understanding in the areas where you feel stuck. Jesus wants you to trust Him enough with your personal struggles. He loves you enough to be willing to teach you and guide you through the unknown. He wants you to take the time to make appointments with Him so that He can teach you new things and give you wise advice because He knows you best.

A soldier is someone who fights for what they love. Your God is a Mighty Warrior who loves you and fights for you daily. No matter what anyone else says, Jehovah says you are worth fighting for. He wants you to know your Protector and to know that you are safe in His hands. He wants you to know that He is Almighty God of Angel Armies and that He is on your side. He is the One who fights for you.

A good father loves, knows, protects, and comforts his children. God is your Father. He wants you to come to Him so He can spend time with you. He loves to hear your voice and see you smile. He is so proud of you and would do anything for you. He doesn't like to see you hurt. He wipes the tears from your eyes and holds you close to His heart. He wants the best for you. How can we go to our Father if we don't know Him? God is our Perfect Father. If we take the time to get to know Him, we will run to Him every time. We will stay close and follow His instructions when we see that He is the Good, Good Father.

A peacemaker looks out for those he loves. We all like to be around peacemakers. They are quiet and kind-hearted. Peacemakers aren't selfish. They are usually more concerned about others. Yahweh is your Prince of Peace. He wants to fill your heart with peace. He doesn't want confusion, stress, or disaster consuming your life. Yahweh wants you to know Him, and He wants to give you peace that passes all understanding.

Most of us aren't going to marry someone that we don't know. I know there are many different cultures, and marriage looks different in each one. If you can, allow yourself to think of marriage as a man and a woman who have spent much time getting to know each other. They become best friends. One day they decide that they want to make a commitment to spend the rest of their lives together as partners. The commitment means that they will forever help each other, look out for one another, and protect each other. They will share a love that no one else in the world could offer. That love keeps them close. The two will help each other make wise choices. They work together as one to make the best of life. One isn't better than the other. They are a team. Their goal is to learn together and teach others what they learn. They work through any circumstance they find themselves in like best friends would do. That's what they are, two best friends, but their hearts are tied together with love. They have something special. Something that can never be taken away from them. It belongs only to them. That is what God longs to have with you. A relationship like that of a best friend, but one that is tied together with a bond of love so strong that nothing can separate it. Nothing can come between you because you are so close together. He longs for an unconditional love relationship with you. He wants that commitment. He wants to hear, *"I do."* He wants to know you truly love Him. As we learn how much He truly loves us, we will surely delight in Him.

To top it all off, have you ever desired to have a hero? One who would come to your rescue, like you see in the movies, just in the nick of time to save your life when you find yourself in a situation with no escape. Just when it's all about to end, the hero comes on to the scene and turns everything around and suddenly...you're safe! You can take a deep breath and let out a sigh of relief as joy rushes over your entire body because you have just been given another chance. What seemed absolutely impossible seconds ago, is now reality. Your Creator, the one who wants to be your Friend, your Comforter, your Counselor, your Teacher, the Lover of your soul, your Partner in life, your Warrior who fights your battles, yes, He is a Hero. He is your personal Hero. He is your Redeemer. He is your Savior. Not only will He save you from the fiery pits of Hell and take you to paradise in Heaven, but He will save you daily right here, right now, on this earth. He wants to be your Hero now. He wants to rescue you from the trap you are in and from the chains you are bound to. He wants to rescue you from depression and anxiety. He wants to rescue you from every dead-end situation you find yourself in. He is a Hero, and He desires to be your personal Savior now and forever.

God has so many wonderful names. From here on out, I may refer to God using many of the different names of His. It may help you develop a deeper relationship with Him. It may even prompt you to ask the Lord if it's okay to call Him by that name. It may also cause you to wonder what the name means leading you to dig deeper.

I could write all day telling you about someone, whether it is about Jesus or someone else that I know. Until you spend time with them and find those things out for yourself, the things I say will only be kind words and knowledge about them to you.

If you think about life and the people you are close to, you will probably recognize that the ones you can trust the most are those who have been there for you when you were broken. They helped you get back to your feet. When you were empty, they gave you hope. When you were lonely, they gave you company. Earlier, I talked about when we don't have the *"want to"* then we say, *"Please make me."* So to sum up this chapter, let's read this section of the psalm again, keeping in mind that Jesus' greatest commands and instructions are to love Him with all of our hearts, souls, minds, and strength.

33 *Teach me your decrees, O Lord;*
I will keep them to the end.
34 *Give me understanding and I will obey your instructions;*
I will put them into practice with all my heart.
35 ***Make me*** *walk along the path of your commands,*
for that is where my happiness is found.
36 *Give me an eagerness for your laws*
rather than a love for money!
37 *Turn my eyes from worthless things,*
and give me life through your word.
38 *Reassure me of your promise,*
made to those who fear you.
39 *Help me abandon my shameful ways;*
for your regulations are good.
40 *I long to obey your commandments!*
Renew my life with your goodness.
(Psalm 119:33-40, emphasis added)

Teach us Lord. Give us understanding. Make us walk along your paths until you don't have to make us anymore. Give us an eagerness until that eagerness becomes natural. Turn our eyes to You. Reassure us of Your promises; one promise being that as we delight in You, you will give us our hearts' desires. Help us abandon our own shameful ways. Renew us as we get to know you. Make us, Lord, until we want to want You, until we need to need You, until we love to love You, until we beg to see You. Please, Lord, keep making us until we understand why we need you so desperately. Until then, we will continue to learn about who You are.

41 Lord, give me your unfailing love,
the salvation that you promised me.
42 Then I can answer those who taunt me,
for I trust in your word.
43 Do not snatch your word of truth from me,
for your regulations are my only hope.
44 I will keep on obeying your instructions
forever and ever.
45 I will walk in freedom,
for I have devoted myself to your
commandments.
46 I will speak to kings about your laws,
and I will not be ashamed.
47 How I delight in your commands!
How I love them!
48 I honor and love your commands.
I meditate on your decrees.

Psalm 119:41–48

8

I Do

Love causes us to do crazy things. Think of the new love relationship between a man and a woman. The man goes out of his way to make sure the woman is happy. The woman can't get him off of her mind. The two are constantly thinking of ways to be together. Conversations go on into the hours of the night, no matter how early they have to be at work the next morning. They give up sleep, money, time, and friends just to be together. They can't stand the thought of being apart. Sooner than later the consuming love the couple has for each other brings them to commit to one another for life, and they both say, *"I do."* The wild romance continues and they live happily ever after. They never have any issues or say anything negative about their lover. Isn't that the way it goes? Probably not. Usually a couple will find out things about their significant other that isn't as pleasing as they thought. Disagreements come around and the fire begins to dwindle.

Does True Love really exist? I mean unconditional, never ending, unfailing, perfect love. Actually, the Bible gives us a definition of true love: *"Love is patient and kind. Love is not jealous or boastful or proud or rude. It does not demand its own way. It is not irritable, and it keeps no record of being wronged. It does not rejoice about injustice but rejoices whenever the truth wins out. Love never gives up, never loses faith, is always hopeful, and endures through every circumstance."* (1 Corinthians 13:4-7)

Is there a man or a woman existing that is always patient, always kind, never jealous, never boastful, never proud or rude, never demands their own way, never irritable, never keeps a record of wrongs, never rejoices about injustice but rejoices when truth wins out, never gives up, never loses faith, always hopeful, and endures through *every* circumstance? I know this may be a little redundant, but I know I have been impatient, unkind, jealous, boastful, proud, rude, demanding, irritable, judgmental, approving of wrongdoing, mad when truth won, I've given up, I've lost faith, I've been hopeless, and I have not endured through every circumstance.

Please don't think that I am saying that you can forget about having a successful marriage. I am very happily married, and we have had our ups and downs. That is because we are two imperfect people. What I am saying is that if you are searching for perfect, unfailing love from another person or waiting for *"the one"* to come along and complete you, you will always be looking for more because we are all imperfect people incapable of completing another person. There is no perfect friendship, no perfect family, and no perfect relationship between two humans. When I say perfect, I mean absolutely flawless through human eyes. Does True Love exist: true as in perfect, pure, unconditional love? Yes, it does, but it will not be found in people or things. Please don't misunderstand what I am saying here. If you call your husband or wife "perfect" or your "true love", then praise the Lord and keep on saying it forever more! My point here isn't to condemn our spouses or our friends, but to look to the One who's love truly is perfect. That True Love is only found in God.

The most important relationship that we can have is one with Jehovah, God. I named some of the crazy things we do when we are in love; like stay up all night, ditch our best friends, spend every penny we have on dates, watch movies we would never go see before, or drive miles just to see each other. We do whatever it takes to experience love. How is this for crazy in love? God, Creator of all things, One who contains all power and authority, One who reigns in Heaven, One who speaks things into existence, He can have anything He desires. This God, whose name alone is Jehovah, can have any wish of His own granted at the blink of His own eye. He holds life and death in His own hands. He can *have* whatever He wants. He can *do* whatever He wants. Possibilities are endless, and *He* is head over heels in love with *YOU*! He is all knowing, which means before He even made *anything*, He knew how it would all turn out. He knew *you* and how *you* would turn out. He knew this world and how it would turn out. He even knew Satan and how he would turn out. Why in the world would He continue on with creation if He knew all of the junk that would come with it? *Because* He loves people, and He *longs* to have a personal relationship with each and every one of us. At any time, He could have wiped us all out and started over until He found a group of people that satisfied Him. But He has so much compassion for *all* people that He is willing to endure through every circumstance so that everyone can have a chance to experience His love.

He could have made us perfect. When He created us, He could have programmed us to do exactly what He wanted us to do, but that wouldn't have satisfied Him because it would have been forced, fake love. He wants someone to love Him because they *want to*, not because they *have to*. He loves us so much that He left absolute serenity and perfect peace in Heaven to be born into this imperfect world as a baby covered in flesh. He knew before we were even created that He would walk this earth and be hated and mocked by His own creation. He knew He would be running on the earth that He made to protect His life from His own people who would chase Him down to kill Him. He knew that He would be tempted by Satan himself. He knew that He would be so scared to the point of sweating drops of blood. He knew that He would be accused, chased, caught, spit upon and laughed at. He knew that He would beg for it to stop. He knew that He would have thorns shoved into His scalp, whips that would rip open His flesh, nails hammered into His hands and feet, and a sword driven into His side. He knew He would suffer in complete darkness and feel the weight of every single sin of each and every person that He Himself gives life to. All our sin, He would take upon Himself. He knew He would face that moment of complete separation from His Father in Heaven and have to walk through the pits of Hell and look Satan in the eye just to overcome death for us.

The craziest part of all of this is that He was *willing* to do it all. Who does that? Would you choose a gruesome death over perfect peace so that someone *might* love you? Would you willingly give up your power and authority so that you could feel the pain of every person and die a criminal's death even for the sake of those that hate you? Only love can drive a person or our Almighty God to do something as radical as that. There is no other way to explain those kinds of actions except for True Love. If you need proof that God is seeking to have a close, personal, intimate relationship with you, there is your proof. Even the crazy things that we do when we are *"in love"* are nothing compared to what He has done!

"Because God's children are human beings—made of flesh and blood—the Son also became flesh and blood. For only as a human being could he die, and only by dying could he break the power of the devil, who had the power of death. Only in this way could he set free all who have lived their lives as slaves to the fear of dying. We also know that the Son did not come to help angels; he came to help the descendants of Abraham. Therefore, it was necessary for him to be made in every respect like us, his brothers and sisters, so that he could be our merciful and faithful High Priest before God. Then he could offer a sacrifice that would take away the sins of the people. Since he himself has gone through suffering and testing, he is able to help us when we are being tested." (Hebrews 2:14-18)

God was made in *every* respect, that means every detail, like us. His name is Jesus. He suffered and was tested and tried *way* beyond what we can even fathom. He *willingly* put Himself through it all so that He could help us. The part that blows my mind about all of it is that He could have put a stop to it at any point.

Jesus said, *"'Do you think I cannot call on my Father, and he will at once put at my disposal more than twelve legions of angels? But how then would the Scriptures be fulfilled that say it must happen in this way?'"* (Matthew 26:53-54 NIV)

Wow! Now that is True Love! I don't know anyone else that would endure all that Jesus did just to have me. Even more so, to say that He did it all *knowing* that it would bring ultimate suffering and death to Himself, and He did it willingly!

When I was younger, I heard the stories about Jesus, the ways He was tempted, how He was treated harshly, the ways that He suffered and died, but I thought that it was easy for Him to go through what He went through because He was God! When you're God, things aren't too hard to handle, are they? I mean, He is the ultimate true Super Hero! That was easy for Him, right? The problem is, thinking of Jesus like that makes it difficult to relate to Him because it can cause one to feel as if Jesus doesn't truly understand a situation or comprehend the pain. We may separate ourselves from Jesus if we feel as if the comparison isn't fair. That kind of view of Jesus can hinder us from taking things to Him or make us feel like our struggle is not something worth bothering God for.

Later, I discovered that my understanding was wrong. *"While Jesus was here on earth, he offered prayers and pleadings, with a loud cry and tears, to the one who could rescue him from death. And God heard his prayers because of his deep reverence for God. Even though Jesus was God's Son, he learned obedience from the things he suffered."* (Hebrews 5:7-8) I pondered those verses and came to the conclusion that if someone is praying and pleading with loud cries and tears in their eyes, then what they are going through is not easy. I thought of the last time I was on my knees begging God to rescue me from the misery I was in. Anyone in that kind of position is struggling. To be moved to tears with loud cries for help, reveals that Jesus was in some pain. *"Since he himself has gone through suffering and testing, he is able to help us when we are being tested."* (Hebrews 2:18) The definition of suffering is the state of undergoing pain, distress, or hardship. To suffer means to experience or be subjected to something bad or unpleasant, to be affected by or subject to an illness or ailment, to become or appear worse in quality, to undergo martyrdom or execution, or to tolerate. Jesus suffered and there is nothing easy in the definition of suffering.

The fact that Jesus cried and tears streamed down His cheeks, tells me that what He went through was not simple. Jesus begging to be rescued, implies that there was something unpleasant about the current situation He was in. Also, the Scriptures say that *even though* He was God's Son, He had to *learn* obedience. The definition of learn is to gain or acquire knowledge of or skill in something by study, experience, or being taught. Hebrews 5:8 tells us that Jesus learned obedience by experience. It doesn't say that Jesus was automatically obedient because He was God's Son. It says *even though* He was God's Son, *He learned* obedience. How did He learn obedience? *Through suffering.*

I realize that I have recorded some passages of Scripture more than once, but it seems like each time I read them there is more depth, more understanding, more proof of His perfect love. *"Though he was God, he did not think of equality with God as something to cling to. Instead, he gave up his divine privileges; he took the humble position of a slave and was born as a human being. When he appeared in human form, he humbled himself in obedience to God and died a criminal's death on a cross."* (Philippians 2:6-8) Breathtaking. God Himself was put in flesh, and even *He* had to learn obedience. Or should I say, He *chose* to *have* to learn obedience.

While we are learning about the character and the love of God, we will also learn from Him. All throughout our Psalm 119 journey, the psalmist has been asking the Lord to teach him His ways. I pray that you, too, are asking Yahweh for understanding. We just read that Jesus *learned* obedience. One of the best ways that *we* can learn is to examine Jesus's life and see how *He* did it. After all, that is one of the reasons He learned it: so that He can help *us* when we are being tested.

Let's examine how Jesus learned obedience.

"Then Jesus, full of the Holy Spirit, returned from the Jordan River. He was led by the Spirit in the wilderness, where he was tempted by the devil for forty days. Jesus ate nothing all that time and became very hungry.

Then the devil said to him, 'If you are the Son of God, tell this stone to become a loaf of bread.'

But Jesus told him, 'No! The Scriptures say, "People do not live by bread alone."'

Then the devil took him up and revealed to him all the kingdoms of the world in a moment of time. 'I will give you the glory of these kingdoms and authority over them,' the devil said, 'because they are mine to give to anyone I please. I will give it all to you if you will worship me.'

Jesus replied, 'The Scriptures say, "You must worship the Lord your God and serve only him."'

Then the devil took him to Jerusalem, to the highest point of the Temple, and said, 'If you are the Son of God, jump off! For the Scriptures say, "He will order his angels to protect and guard you. And they will hold you up with their hands so you won't even hurt your foot on a stone."'

Jesus responded, 'The Scriptures also say, "You must not test the Lord your God."'

When the devil had finished tempting Jesus, he left him until the next opportunity came." (Luke 4:1-13)

The first few verses state that Jesus had just returned from the Jordan River full of the Holy Spirit then He was led *by the Spirit* into the wilderness where he was tempted by the devil. Did you catch that? *Who* led Him to the wilderness? The Holy Spirit led Him there! Why? Perhaps it was part of His learning obedience. Take note that God didn't do the tempting. That was all Satan, but God did lead Him there to take the test with the intention of training and strengthening Jesus's character.

For forty days Jesus had to put up with Satan's constant tempting. Forty days! When I have to deal with him for *one* day, I think it's the end of the world! Now remember, just because He was God, it doesn't mean it was easier for Him. He was made like us in every way. Therefore, He *felt* everything just like we do in *every* way.

The fact that He was full of the Holy Spirit might lead to the conclusion that He was extra strong. We might assume that the Holy Spirit would give Him mighty, supernatural, physical strength, but the Scriptures say He didn't eat for forty days, and He was hungry! Very hungry! Even though He was full of the Spirit, He still felt the weakness of His physical body.

The sly devil tempted Jesus where He was weak and dared Him to turn a stone into bread. How tempting that must have been! I know when I'm hungry, all I can think about is what I'm going to eat and how I'm going to get it. I get cranky, I can't think very well, I get weak if I wait too long, and so many times I've said, *"I'm starving. I could eat anything right now!"* How tempting it must have been to turn a stone into bread. That was a *big* deal for Jesus. No food for forty days. He was extremely hungry in a fully human body. He felt everything that we would feel without food for forty days. By the way, He wasn't the only one that fasted that long. The Bible tells us that Moses (Exodus 34:28, Deuteronomy 9:18) and Elijah (1 Kings 19:8) did as well. That proves further that it is possible for humans other than Jesus. I don't know that it would be possible without God, but with God it is possible. So here we have Jesus, who was very hungry; Jesus who can turn anything into food at any time, and Satan tempting Him to do so. Notice what Jesus did to resist the temptation. *"Then the devil said to him, 'If you are the Son of God, tell this stone to become a loaf of bread.' But Jesus told him, 'No! The Scriptures say, "People do not live by bread alone."'"* (Luke 4:3-4) Jesus used truth from the word of God to resist the devil. He fought him off with Scripture. Not only did He do it once, but every time Satan tempted Him with something that could have ended His suffering, He fought off the temptation with Scripture.

Jesus lived in a way that reveals God's design for us. Remember, we have a body, a soul, and a spirit. Jesus did too. Jesus was connected with God the Father through the power of the Holy Spirit. In the story of temptation, we read that Jesus was being led by the Spirit. By allowing the Holy Spirit to lead Him, Jesus was able to live out of the right mind, the right will, and the right emotions that He needed implanted in His soul so that He could physically act out and walk in God's ways. The pattern shown here is the spirit guiding the soul, which enables the body to act accordingly. God's design is for us to walk in the Spirit so that He can fill us with His mind, His will, His emotions, and His strength. Then our soul is aligned with God's. In doing so, we are physically able with our bodies to act out and go in the ways of God. God has a specific design for us, and that is for us to live from the inside out, Spirit- Soul- Body. When we live from the outside in, Body- Soul- Spirit, we set ourselves up for making unwise choices.

Just think if Jesus had lived from the outside in. If He chose to please His body first, He would have listened to Satan and turned the stone into bread to satisfy His hunger. He would have listened to Satan and worshiped Him so that He could instantly have all the kingdoms of the world to Himself instead of waiting for His death sentence to receive it. If Jesus chose to please His body first, He would have tested God and jumped off of the highest point of the Temple and let the angels catch Him just to show Satan that He could. But Jesus chose to live in the way that God designed for us to live, humbly from the inside out.

Here are some examples of what it looks like to live from the outside in.

"The serpent was the shrewdest of all the wild animals the Lord God had made. One day he asked the woman, 'Did God really say you must not eat the fruit from any of the trees in the garden?'

'Of course we may eat fruit from the trees in the garden,' the woman replied. 'It's only the fruit from the tree in the middle of the garden that we are not allowed to eat. God said, "You must not eat it or even touch it; if you do, you will die."'" (Genesis 3:1-3)

Satan started off with a question just like he did with Jesus. Eve came back with truth, God's word, Scripture, just like Jesus did. So far, so good, Eve!

The devil wasn't finished with Eve just like we saw in the temptation of Jesus; *"When the devil had finished tempting Jesus, he left him* ***until the next opportunity came.****"* (Luke 4:13, emphasis added) As long as we are living on this earth, Satan isn't finished. He is always looking and waiting for that next opportunity.

Satan continued, *"'You won't die!' the serpent replied to the woman. 'God knows that your eyes will be opened as soon as you eat it, and you will be like God, knowing both good and evil.'"* (Genesis 3:4-5)

The devil tried again. This time he told Eve half truth, half lie. She may not have died immediately, but eventually she would. To be like God sounded great to Eve, but what she didn't know, was that to "*know evil*" was not a good thing. *"The woman was convinced. She saw that the tree was beautiful and its fruit looked delicious, and she wanted the wisdom it would give her. So she took some of the fruit and ate it. Then she gave some to her husband, who was with her, and he ate it, too."* (Genesis 3:6)

Satan dangled that fruit in front of her eyes until her mouth began to water. He kept drawing Eve's eyes to something that was pleasing to her body. He continued to point out the one thing that she was told she couldn't have. She wanted to taste the fruit and the wisdom it would give her so badly that her physical body persuaded her mind. She thought about the fruit until she convinced herself that it would be okay to taste it. She reached out and touched it and saw that it looked good and felt good in her hands. At that point, her body was controlling her will. Then she had her *own* will. Her body controlled her emotions and she longed to have what she knew wasn't right, but the emotions within her were strong. The fact that Eve allowed her body to be in control, caused her to act on what was not right. Adam, too, followed Eve's lead, living from the outside in. *"At that moment their eyes were opened, and they suddenly felt shame at their nakedness. So they sewed fig leaves together to cover themselves."* (Genesis 3:7) Shame and guilt came over their beings because they allowed their bodies to take control. *"When the cool evening breezes were blowing, the man and his wife heard the Lord God walking about in the garden. So they hid from the Lord God among the trees."* (Genesis 3:8)

Can you see Satan's trick? He had a plan, and it was to get their eyes physically focused on things of this world, leading them to act on ungodly motives, separating their spirit from God, causing them to want to hide from His presence. Satan's strategy is to get us to live to please our body first so that our souls; our mind, will, and emotions, will do what pleases our flesh. His ultimate intention is leading us to have a self-pleasing spirit that does not know how to connect with our Heavenly Father because of the demands of this world.

God's design is just the opposite. He created us in His image to connect with Him first so that our eyes are focused on Him and not the world. Then He will line up our thoughts, motives, and desires so that they are in sync with His, like He did with Jesus. By doing that, we have the ability to act out in ways that are pleasing to God, and ultimately, to us as well. That is how Jesus was able to resist temptation in times of evil and stay pure. *"In flesh was he revealed to sight,* ***kept righteous*** *by the Spirit's might..."* (1 Timothy 3:16 ISV, emphasis added)

I used to think, *"But that was Jesus. He was full of the Holy Spirit, and He was led by the Spirit. I don't know how to do that."* I desperately wanted to know how to live by God's design, but how could I have God's mind?

"Oh, how great are God's riches and wisdom and knowledge! How impossible it is for us to understand his decisions and his ways! For who can know the Lord's thoughts? Who knows enough to give him advice?" (Romans 11:33-34)

"That is what the Scriptures mean when they say, 'No eye has seen, no ear has heard, and no mind has imagined what God has prepared for those who love him.'" (1 Corinthians 2:9)

"'My thoughts are nothing like your thoughts,' says the Lord. 'And my ways are far beyond anything you could imagine. For just as the heavens are higher than the earth, so my ways are higher than your ways and my thoughts higher than your thoughts.'" (Isaiah 55:8-9)

After reading those Scriptures, it sounds like it's impossible for us to know the ways of the Lord, let alone hear His thoughts. If that's the case, how can we be led by Him?

"Don't you realize that your body is the temple of the Holy Spirit, who lives in you and was given to you by God?" (1 Corinthians 6:19)

Stop and let that sink in. If you are a child of God, your body is His temple. Your body is the place that the Spirit of God, the Holy Spirit, lives. You contain the same Spirit that Jesus contained. There isn't anything that you or I have done to earn it. God gave it to us. He gave part of Himself to you. To live in you.

We just read above that no eye has seen, no ear has heard, no mind has imagined what God has prepared for those who love him, and following that verse are these words: *"But it was to us that God revealed these things by his Spirit. For his Spirit searches out everything and shows us God's deep secrets. No one can know a person's thoughts except that person's own spirit, and no one can know God's thoughts except God's own Spirit. And we have received God's Spirit (not the world's spirit), so we can know the wonderful things God has freely given us.* (1 Corinthians 2:10-12)

His Spirit searches out everything and shows us God's deep secrets! Really? It's possible! No one can know God's thoughts except His own Spirit, and we have His Spirit so we can know His thoughts! Mind blowing, right?

"When we tell you these things, we do not use words that come from human wisdom. Instead, we speak words given to us by the Spirit, using the Spirit's words to explain spiritual truths." (1 Corinthians 2:13)

Wow! The Spirit gives us words to speak!

"But people who aren't spiritual can't receive these truths from God's Spirit. It all sounds foolish to them and they can't understand it, for only those who are spiritual can understand what the Spirit means. Those who are spiritual can evaluate all things, but they themselves cannot be evaluated by others. For, 'Who can know the Lord's thoughts? Who knows enough to teach him?' ***But WE understand these things, for WE have the MIND of CHRIST.****"* (1 Corinthians 2:14-16, emphasis added)

Wait a minute. Did it say that we have the mind of Christ? Yes, it did! That's a lot to take in! I love verse 15. *"Those who are spiritual can evaluate all things, but they themselves cannot be evaluated by others."* Because we have the mind of Christ, all things can be examined and checked out, and we cannot be evaluated by others. Others can't judge us! Those who don't have the mind of Christ will never get to understand what a person with the mind of Christ sees and knows. This is such an amazing truth! It's like we get to be a part of a whole new world!

We have been freely given the power of the Holy Spirit. We have the same power that raised Jesus's dead body from the grave living inside of us, and that same power gives us the ability to have the mind of Christ! That is so huge, and I don't even know what to do with it! Teach me Lord!

Jesus Himself said that He didn't speak or do anything on His own but only what He saw and heard His Father doing. The Holy Spirit is what kept Jesus in line with the will of God instead of His own human will. We can look at another example of Jesus when He was struggling and see clearly that He was led by the Spirit. Let's read what Luke recorded, then we will read what Matthew recorded about the same account.

"Then, accompanied by the disciples, Jesus left the upstairs room and went as usual to the Mount of Olives. There he told them, 'Pray that you will not give in to temptation.'

He walked away, about a stone's throw, and knelt down and prayed, 'Father, if you are willing, please take this cup of suffering away from me. Yet I want your will to be done, not mine.' Then an angel from heaven appeared and strengthened him. He prayed more fervently, and he was in such agony of spirit that his sweat fell to the ground like great drops of blood." (Luke 22:39-44)

"Then Jesus went with them to the olive grove called Gethsemane, and he said, 'Sit here while I go over there to pray.' He took Peter and Zebedee's two sons, James and John, and he became anguished and distressed. He

told them, 'My soul is crushed with grief to the point of death. Stay here and keep watch with me.'

He went on a little farther and bowed with his face to the ground, praying, 'My Father! If it is possible, let this cup of suffering be taken away from me. Yet I want your will to be done, not mine.'

Then he returned to the disciples and found them asleep. He said to Peter, 'Couldn't you watch with me even one hour? Keep watch and pray, so that you will not give in to temptation. For the spirit is willing, but the body is weak!'

Then Jesus left them a second time and prayed, 'My Father! If this cup cannot be taken away unless I drink it, your will be done.' When he returned to them again, he found them sleeping, for they couldn't keep their eyes open.

So he went to pray a third time, saying the same things again." (Matthew 26:36-44)

In the garden of Gethsemane, Jesus was severely weak and dreading what was going to happen to Him. He knew He was about to be tortured and would suffer greatly, beyond what any of us can imagine. He knew every detail of what was coming for Him. He suffered severe anxiety in His physical mind to the point of sweating drops of blood. He, *though He was God*, chose to be fully human so that He could help us. Jesus, the Son of God, begged for another way. He pleaded with the Father to take the suffering away, but He was also willing to say that if it must be done, let it be done. He asked not only once, but three times according to the account of Matthew! When you hear people say, *"Jesus went through all the things that we have gone through,"* it is true. Even severe anxiety, pain, and rejection. He knows every pain, every fear, and every hurt. There is not one thing that Jesus does not understand. That is why He came to live in a human body.

Once again, Jesus displays an example of living by God's design: Living from the inside out- Spirit, Soul, Body. Jesus said His soul was crushed with grief to the point of death. When we are in a state of mind like that, it is so easy to give into temptation! That is why Jesus said to His disciples, *"'Keep watch and pray so that you do not give in to temptation. For the spirit is willing, but the body is weak!'"* (Matthew 26:41) Jesus was warning them not to live out of fleshly desires. He was telling them that they must stay alert and pray. Praying is how we align our spirits with God's Spirit. Jesus showed us that our spirit is willing to keep going, but our bodies are not. We must go to God so that He can give us new strength, His strength.

Jesus was honest, too! He did not pretend. He begged three times for the suffering to be taken away. That was His body begging, but then His Spirit said, I want Your will to be done, not mine. The account in Luke tells us that after He prayed, and angel came and strengthened Him. We must remember to live from the inside out. Spirit first. God's Spirit will lead the soul and strengthen the body. If we live the other way around, outside in, body first, we will crumble.

Jesus. He has experienced everything that a human can go through. He, of all people, understands us best. He was born from a woman's womb. There was a time when your Almighty God was held in the hands of an unmarried teenage girl, and He cried as every other baby does. Our God could not talk, He had His cloth diapers changed, He went through the teething stage, and He had to learn to walk. He grew up just as you and I have. He had to be obedient to His earthly parents, He had to work, and He went through struggles just like us.

Remember we read in Hebrews 10 that Jesus is our mediator. Because He has experienced it all, He can sit at the right hand of the Father and say, *"You know, Dad, that's really tough."* He has compassion for us. He feels what we feel. So many people take situations that are unexplainable and say, *"If God is so passionate and merciful then why has He allowed this to happen?"* Our compassionate and merciful God chose to be born a man so that He could live in this world that we live in and come face to face with its problems. He did it all knowing He was going to be mocked, hated and beat so severely that His face would be unrecognizable, hung as if He had done something wrong, and suffer to the very last drop of blood on the cross. Then He literally went through the real Hell, after going through Hell on earth, so that you and I could have everlasting life. *True Love.*

It was only by the power of the Holy Spirit and the close relationship that He had with His Father that got Him through it all. His words were, *"'Keep watch and pray so that you will not give into temptation. For the spirit is willing, but the body is weak!'"* (Matthew 26:41) We must live led by the Spirit first, then soul, then body. If we allow our body to lead, we will fall because the body is weak. You and I have access to the same Spirit and the same Father because of Jesus. Because of Him, we have eternal life. We have forever to look forward to.

It is those kinds of truths that draw me close to the Lord and allow me to love Him with more of my heart, soul, mind, and strength. This chapter is titled *I Do*. We have covered a lot, and what does it all have to do with saying, *"I do"*? Before you say, *"I do,"* don't you want to know what and who you are committing to? If you are looking for True Love, Jesus is the answer. He did all of that for you, and He made a way for you to know the secrets of God and to have the mind of Christ. He created you with a design. A design to always be connected with Him through His Spirit and your spirit being together as one so that you can live life boldly and abundantly. He designed you to be able to get through anything as long as you stay connected with Him. Just like when two people fall in love, when God reveals His unfailing love and captures your heart, your response to Him will be, *"I do."*

"Indeed, your husband is your Maker—His name is Yahweh of Hosts— and the Holy One of Israel is your Redeemer; He is called the God of all the earth." (Isaiah 54:5 HCSB) Have you ever thought of God as your husband? I know it may be strange to think about, especially for a man. The significance of it is the type of relationship that it is. We know that Jesus calls us His friends; *"'I no longer call you slaves, because a master doesn't confide in his slaves. Now you are my friends, since I have told you everything the Father told me.'"* (John 15:15) We call Him our Savior; *"Furthermore, we have seen with our own eyes and now testify that the Father sent his Son to be the Savior of the world."* (1 John 4:14) We call Him Father, Counselor, Mighty God, Prince of Peace; *"For a child will be born for us, a son will be given to us, and the government will be on His shoulders. He will be named Wonderful Counselor, Mighty God, Eternal Father, Prince of Peace."* (Isaiah 9:6) It's one thing to think of God as your Friend, or Teacher, or Father, but to think of Him as your spouse puts a whole new level of intimacy on it. Marriage is the most intimate of all human relationships, uniting a man and a woman in a "one-flesh" union. Marriage involves "leaving" one's family of origin and "being united" to one's spouse, which signifies the establishment of a new family unit distinct from the two originating families. Marriage is a relationship of free self-giving of one human being to another. The marriage partners are to be first and foremost concerned about the wellbeing of the other person and to be committed to each other in steadfast love and devotion. That involves the need of forgiveness and restoration of the relationship in the case of sin. Marriage is not only permanent, sacred, intimate, and mutual; it is also exclusive. That means that no other human relationship must interfere with the marriage commitment between husband and wife.

Spiritually speaking, if our Maker is our "Spouse", then we should seek to know God better than we know anyone else, and we should make our relationship with Him our priority. When you asked Him to come into your heart and be your Savior, you and He became one. As we understand the amount of love that He lavishes on us, then our natural response to Him will be, *"Yes. I do."*

When we experience His love, then we can do anything. The awareness of His Great Love allows us to live led by His Spirit. The more we know Him, the more we love Him, and the more we can hear His voice and follow Him. Living led by the Spirit doesn't have to be only for Jesus. It doesn't have to be for a few special people. It is a privilege given to all of us, and the way to get there is simply knowing Yahweh.

God's Love changes everything. Until we understand how much our Lord truly loves us, we won't be able to allow the words of the psalmist to be our own. My prayer is that you will see God in new and deeper ways. I hope that His love is growing on you, and you are falling for Him in ways you didn't know were possible. He is the One and Only True Love. If you believe it is true, speak these words to Him from your heart to His.

41 *Lord, give me* ***your unfailing love,***
the salvation that you promised me.
42 *Then* ***I can*** *answer those who taunt me,*
for ***I trust*** *in your word.*
43 *Do not snatch your word of truth from me,*
for your regulations are my only hope.
44 ***I will*** *keep on obeying your instructions*
forever and ever.
45 ***I will*** *walk in freedom,*
for ***I have devoted myself*** *to your commandments.*
46 ***I will speak*** *to kings about your laws,*
and ***I will not be ashamed.***
47 *How* ***I delight*** *in your commands!*
How ***I love*** *them!*
48 ***I honor and love*** *your commands.*
I meditate *on your decrees.*
(Psalm 119:41-48, emphasis added)

"I do."

49 Remember your promise to me;
it is my only hope.
50 Your promise revives me;
it comforts me in all my troubles.
51 The proud hold me in utter contempt,
but I do not turn away from your instructions.
52 I meditate on your age-old regulations;
O Lord, they comfort me.
53 I become furious with the wicked,
because they reject your instructions.
54 Your decrees have been the theme of my songs
wherever I have lived.
55 I reflect at night on who you are, O Lord;
therefore, I obey your instructions.
56 This is how I spend my life:
obeying your commandments.

Psalm 119:49–56

9

Your Promise to Me

We know now without a doubt that Jesus loves us. Not only because the song says "Yes, Jesus loves me, the Bible tells me so," but because of the ridiculous amount of patience, pain, and suffering that He willingly chose to endure to save us. He cares so deeply for us that He tasted death so that we could have eternal life with Him. He is so full of mercy and grace that He purchased our freedom with His blood. He totally sacrificed His life because He longs for you to be drawn to Him. He wants you to know how much He truly loves you.

His loves never fails and never gives up, but does that mean that this life we live here on earth is problem free? No, but True Love is what gets us through the struggles.

Just before Jesus was tortured and killed, He was talking with His disciples, *His friends*, and preparing them for what was about to happen. *"Jesus asked, 'Do you now believe? But the time is coming—indeed it's here now—when you will be scattered, each one going his own way, leaving me alone. Yet I am not alone because the Father is with me. I have told you all this so that you may have peace in me. Here on earth you will have many trials and sorrows. But take heart, because I have overcome the world.'"* (John 16:31-33)

Jesus is asking, *"Do you really believe Me? If everyone around you scatters and leaves you, do you really believe that you aren't alone? Do you know that I am with you? Do you have peace in Me? In this world you won't have peace, but I can give you peace because I have overcome the world and all it contains. Do you really believe that I want peace for you? Do you believe Me?"*

If He has already overcome the world, then why are bad things still happening? Let's go back to the beginning. When God created us and the angels, He gave us all free will. Why? Because He wants each of us to be able to choose what we want. He didn't create angels and people to be programmed to do only what He wishes. Instead, He created us in His image with the ability to know all about Him and with the capacity to love Him with all our heart, soul, and mind. He created us so that He could love us unconditionally with a desire that we would love Him too. He gave us free will because He wants our love for Him to be real. He never forces us to do what He wants.

Let's take a look at the creation of Lucifer, who is most often called Satan.

"'You were the model of perfection,
full of wisdom and exquisite in beauty.
You were in Eden,
the garden of God.
Your clothing was adorned with every precious stone—
red carnelian, pale-green peridot, white moonstone,
blue-green beryl, onyx, green jasper,
blue lapis lazuli, turquoise, and emerald—
all beautifully crafted for you and set in the finest gold.
They were given to you
on the day you were created.
I ordained and anointed you
as the mighty angelic guardian.
You had access to the holy mountain of God
and walked among the stones of fire.
You were blameless in all you did
from the day you were created
until the day evil was found in you.
Your rich commerce led you to violence,
and you sinned.
So I banished you in disgrace
from the mountain of God.
I expelled you, O mighty guardian,
from your place among the stones of fire.
Your heart was filled with pride
because of all your beauty.
Your wisdom was corrupted
by your love of splendor.

So I threw you to the ground
and exposed you to the curious gaze of kings.
You defiled your sanctuaries
with your many sins and your dishonest trade.
So I brought fire out from within you,
and it consumed you.
I reduced you to ashes on the ground
in the sight of all who were watching.
All who knew you are appalled at your fate.
You have come to a terrible end,
and you will exist no more.'"
(Ezekiel 28:12b-19)

"How you are fallen from heaven,
O Lucifer, son of the morning!
How you are cut down to the ground,
You who weakened the nations!
For you have said in your heart:
'I will ascend into heaven,
I will exalt my throne above the stars of God;
I will also sit on the mount of the congregation
On the farthest sides of the north;
I will ascend above the heights of the clouds,
I will be like the Most High.'"
(Isaiah 14:12-14)

Satan was beautiful! He was put in charge as a mighty angelic guardian, full of wisdom, modeling perfection. Can you believe it? It sounds like he had it made, but Satan allowed his beauty and wisdom to give him a big head, and he began to think highly of himself.

Satan was the first to sin. He was the first to look away from God and try to do things his own way. He became full of pride and jealousy and wanted what God had. He decided that he wanted to be better than God. He wanted a higher rank, all the praise for himself, power, and control.

Have you ever wondered why God didn't just get rid of Satan? Wouldn't that have taken care of everything? If God would have just erased Satan's life from the heavens and earth, He would have interfered with free will and His love for all He created. If God just ended the life that He created because of disobedience, then, in a sense, we are being controlled. *"If you don't do this, your life is over."* That isn't the nature or the desire of God's heart.

I wonder, if Lucifer hadn't been the first to turn away from God and sin, would there have been someone else who would have? Satan wasn't the only one that was cast out of heaven. He had followers. *"This great dragon—the ancient serpent called the devil, or Satan, the one deceiving the whole world—was thrown down to the earth with all his angels."* (Revelation 12:9) We might not know the answer to that thought as long as we are here on earth, but my point is that if God just zapped a person every time they chose to do something against His will, then the only people that would be left would be the ones who were staying with God out of fear of their life ending. Obligation and fear would rule our existence. There may be a few who would stay because they genuinely loved Him, but my assumption is that if God were that way, when people began to see the lack of mercy in Him, their actions may have stayed right, but their hearts would have fallen away from His. Then God would have had a group of people who loved Him because rules told them they had to. Their actions and their mouths would have professed that they loved Him, but their hearts would have been far from Him. It would have ended in fake, forced love. That is not the heart of God.

"And so the Lord says, 'These people say they are mine. They honor me with their lips, but their hearts are far from me. And their worship of me is nothing but man-made rules learned by rote.'" (Isaiah 29:13) We can learn from this Scripture that fake, forced love is not God's desire, yet, it still happens.

God chose to create all things, Satan being part of that creation, and then He granted us the freedom to do what we want, with high hopes that we would choose to follow and obey Him because He knows and has what is best for us. For God to simply remove Satan's existence, would be the same as interfering with free will.

God does put a limit on evil, and there are consequences for evil actions as we read in the Scriptures about Lucifer. He banished Satan and threw him out of Heaven. Now Satan is paying for his actions. The sad part is, because I know that God is Love and He is full of mercy and grace, Satan could turn from his wicked ways and repent and return his heart to the Lord, but he won't do it, and God knows that.

Nothing goes unseen, and it doesn't mean that God doesn't care. The truth is that He cares so much that He allows us the freedom to do and choose what we want even though it may hurt Him or His children, but He promises that He will work everything out for our good. *"And we know that God causes everything to work together for the good of those who love God and are called according to his purpose for them."* (Romans 8:28)

Jehovah isn't a God that says, *"If you don't do what I say then you will be punished. You better listen to me or else..."* That isn't Love's tone. God's tone sounds more like, *"If you will listen to My words, you will have peace. But this world isn't going to be an easy place to live because many have chosen their own way. When people choose to reject me then they do things that hurt My children. I won't force them to come to know Me, but they will have consequences for their actions in hopes that they will long for Me. That is up to them, and it's up to you."*

We may have a hard time grasping the rules of free will when tough things happen like little children being abused and sometimes even murdered. We must understand that it was man that chose to do that to the little child, not God. God didn't stop it from happening, but we have to remember that every person has free will and God doesn't force people to do what pleases Him. God will judge the one who performed the evil acts and he or she will have consequences to pay. The judgement is up to God, and we can trust that He will take care of it. That person will also have the option to turn from their wicked ways and choose to follow the ways of God. If they choose not to turn away from evil, they will forever have consequences to pay because of the harm and the hurt they cause others. It breaks God's heart to see His people hurting His people. He wants so badly for everyone to have the opportunity to have everlasting life and peace with Him and His children. If He takes the life away from every person that commits an evil act, then He would also be taking away that person's opportunity to change their ways and come to Him and receive everlasting life. God represents a crazy amount of grace that we will never fully understand.

"The Lord isn't really being slow about his promise, as some people think. No, he is being patient for your sake. He does not want anyone to be destroyed, but wants everyone to repent." (2 Peter 3:9)

We have to trust, also, that He will bring something good out of the bad for those who are hurt. If a child's life was taken, then the good would be that they are now with Jesus in a safe and wonderful place, free from sorrow and pain, living everlasting life. If the child is still here on this earth, we can trust that God will use what Satan intended for harm, for good somehow. We don't have to understand how, but we can know that He will because it is one of His promises to those who love Him. He hates it when violence and perversion take hold, but He knows how to turn things around and take something that is broken and make it whole. He turns ashes into beauty.

What happened to Jesus was horrible and heartbreaking, but the good that came out of it is that we can now know God better because of what He did through Jesus. Jesus was raised from the dead and able to be with His Father again, and we have been cleansed from our sins and have access to everlasting life. He overcame the world and the mess that it brings to free us from sin and death. God allowed the gruesome death to happen and because of that one death, many lives are saved.

The example of the life of Jesus shows us how God takes bad things and uses them for the good of those that love Him. Jesus ultimately got His life back in Heaven, and anyone who chooses to believe and accept Jesus as their Savior will also live forever. Only God can take a violent, gruesome, heart wrenching death like the one of His Son, Jesus, and turn it around in such a perfect way that we can even have the heart to say, *"His death was a good thing."* Only God.

If we don't believe that God is Good, then we will never experience His true peace. It is His True Love that gets us through the tough places. I can be stuck in a bad situation, and everything around me seems to be crashing in. I may be scared, worried, hurt, confused, exhausted, and hopeless, but, even in the midst of it all, if someone reaches out to me to show compassion or support, it's as if that little taste of love gives me the strength to keep moving on. We can't always count on someone to be there to love us, but one thing we can count on is the love of Jesus.

The psalmist says to God, *"Remember your promise to me. It is my only hope. Your promise revives me. It comforts me in all of my troubles."* (vs. 49, 50) When life gets tough, we must hold on to the things that God has promised us. His word is full of them. At the beginning of this book we read Scriptures that say God cannot lie, and all Scripture is inspired by God. *"And because of his glory and excellence, he has given us great and precious promises. These are the promises that enable you to share his divine nature and escape the world's corruption caused by human desires."* (2 Peter 1:4) Notice where the world's corruption comes from according to 2 Peter 1:4: *human desires*. It is not God's doing. God's promises enable us to *escape* the corruption of the world! How? By enabling us to share His divine nature; meaning that the things of God become yours as you rest in His promises. When His promises become real to you, then you can escape the chaos caused by sin and people and the things of this world.

One of the greatest promises of God is the promise of the Holy Spirit. I have thought at times that it would have been easier to live during the time that Jesus physically lived and walked on this earth, but Jesus said to the people that were with Him, *"'But I tell you the truth, it is to your advantage that I go away; for if I do not go away, the Helper will not come to you; but if I go, I will send Him to you.'"* (John 16:7 NASB) *"'But the Helper, the Holy Spirit, whom the Father will send in My name, He will teach you all things, and bring to your remembrance all that I said to you.'"* (John 14:26 NASB) Jesus said that it was better for Him to go so He could send us the Helper. If the Helper, which is the Holy Spirit, is going to teach us all things, then that means there has to be some level of communication going on between us and the Holy Spirit or we wouldn't be able to learn from Him.

Jesus says, *"'There is so much more I want to tell you, but you can't bear it now. When the Spirit of truth comes, he will guide you into all truth. He will not speak on his own but will tell you what he has heard. He will tell you about the future. He will bring me glory by telling you whatever he receives from me. All that belongs to the Father is mine; this is why I said, "The Spirit will tell you whatever he receives from me."'"* (John 16:12-15)

The promise of the Holy Spirit is amazing because Jesus speaks to us through the Holy Spirit. Did you know that you can hear God's voice? Receiving this truth, believing that God speaks to you, just might be the most life changing truth that you will ever receive. You might be thinking the promise isn't for everyone. Maybe you believe that the promise of the Holy Spirit was only for Jesus's disciples that were living with Him at that time: the ones He was literally talking to. How do we know that the promise is for us and not only for them? If we go to John chapter 17, we will find a prayer that Jesus prayed. For one thing, it's absolutely mind-blowing that Jesus was about to be killed violently, yet He was taking the time to pray for others. Secondly, read who He was praying for: *"'I am praying not only for these disciples but also for all who will ever believe in me through their message. I pray that they will all be one, just as you and I are one--as you are in me, Father, and I am in you. And may they be in us so that the world will believe you sent me.'"* (John 17:20-21) That's you and me and anyone who believes in Him!

After Jesus's death, He was raised from the grave, praise God, and He revealed Himself to many on the earth before He ascended back to Heaven. *"During the forty days after he suffered and died, he appeared to the apostles from time to time, and he proved to them in many ways that he was actually alive. And he talked to them about the Kingdom of God.*

Once when he was eating with them, he commanded them, 'Do not leave Jerusalem until the Father sends you the gift he promised, as I told you before. John baptized with water, but in just a few days you will be baptized with the Holy Spirit.'" (Acts 1:3-5)

God told the prophet, Joel, a *long* time ago, *"'In the last days,' God says, 'I will pour out my Spirit upon all people. Your sons and daughters will prophesy. Your young men will see visions, and your old men will dream dreams. In those days I will pour out my Spirit even on my servants—men and women alike—and they will prophesy.'"* (Acts 2:17-18)

If you are a man reading this book, then you are someone's son. If you are a woman, then you are someone's daughter. God clearly states that He will pour out His Spirit on *all* people. Not only that, but because of it, all people can prophesy. If God says that we can *all* prophesy, then what must take place before we can prophesy?

Definition of prophesy- to predict something or to utter something inspired by God. If we have the ability to prophesy, then we can hear God. In fact, we *must* hear God before we can prophesy.

When the Holy Spirit had been poured out for all to witness, Peter spoke of the promise. *"God raised Jesus from the dead, and we are all witnesses of this. Now he is exalted to the place of highest honor in heaven, at God's right hand. And the Father, as he had promised, gave him the Holy Spirit to pour out upon us, just as you see and hear today."* (Acts 2:32-33)

"This promise is to you, to your children, and to those far away—all who have been called by the Lord our God." (Acts 2:39)

The promise of the Holy Spirit is for *all* who have been called. That includes you. If you believe in Jesus, the Holy Spirit has been given to you by Him as a gift. If you choose to unwrap the gift and receive it as yours, then you have received the gift and the promise of God's voice. You can hear His voice*!*

A wonderful example of Jesus speaking through the Holy Spirit is recorded in Revelation. The title of the book almost explains it itself. Revelation means a surprising and previously unknown fact, especially one that is made known in a dramatic way: the making known of something that was previously secret or unknown.

John, the apostle, wrote the book of Revelation. He was exiled to an island for preaching the word of God and for sharing his testimony about Jesus. One day he was worshiping in the Spirit, and behind him he heard a loud voice that said, *"Write in a book everything that you see."* John saw God in a vision, and that is how we have the book of Revelation. John said, *"When I saw him, I fell at his feet as if I were dead. But he laid his right hand on me and said, 'Don't be afraid! I am the First and the Last. I am the living one. I died, but look—I am alive forever and ever! And I hold the keys of death and the grave.'" (*Revelation 1:17-18)

We just read the words of Jesus, the red letters in the Bible, yet He was no longer physically living on the earth. He spoke to John through the Spirit. What God said to John, through the Holy Spirit, was worthy enough and so real that it made it in the Bible in red letters!

Jesus often said to those who were living with Him during His life here on earth, *"Anyone with ears to hear should listen and understand."* (Mark 4:9) He was talking about His physical voice. He said anyone who hears Me should listen and understand.

Jesus made it clear that He would continue to speak to us even after He ascended back to Heaven, and He would do so by sending us the Holy Spirit to teach us and tell us what He says. He tells us the same thing He told those who were physically living with Him on the earth, except the statement changed just a little. This is what He says to us today, *"Anyone with ears to hear must listen to the Spirit and understand what he is saying to the churches."* (Revelation 2:7a emphasis added) Jesus promised us the Holy Spirit, and He speaks to us through the Spirit.

Hearing Jesus's voice is what makes all the other promises of God come alive. We can read about His promises all day long and try to force ourselves to truly believe that they are true, but when we *hear Jesus* tell us the promise, it changes everything! His voice heals our broken hearts. Think about it. Which means more? Reading in a book that God loves you, or hearing the voice of Jesus saying personally to you that He loves you? There's no doubt that the personal word is going to touch your heart in a way that only reading it can't.

Combine the voice of God with the promises of God, and we will have a good foundation to stand on. At different times in my life, I have held on to different promises. Do you know what Jehovah's promises are? What are you holding on to? If you don't have a promise to hold on to, I encourage you to find one. Here are just a few of them that we can read together. If something here grabs your heart, hold on to it and take it straight to Jesus and ask Him to speak it to your heart with His voice. You can ask with confidence because Jesus wants to speak. He is the one who said He would guide you into all truth and speak to you. Don't be afraid to ask and ask boldly. Jesus wants to talk to you!

"'But all who listen to me will live in peace, untroubled by fear of harm.'" (Proverbs 1:33) Are you living in fear of danger today? God's word says listen to Him, hear Him, and you will live in peace.

"'I am leaving you with a gift—peace of mind and heart. And the peace I give is a gift the world cannot give. So don't be troubled or afraid.'" (John 14:27) Do you have a troubled heart and mind? Jesus has a gift for you-peace. It's a gift you will not find in the world. It can't be earned. It's freely and gladly given.

"'For I know the plans I have for you,' says the Lord. 'They are plans for good and not for disaster, to give you a future and a hope.'" (Jeremiah 29:11) Are you afraid of what your future holds? The Lord says He has good plans in store for you. His ways are inconceivable.

"Then Jesus said, 'Come to me, all you who are weary and burdened, and I will give you rest. Take my yoke upon you and learn from me, for I am gentle and humble in heart, and you will find rest for your souls.'" (Matthew 11:28-29) Are you weary and broken? Jesus says come to Him. There's no reason

to hesitate to go to Jesus because He is gentle and humble. If you go to Him, He will give you rest.

"He gives power to the weak and strength to the powerless. Even youths will become weak and tired, and young men will fall in exhaustion. But those who trust in the Lord will find new strength. They will soar high on wings like eagles. They will run and not grow weary. They will walk and not faint." (Isaiah 40:29-31) Do you feel weak? Do you feel powerless? Are you exhausted? There is hope. God's word says trust in the Lord, and you will find new strength. If you ask Jesus how He sees you, you may be surprised what the answer will be.

"If you confess with your mouth that Jesus is Lord and believe in your heart that God raised him from the dead, you will be saved." (Romans 10:9 ESV) Are you lost? Are you afraid you won't make it to Heaven? Are you confused about how your soul can be saved because one person says this and the other says that? God's word is all truth. He says if you say with your mouth that Jesus is Lord, and in your heart you know and believe that Jesus was raised from the dead, you are saved. Simple. It's an act of faith. Faith is all it takes. Jesus did the hard part. All you have to do is accept it.

"Cast all your anxiety on him because he cares for you." (1Peter 5:7 NIV) Are you feeling worried and like nobody cares? Jesus cares for you, and He wants to take the weight off of your shoulders and carry it for you.

"Do not be afraid or discouraged, for the LORD will personally go ahead of you. He will be with you; he will neither fail you nor abandon you." (Deuteronomy 31:8) Feeling alone? Scared? Hopeless? You have a God who is always with you. He never fails you or leaves you alone. He is not far from you. In fact, He *personally*, meaning specifically for ***you***, goes before you. There is no place you will go that Jesus has not already been. He is always with you to guide you through every step. You're never alone. Would you be willing to ask Jesus to reveal Himself to you in a way that is personal and real; in a way that shows you that you aren't alone?

"The LORD is close to the brokenhearted and saves those who are crushed in spirit." (Psalm 34:18 NIV) Are you crushed and brokenhearted? The Lord is very close to you and is ready to save you. Will you ask Him how much He loves you?

"He heals the brokenhearted and binds up their wounds." (Psalm 147:3 ESV) Is your heart wounded and feeling beyond repairable? Jesus heals. That's what He is best at: healing your heart, binding it up, making it new again.

"And God shall wipe away all tears from their eyes; and there shall be no more death, neither sorrow, nor crying, neither shall there be any more pain: for the former things are passed away." (Revelation 21:4 KJV) Are you tired

of this world and the pain that it causes? There's good news. This world won't last forever. There is a new beginning, one that will never end. It is a perfect place, and, if you belong to Jesus, you will inherit paradise!

"My soul, praise the Lord, and do not forget all His benefits. He forgives all your sin; He heals all your diseases. He redeems your life from the Pit; He crowns you with faithful love and compassion." (Psalm 103:2-4 HCSB) Feeling shame? Jesus forgives. Feeling sick? Jesus heals. Feeling unworthy? Jesus redeems. Feeling rejected? Jesus loves faithfully and pours out compassion. His benefits to you are great.

"'My grace is all you need. My power works best in weakness.'" (2 Corinthians 12:9) You don't have to be strong for Jesus. You don't have to have it all figured out. All the strength you need is found in the grace of Jesus. His great love is what fuels our souls. His grace is all you need. If you feel like you have nothing and your life is going nowhere, you are in a great place because there is only one thing you need, and it is Jesus. There are no requirements you need in order to have Him. You don't have to go anywhere to find Him, and you don't need any money to buy Him. He is all yours right now. Let your heart and mind be fixed on Him and you will see that He is all you need.

"And this same God who takes care of me will supply all your needs from his glorious riches, which have been given to us in Christ Jesus." (Philippians 4:19) Everything that God has, He has given to you. There is nothing you will lack when you give your heart to Him.

"'My child, pay attention to what I say. Listen carefully to my words. Don't lose sight of them. Let them penetrate deep into your heart, for they bring life to those who find them, and healing to their whole body.'" (Proverbs 4:20-22) His words bring life and healing to your whole body! This promise makes me want to know more about Him and hear His voice.

Find a promise that you really need right now. Circle one of the promises above or write down your own and claim it. Let it penetrate deep into your heart. It may not seem like it's a promise you can receive. You may feel like it's one that will never be true for you, but find what you need and claim it anyway, whether it feels true or not. Then spend time actually talking to Jesus about it. Be honest with Him. Say, *"Jesus, this is your promise to me, but it doesn't feel true. What am I missing? Where are you, and how do you see me?"* Talk to Him. Even if you feel like a crazy person talking to an imaginary friend, do it! It is totally worth it!

When life gets you down, His promise will comfort you, revive you, and give you hope. Isn't it amazing that He doesn't require us to be perfect before we can claim His promises? He isn't waiting for you to get everything correct before He loves you. In fact, He showed us His greatest act of love before we were even born. He went ahead and took care of our mess before we even made it. He has always been there holding out His arms saying, *"Come to me. I love you. Always."*

We often have it backwards. We think when we can become a better person, then we will be able to be closer to God. Many of us have bad habits that we need to get rid of, and because we haven't given them up, we feel unworthy of His acceptance. If that were how it really worked, then God's love would be conditional. Truth is, His love is Unconditional. It is Unfailing Love. Believe it or not, He loves you no matter what. That is why He died for you. Instead of focusing on what you can do to be a better person or dwelling on what you've done wrong and allowing shame to pull you down, do as the psalmist did and, at the end of the day, reflect on who He is. Notice what happened when he did this:

"I reflect at night on who you are, O Lord;
therefore, I obey your instructions."
(Psalm 119:55)

Did you catch that? When we reflect on who He is, the response we have is to obey His instructions. Love makes us do crazy things. When we fall in love with our Savior, our Father, our Friend, Jehovah our God, our True Love, we can't help but do what pleases Him.

"This is how I spend my life:
obeying your commandments."
(Psalm 119:56)
"Because I love you."

49 *Remember your promise to me;*
it is my only hope.
50 *Your promise revives me;*
it comforts me in all my troubles.
51 *The proud hold me in utter contempt,*
but I do not turn away from your instructions.
52 *I meditate on your age-old regulations;*
O Lord, they comfort me.
53 *I become furious with the wicked,*
because they reject your instructions.
54 *Your decrees have been the theme of my songs*
wherever I have lived.
55 *I reflect at night on who you are, O Lord;*
therefore, I obey your instructions.
56 *This is how I spend my life:*
obeying your commandments.

(Psalm 119:49-56)

His love and His promises have an effect on us. They change us more and more into the image of Christ.

57 Lord, you are mine!
I promise to obey your words!
58 With all my heart I want your blessings.
Be merciful as you promised.
59 I pondered the direction of my life,
and I turned to follow your laws.
60 I will hurry, without delay,
to obey your commands.
61 Evil people try to drag me into sin,
but I am firmly anchored to your instructions.
62 I rise at midnight to thank you
for your just regulations.
63 I am a friend to anyone who fears you—
anyone who obeys your commandments.
64 O Lord, your unfailing love fills the earth;
teach me your decrees.

Psalm 119:57–64

10

I Surrender

We have a God that cares for us and has plans for our good. He desires to give us a future and a hope. He forgives us. He stands by our side. He heals the brokenhearted. *"And we know that all things work together for good to them that love God, to them who are the called according to his purpose."* (Romans 8:28 KJV)

Do you believe it? Do you believe that He loves you so much that He purposely died for you? Do you believe that He works all things together for the good? *ALL* things. You may believe that He does that for those who know the Bible thoroughly, for the "good ones" that live a pure life, for those who go to church every Sunday, for the ones that don't fight with their spouses or yell at their kids, for those that do well in school and never get in trouble, and so on. You fill in the blank. According to Romans 8:28, who does He work out *ALL* things for? *Those that love Him.*

We don't have to have it all together to love God, but loving Him drives us to want to do good. Even if I can't wrap my head around it, and I can't seem to understand how in the world my situation could ever bring about *anything* good, I can trust in His word.

"'My thoughts are nothing like your thoughts,' says the Lord. 'And my ways are far beyond anything you could imagine. For just as the heavens are higher than the earth, so my ways are higher than your ways and my thoughts higher than your thoughts.'" (Isaiah 55:8-9)

You and I can trust that He has nothing but good planned for us. He can take anything and turn it into good. We can trust that we will be blessed by loving and pursuing Him. God says, "*'Don't be afraid, for I am with you. Don't be discouraged, for I AM YOUR GOD. I WILL strengthen you and help you. I WILL hold you up with my victorious right hand.'"* (Isaiah 41:10, emphasis added) What do we have to lose? When I surrender my life to Him and trust in His ways even when I can't understand, then I can say the words written from the psalm at the beginning of the chapter. *"Lord, you are mine! I promise to obey your words!"* (vs. 57) How can one be so bold to promise that?

Remember, His greatest commandment is to love Him with all our heart, soul, mind, and strength, and everything else hangs off of that. If loving Him is our focus, then we will be able to say, *"You are mine. I will obey you. I will love you the best I know how to."* After discovering how deeply He loves us, we can't help but to love Him back.

Next, we can say along with the psalmist *"With all my heart I want your blessings. Be merciful as you promised. I pondered the direction of my life, and I turned to follow your laws."* (vs. 58,59)

Notice the words *"I turned."* This part is important. I have always known that Jesus loves me because the Bible tells me so, but it wasn't until I was in a pit, literally begging for a way out, that I realized that the Lord was revealing His love to me in a tangible way. I needed to be rescued because, in my own misery, I had chosen my own way out of the pit. I made up my mind and made a decision. It was a good thing that I didn't take immediate action because in between the time that I was waiting to follow through with a life changing decision that I had made, the Lord showed me that what I wanted to do, and what I was planning to do, was not what He had in mind for me. Remember that verse? *The Lord* has plans for us. *We* also have plans for us. When our own plans don't agree with His plans, we find ourselves struggling. God clearly showed me that He had a plan for me, and it was not the same plan that I had for me. Ouch! That is tough!

I heard the Lord's voice. He spoke to me through another person who was strong in the Lord and who could be trusted for wise, godly counsel. Because of my trust in God's word, and because I believed that anything He had planned for me was better than even the best plan that I could ever come up with, I chose to literally *turn* from my own desires to follow Him.

His way did not look good to me. I couldn't see any good in that direction, but I trusted His voice. *"'My thoughts are nothing like your thoughts,' says the Lord. 'And my ways are far beyond anything you could imagine. For just as the heavens are higher than the earth, so my ways are higher than your ways and my thoughts higher than your thoughts.'"* (Isaiah 55:8-9) Because of my faith in His promises through those verses, I was able to surrender to *His will.* Surrendering isn't easy, but strangely, the moment I made the decision to let go and give my life and desires to Him, there was peace. Not peace like "everything is fixed, my life is perfect, I couldn't be happier," but peace in the midst of it. Peace of mind and heart. Jesus says, *"'I am leaving you with a gift-- peace of mind and heart. And the peace I give is a gift the world cannot give. So don't be troubled or afraid.'"* (John 14:27)

The world tells us to be a good person and do what is right and then you will be accepted and loved by God. *God says* get to know Him and love Him, and all the laws hang from that. His love is not earned. It is free. He does not want our works and our sacrifices. He wants our love.

True Love changes things. It should be pretty obvious to pick out those that you truly love you because you will notice that you automatically and willingly do what pleases them. Same with God. When we really know Him and deeply love Him, our hearts desire is to please Him.

True Love responds like this: *"I will hurry, without delay, to obey your commands. Evil people try to drag me into sin, but I am firmly anchored to your instructions. I rise at midnight to thank you for your just regulations. I am a friend to anyone who fears (respects) you— anyone who obeys your commandments. O Lord, your unfailing love fills the earth; teach me your decrees."* (Psalm 119:60-64, emphasis added)

When you love Him, He changes you. In turn, you willingly accept the changes. When you love Him, the temptations that are placed in front of you by the people trying to drag you into sin, won't be so hard to resist any longer because you will be anchored to His instructions. The old ways of living will gradually begin to not taste right. It's as if they are being slowly and gently erased from your desires. His love changes you from the inside-out. That is what we call True Love. His True Love purifies.

Do you desire to love God more, but you aren't quite sure how? In the last chapter we talked about how we can hear God's voice. I believe that we can talk and search and discover all these wonderful things about Jesus, but if we don't hear Him speak to us personally, then what we will have is a distant relationship with an amazing God. We might know of Him, but not know Him personally.

Merely hearing about personality traits and stories about a person makes them only an acquaintance. Let's say your friend tells you about a man named John, and someone asks you, *"Do you know John?"* You could say, *"Well I've heard a lot about him. I hear he's a really good person. He cares about other people, and he would go out of his way to meet the needs of others, but I've never actually met him. I'd sure like to."* We can do the same with Jesus. Sure, I have learned great things about Him, like the amazing miracles He has done. I have read of Him in the Bible, listened to sermons at church about Him, and heard of other's "*God*" stories. Even with all of that, I can still lack experience and relationship of my own.

My desire is that you know Jesus because *you* have met with Him, and *you* have spoken with Him. It all comes back to faith. Do you dare to believe that what the Bible says is true, and if you do, do you dare ask Jesus to speak to you? That is where relationships begin.

When two people begin a new relationship, first they get to know each other. Each of them will spend time sharing a little about themselves, letting the other know who they are and what they like. Throughout this entire book, we have spent time getting to know who Jesus is and what He is like. We know that He knows who we are and what we are like, so what's next? If you think about a new relationship, after the two have somewhat figured out what each person is like, the next step is usually words of affirmation. Things like, *"I love spending time with you. You are the best part of my day. You are such a hard worker, and I admire your diligence,"* with a response like, *"Thank you. You're so beautiful, and you are the best part of my day, too. I can't wait to spend more time with you."*

Whether we realize it or not, we are fueled by the loving words of encouragement from others. If that's the case, then what happens when we don't receive those words from anyone? We might experience depression, sadness, or hopelessness. The truth is, we don't have to wait on *people* to fill that void in our hearts. We can talk with *Jesus*.

Just when I was at the point that I thought I had discovered the depths of where a relationship with Jesus could go, God placed a book in my path that changed my life with Jesus forever. It is called *4 Keys to Hearing God's Voice* by Mark and Patti Virkler. Through that book, I was taught that I could hear God's voice every day! I was used to hearing His voice once every three months or maybe once a week. I didn't realize that God was talking and wanted to talk to me every single day! It wasn't over night that I learned how to hear Him. It took some time. In fact, I have actually read that book five times now by the Lord's prompting because that's how important it is to God that I know His voice. He wants someone to talk to. He wants to talk to you, too. Every day!

Just like a relationship between two friends, it takes time and effort on both ends. God is always doing His part. He surrounds us with His creation, the sunrise and the sunset. He paints the sky differently every day. The wind. The rivers. The oceans. Animals. People. He is everywhere, constantly pursuing us. We have to do our part.

Mark Virkler's four keys to hearing God's voice are: Be Still, Tune to Spontaneity, Vision, and Journaling. To very quickly sum the four keys up, you find a time to get still with God, talk to Him and ask Him a question, then sit quietly and listen for His answer. Your answer from Him won't be an answer like you hear from a friend where you hear an audible voice. Now, of course,

He is God, so He *can* answer you in an audible voice if that is the way He chooses to. More than likely, He will answer you through spontaneous thoughts in your mind or through pictures in your mind. When He speaks through your thoughts or pictures in your mind, the last key is to allow the thoughts or pictures to finish and write down what you see or hear.

Journaling has so many benefits. Writing helps you focus only on what you are recording. It keeps you from being distracted by the things you have to do later or from thinking about something else. Journaling is a written record so it will help you remember it later. Recording your thoughts is also important because it may be confirmation for something down the road that Jesus will show you later. Writing down your conversations with Jesus might be one of the most valuable things you do in your walk with Him.

When I was first introduced to journaling, to be quite honest, I didn't want to do it. Journaling wasn't something I did nor was it something I was interested in. It just wasn't part of my life. To me it was one more thing I had to keep up with. I know there are many men and women that keep a record of things and journal in their own way, and I love that it's a hobby and a passion for many of you out there. For you who are already in the habit of writing, this journaling with Jesus part won't be so difficult for you. If you are like I was and have no interest in journaling, this will be a challenge worth disciplining yourself to do. If you are a man and that word "journal" completely throws you off, then you can call it a notebook or a log or find title that suits you.

What really got me hooked was seeing proof of how important it is to God. First of all, I came to realize that if it wasn't for men recording the things that God said, then we would not have the Bible. We have the Bible today because God inspired men to write the things that He showed them. Out of curiosity, I started from the beginning of the Bible to see how often the Lord spoke, and I was amazed at how often it said *"then the Lord said"* or that God spoke in a dream or through a vision. It's everywhere in the Bible! You can look for yourself. He spoke all the time, and He is still speaking all the time.

One of my favorite examples in the Bible is, *"I will stand upon my watch, and set me upon the tower, and will watch to see what he will say unto me, and what I shall answer when I am reproved.*

And the Lord answered me, and said, Write the vision, and make it plain upon tables, that he may run that readeth it." (Habakkuk 2:1-2 KJV)

Habakkuk went to a secluded place, he asked the Lord a question, then he waited to see what the Lord would say and how He would answer him. In this case, the writer received his answer from God in a vision. God had given him a picture, a vision, and he recorded what he saw and what the vision meant.

It is biblical that we can hear God's voice, and it's beneficial to us that we write down what God inspires us to write. I am not at all saying that you are writing Scripture or suggesting that you add to the Bible, just to make that clear. That is not okay at all. I am saying that we use the Bible as our guide. The Bible teaches us what His voice is like and the different ways that He speaks to us. I am suggesting that you write down what you say to the Lord and what you believe He says to you, not so you can tell others what to do, but to benefit your own personal life and your own personal relationship that you have with Jesus. The journal or log is a record of conversations between you and God.

To learn more specifically about hearing the voice of God, a couple of books that I have found to be tremendously beneficial are *4 Keys to Hearing God's Voice* by Mark and Patti Virkler and *Frequency* by Robert Morris.

My challenge to you is to consider yourself to be in a relationship with Jesus. It might be a friendship that you would like to grow deeper into, a companionship, or a Father/child relationship. Maybe you don't even know what to expect or look for in a relationship with Jesus. Regardless of how you view your relationship with Him, simply view Him as someone you know you should know better.

I greatly encourage you to get a notebook of some sort and start out by writing a letter to Jesus telling Him what you respect about Him. Write what you admire about Him. What do you love about Him? Write it out directly to Him. It might seem strange, but the ways of God are not what the world considers "normal." It might seem like you're writing to an imaginary person, but Yeshua is real. He is the reason why you have breath in your lungs right now. This is how we do our part. We start by surrendering ourselves to Him and begin to pursue Him. The psalmist did a great job at giving us examples of what letters to God might look like. Let's refresh our minds with the portion from the beginning of this chapter:

57 *Lord, you are mine!*
I promise to obey your words!
58 *With all my heart I want your blessings.*
Be merciful as you promised.
59 *I pondered the direction of my life,*
and I turned to follow your laws.
60 *I will hurry, without delay,*
to obey your commands.
61 *Evil people try to drag me into sin,*
but I am firmly anchored to your instructions.
62 *I rise at midnight to thank you*
for your just regulations.

63 *I am a friend to anyone who fears you—*
anyone who obeys your commandments.
64 *O Lord, your unfailing love fills the earth;*
teach me your decrees.
(Psalm 119:57-64)

Now write your own letter to Him. It doesn't need to sound anything like what you read above. Just be honest. Be you. Write to Him, the one who gave up His life for you. Maybe you have done this before and if you have, you know that you can't write to Him too much. I encourage everyone: those who are brand new at this, those who have tried it but not kept up with it, those who are experienced, everyone: men and women alike. I encourage you to write to your Heavenly Father because it is your own personal experience that matters most to you. Follow the example from Habakkuk, and when you are finished writing to God, take some time to be still and listen to what He might want to say back to you. If you feel like He is giving you pictures or thoughts, write them down. That just might be His letter back to you. It may feel like it's you, making up your own thoughts, but don't question it at first. For now, just write it down. That is where our relationship and conversations with God begin. Go find you a quiet time and place and talk with Him. You might begin by saying, *"Lord, this is how I see you...."* Then ask Him, *"How do you see me?"* and let Him tell you.

If you would like to have an example of what two-way journaling with the Lord can look like, I have written a book that simply contains my own personal journaling records with Jesus with the hope and desire that it would help and encourage others to hear God's voice speaking personally to them. The title of the book is called *33:3 Ask Me*. Journaling has been one of the greatest treasures that I share with Jesus and I would love to share it with you. Now go write!

65 You have done many good things for me, Lord,
just as you promised.
66 I believe in your commands;
now teach me good judgment and knowledge.
67 I used to wander off until you disciplined me;
but now I closely follow your word.
68 You are good and do only good;
teach me your decrees.
69 Arrogant people smear me with lies,
but in truth I obey your commandments with all my heart.
70 Their hearts are dull and stupid,
but I delight in your instructions.
71 My suffering was good for me,
for it taught me to pay attention to your decrees.
72 Your instructions are more valuable to me
than millions in gold and silver.

Psalm 119:65–72

11

More than Millions

For a big portion of my life, I would only think to call on God when things got rough. I waited until I was desperate before I cried out to Him for help and hit my knees when it was my last resort. I used to live so much of my daily life without God. I made decisions without Him. I made my own plans and took control without feeling a need to ask the Lord for direction. Thankfully, the Lord pulled me out of that reality.

I believe we all have a desire within us to want to be closer to God, to want to spend more of our time with Him, but we can be so busy and easily distracted that it gets smothered out by other obligations.

What is it that brings us from that stage to the next level? I believe it only happens to those who experience the unfailing love of God. Notice I said "experience." Not the knowledge of His unfailing love, but the experience of His love. This experience is available for anyone, but only those who search will find the treasure. Without knowing and feeling how much He *personally* loves you, it's easy to drift away and put Him on a shelf. It's easy to get sidetracked and focused on other things when there is a lack of passion. If we don't understand the awesome, crazy love that He wants to share with us, then it's easy to put a hold on the relationship and only call Him when we need Him.

Love is what drives us to dig deeper, takes us to new levels, and keeps us persevering. Love is the reason we do things for someone when we don't even feel like doing it. Love is a sacrifice, and Jesus gave the ultimate sacrifice just to have you.

Paul says in the Scriptures, *"If I could speak all the languages of earth and of angels, but didn't love others, I would only be a noisy gong or a clanging cymbal. If I had the gift of prophecy, and if I understood all of God's secret plans and possessed all knowledge, and if I had such faith that I could move mountains, but didn't love others, I would be nothing. If I gave everything I have to the poor and even sacrificed my body, I could boast about it; but if I didn't love others, I would have gained nothing."* (1 Corinthians 13:1-3)

Imagine that you could speak every language, you could prophecy, you understood all of God's secret plans, contained *all* knowledge, moved mountains with your faith, gave everything you had to the poor, and sacrificed your body. That's a lot! I would think that a person with those abilities would be quite beneficial to this world, but Scripture tells us that even those great things *without love* are *nothing!* I don't know any human alive that can do all of that awesomeness, but I do know that Jesus was human, and He was capable of every bit of that. Jesus didn't perform miracles so He could be popular and look cool. He didn't walk on water just because He could. He didn't sacrifice His body so that He could boast about it. He did it all because He loves us, and if He did it for any other reason, He would have gained nothing.

"Prophecy and speaking in unknown languages and special knowledge will become useless. But love will last forever! Now our knowledge is partial and incomplete, and even the gift of prophecy reveals only part of the whole picture! But when the time of perfection comes, these partial things will become useless. When I was a child, I spoke and thought and reasoned as a child. But when I grew up, I put away childish things. Now we see things imperfectly, like puzzling reflections in a mirror, but then we will see everything with perfect clarity. All that I know now is partial and incomplete, but then I will know everything completely, just as God now knows me completely. Three things will last forever—faith, hope, and love—and the greatest of these is love." (1 Corinthians 13:8-13, emphasis added)

All Scripture is inspired by God, so who do you think wrote those words on Paul's heart? Yes, you are right. Yahweh Himself. Did you know that you had such a romantic God? He is all about Love! Now if you are a man, I imagine it may be hard to picture God as romantic, but maybe you can relate to Him as your best friend or the perfect Father. Love can be expressed in many forms. I challenge you to ask the Lord to reveal Himself to you. Ask Him how He wants you personally to experience Him and see Him.

My dad loves animals, and God knows that. One way that God will catch his attention is by allowing him to see animals in three's. Instead of one bald eagle, he will see three. Instead of one woodpecker, three of them show up.

He catches my mom's attention with blue butterflies. Every time she sees a blue butterfly, she is reminded of the presence of Jesus going with her. God goes beyond your expectations, and He speaks in *your* language. If you love music, He will speak through music. If you love sports, He will speak through sports. If you love hunting, He will speak through your hunting experiences. If you love the ocean, He will speak through the ocean. He will show His love to each one of us in our own unique way. He's that cool! And remember what the Scriptures above said, *"He knows you completely."* He's going to speak to you in a way that *you* can hear and understand Him.

Let's ponder the words in our psalm for today. *"You have done many good things for me, Lord, just as you promised. I believe in your commands; now teach me good judgment and knowledge."* (vs.65,66)

In those two verses you can hear faith in God and a desire to change. He started by acknowledging that God has done many good things and confessed that he believed in Him. Do you believe in Him? Do you believe that He will follow through with His promises? Next, the psalmist asked the Lord to teach him good judgement and knowledge. It's important that we ask the Lord to help us to make wise decisions and to see things how He sees them. Alone, we only see things from a human point of view, but with His help we can see things differently.

God can help us see things as if we are looking through a microscope. He may show us the inner places of ourselves or of others; places that, with the naked eye, are unseen. God will open our eyes to see things so that we may be healed or so that we may understand others better. We all have deep and hidden things that only God knows about, and when He can give us just a glimpse of what's going on within us, it can change our whole perspective about ourselves or another person. Sometimes we need God's view like a magnifying glass so we can zoom in and see things a little more clearly. Other times we need a telescope so we can see the dreams and the desires of our hearts or others' hearts. God possesses the correct lenses that we need to view things from His perspective. We need His wisdom, His knowledge, not our own limited sight. *"Teach us good judgement and show us what you see, Lord."*

"I used to wander off until you disciplined me; but now I closely follow your word. You are good and do only good; teach me your decrees." (vs. 67,68)

I can claim that whole first line. *I used to wander off until God disciplined me.* I lived my life in my own way until I found myself in a place that I knew I shouldn't be. Realizing I had gotten myself in a mess that I couldn't get out of on my own, I would cry out to God to help me.

It's kind of like when children get to the age of wanting to do things on their own. They might begin to make decisions that their parents probably warned them about and advised them not to do. If so, they will eventually find themselves in a bind and have nowhere to turn to except for Mom and Dad. That feeling is awful because it's extremely hard to have to go ask Mom and Dad for help when you know they warned you not to travel the road that you chose to take. Then you tell them that you're sorry, and you'll never make that mistake again, only to find yourself down the same road again sometime later.

We are prone to wander away from God. We wander off until we are disciplined. Wander off until we are disciplined. Wander off until we are disciplined. Are you tired of that cycle? The way to break that cycle is to closely follow His word. The only reason that I stay close to Him and follow His word now, is because I discovered that He is irresistible! I can't believe how much He loves me and wants to be my partner in life and not just an occasional acquaintance. Not only that, but He is completely Holy! He is all powerful. He is the One and only Almighty God! This Holy, Powerful, Mighty God desires to have a personal relationship with me! And He wants the same with you, too.

As we experience His love, we experience the healthy fear of God. I'm not talking about *scared of Him* fear, but fear as in *reverence and respect for Him.* Because He is Holy, I want to respect that and do what pleases Him. Because of who He is and what He has done for me, I don't want to do anything that would go against Him. Fear of God isn't a fear of punishment, rather it is a fear of allowing anything to come between His heart and mine. I want to be as close to Him as I possibly can be, and I fear being away from Him.

We have to remind ourselves that God is good and does only good. If we can allow Jesus to engrave that truth on our hearts, then we won't want to wander off and abandon Him until we find ourselves on our knees again because we will trust in His plans for us. Therefore, we will not only desire to stay close to Him, but we will closely follow His word.

"Arrogant people smear me with lies, but in truth I obey your commandments with all my heart. Their hearts are dull and stupid, but I delight in your instructions." (vs. 69,70)

When we become true followers of Christ, sometimes we discover that what we once thought was good company, may not be such good company after all. There are some people that, as the Scriptures say, smear us with lies. For instance, in my past, I could be easily persuaded to go to a party and drink or even be the one to host the party. As the Lord began to change me from the inside out, I noticed that the party lifestyle was starting to become unappealing to me. I still put myself in that atmosphere and tried to fight off the temptation. When I would say no, I would hear things like, *"Well Jesus drank wine. He even made water turn into wine when they ran out at the wedding ceremony."* Well, that may be true, but if I didn't know Scripture, I wouldn't have known that God tells us that drunkenness and wild parties are sins. If I drink to the point that I am no longer in control of my body and actions, then I am living from the outside-in and allowing my body to do the leading, which is not the way that God designed me. The reason God said not to be part of drunkenness and wild parties was not to condemn me, but to protect me from its harm. If you have witnessed the outcome of parties that involve people that are far from sober-minded, it does not take long to notice the really dumb choices that are made when in that state of mind. For me, it always seemed fun and exciting while in the moment, but the next day I lived in shame and felt physically beat and mentally exhausted. As I sought the Lord, my ways began to change. Others may have called me names and put me down for standing my ground. The new me was boring and no fun to that crowd anymore. I was probably considered a fool in the eyes of others.

Some people will smear you with lies, but when you know the Author of Truth personally, you will choose to obey Him with all your heart. The Bible describes arrogant people as having dull and stupid hearts. I don't think it is saying that people are stupid. The word stupid means foolish or unwise, to make poor judgement. The intentions of their hearts are unwise. I don't want a dull and stupid heart, do you? I used to be that way, but I have found True Love, and I no longer want to settle for dull and stupid! There is so much more to life than that.

Discovering the great love that God has for you will give you the strength to say *"no"* when you need to. *"My suffering was good for me, for it taught me to pay attention to your decrees. Your instructions are more valuable to me than millions in gold and silver."* (vs. 71,72)

Oh, how I bet He smiles over the one that says, *"My suffering was good for me, for it taught me to pay attention to YOU."* Good parents don't discipline their children because they get a sick sense of humor out of seeing them suffer. They discipline because they don't want to see their child hurt themselves and because they love them. Finally, it makes sense why my parents said, *"I'm punishing you because I love you."* The intention of our heavenly Father's discipline is for our good.

God isn't mad at us if we are stuck in the phase of only calling on Him when we need Him. He isn't like us. He doesn't give up and say, *"Sorry. I'm tired of being used. You're not really my friend. You only think about me when you need me so you're on your own."* No, God is True Love. He never gives up and endures through every circumstance. He never leaves you or forsakes you. He isn't mad, but He does long for you to stay close. His heart aches for our love. That is why He made us.

Love changes everything. Love allows us to be thankful for the struggles because, in them, we find True Love. Honestly, one can be the richest person on earth and contain millions of dollars, but if that person does not have love, the money means nothing except for freedom to buy whatever they want. Unfortunately, money cannot buy True Love. Without love, we are hopeless people.

Our relationship with God is more valuable than millions in silver and gold because it is the one relationship that will never fail you. I pray that you and I can experience the love of God as the psalmist did.

"Your unfailing love is better than life itself; how I praise you!" (Psalm 63:3) If you can say that *love* is better than *life* itself, I would say that is *True Love.*

"Jesus, your love is more than millions in silver and gold, better than life itself. We want to know You and to feel You because You are all we truly need, Jesus. As we draw near to you, draw nearer to us."

73 You made me; you created me.
Now give me the sense to follow your commands.
74 May all who fear you find in me a cause for joy, for I have put my hope in your word.
75 I know, O Lord, that your regulations are fair;
you disciplined me because I needed it.
76 Now let your unfailing love comfort me,
just as you promised me, your servant.
77 Surround me with your tender mercies so I may live,
for your instructions are my delight.
78 Bring disgrace upon the arrogant people who lied about me; meanwhile, I will concentrate on your commandments.
79 Let me be united with all who fear you,
with those who know your laws.
80 May I be blameless in keeping your decrees;
then I will never be ashamed.

Psalm 119:73–80

12

Surround Me

Keep in mind when we read these psalms, that the words decrees, regulations, and commands, should bring to our minds the greatest commandment first. You know that by heart now, right? Love God with all your heart, soul, mind, and strength. If we think of all of the other things we need to be doing first, like don't lie, don't hate, don't have foul language, don't act like that, don't hang out there, don't do that, and so on and so on, then we set ourselves up to feel like a complete failure. As a result, we either give up trying, or we try so hard we become exhausted and ultimately feel hopeless.

Our relationship with God should not be defined by how much we do for Him, nor should it be evaluated by another's opinion. Before I realized that Jesus wanted a real relationship with me, I would feel guilty that I wasn't doing enough for Him. That guilty feeling only resulted in me acting out of obligation.

Jesus isn't after how much we can do for Him because if we are doing it out of obligation, then the love behind it is absent and the results go nowhere. Remember, we can do all kinds of amazing things, but if love isn't the motivator, then it means nothing. He wants to spend quality time with you. He wants you to get to know Him. Relationships require that you get to know the other person as they also get to know you. The difference in our human relationships and our relationship with God is that He already completely knows us. In fact, He knows you better than you know you. But even though *He* knows you already, He wants to tell *you* what He knows, how He sees you, and make sure that *you* know how much He loves you. Believe it or not, you may be believing things about yourself that aren't true in the eyes of Jesus, and He wants to tell you what He believes about you.

In the earlier stages of building my relationship with God, I can remember saying, *"Use me, Lord. Use me."* I constantly felt like I needed to be doing something for Him. After all, `the things He has done for me, I felt like I needed to be returning the favor to Him by being useful in some kind of way. The Lord had to train me to be still and rest in His presence.

I can remember a time that I was just waiting for Him to show me what I could do, and I kept getting message after message through my devotionals, through my teachers, and in journaling to *"rest in Him."* At first it felt uncomfortable because I wasn't used to just sitting and talking with God, but after I did it, I realized how God just wanted to sit and get to know one another. Sometimes a song would come to mind, and when I played it, I was moved to tears. Other times when I closed my eyes, I could see Him and me sitting on a beach somewhere not even saying a word, just simply enjoying the atmosphere.

There was one particular morning that I was feeling very lonely. I was longing to feel what it feels like when one person loves another. You know that feeling that courses through your body when someone touches your hand for the first time, or even deeper, the first time someone presses their lips against yours? That's the feeling I was craving. That morning I got up to spend time with the Lord, but I was feeling empty. I knew that life with God is good, but what about the physical part? How can God fill that longing? I was so desperate that I was crying. Then I read a short devotion, and the Lord spoke to me through the words on the page. Of all the things that could have been said through any devotional book, this one was speaking of God's tangible Love. God was expressing how high, how deep, how long, and how wide His love is. His love is so powerful that it would be too much for us to handle if He released it in its fullness right now. The manifestation of God's love is so rich that it could overwhelm us to the point of feeling crushed. The presence of His love is like the purest high one can contain. Once again, through the words in the devotion, He was inviting me to rest in His presence. Nothing more than just being with Him.

After reading the devotion, I closed my eyes to ponder those thoughts, and it was as if I could tangibly *feel* God's presence on me. He said that one day I would experience unrestricted ecstasy, but in that moment, He granted me a taste of that ecstasy. If I had been standing, I believe I would have gotten weak in the knees and fallen down. It was so overwhelmingly amazing that I think my heart forgot to beat for a moment. It was better than butterflies, better than the first touch of a hand, better than a first kiss. Indescribable. Unexplainable. Ecstasy is the best word for it. Not like the drug. I don't even know what that's like. This was pure ecstasy, which is defined as: a rapturous delight; an overpowering emotion or exaltation; a state of sudden, intense feeling.

That morning God showed me that He had *everything* that I longed for, even physical, tangible love that I believed I could only find in man. I believed it was something that God didn't understand and that it was the one thing that He couldn't offer me. He proved me wrong. He gave me a taste of what His tangible love is like, and He was right when He said through the devotion that if I were to experience the completeness of His love right now, that it would overwhelm me to the point of being crushed! He allowed me to experience just enough of it to show me that He *can* fulfill my every need. I no longer felt empty, depressed, or lonely. He filled my heart so full of His tangible love that I couldn't help but be joyful!

It is simple moments like those that allow the bond between God and me to grow stronger. He placed an unexplainable joy in my heart that only He could give me. It wasn't through works that I experienced those treasures, it was by spending quality time with Jesus and getting to know Him personally. The only thing I had to do was set aside the time to spend with Him. I could have easily just stayed in bed. I could have given in to the thought that it would be a waste of time. I was already feeling lonely and doubtful that God could fill the desire that I was having anyway. Staying in bed to sleep off more of the day would have made sense, but I was obedient to Yeshua's desires, and I got up to spend time with Him. That one act of diligence made all the difference. The only work I had to do was get out of bed and go sit on my couch to be with Jesus and think about how lonely I felt. Then Jesus took over and captured my heart from there!

He builds the passion up in me. He lights the fire in my soul as He begins to reveal Himself to me in ways that I didn't even know were possible. He says, *"Seek me wholeheartedly and you WILL find me."* He does that in ways that are unthinkable, unexpected, unexplainable, and so personal. When it happens, I can't help but want to tell someone. I want to share His love with others. Sometimes I don't even know how I'm going to do that because people might think I am crazy! But I don't care because I know it's real! I know that it is the key to living life abundantly like Jesus promises, and I want others to find it.

God's Love is essential. Without understanding the amazing love that He has for us, we cannot be effective for Him. Once we tap into the realization of His True Love, then He will begin to use us. No longer will we be a servant, serving our master out of duty, but we will serve because we love Him, and we want others to have what we have. We will give up things for Him because we know He is worth it. We will serve with a willing heart.

Jesus said, *"'If any of you wants to be my follower, you must give up your own way, take up your cross daily, and follow me. If you try to hang on to your life, you will lose it. But if you give up your life for my sake, you will save it. And what do you benefit if you gain the whole world but are yourself lost or destroyed? If anyone is ashamed of me and my message, the Son of Man will be ashamed of that person when he returns in his glory and in the glory of the Father and the holy angels. I tell you the truth, some standing here right now will not die before they see the Kingdom of God.'"* (Luke 9:23-27)

Before I understood the depths of God's heart, I felt a little angry after reading that passage. I thought to myself, *"Why should I have to give up my own ways? Why should I have to lose my life in order to save it?"* I knew that Jesus wants us to live life to the fullest and live it abundantly, so for me to give up my life in order to follow Him sounded like it would be no fun and hard! It didn't sound like the full and abundant life that He promises. But now that I know Him, it's easier for me to give up my own ways and control of my life because I know that every plan He has for me is *way* better than any plan I can come up with even if, by my own human understanding, it seems as if there is no other way.

I know now that I am much better off if I let Him have control because He is for me and not against me, and His thoughts are higher than my thoughts. Now, when I read *"If you give up your life for my sake, you will save it,"* it makes sense. The plans that He has for you and me are in our best interest. We have to trust in True Love. He's not asking us to lose our life because He wants to take away what we have or what we want. He wants us to give up control because what we don't realize is that we are the ones hindering ourselves from having what's best! Giving up our own ways and giving Jesus control sounds like foolishness to the human mind, but it's actually freedom and abundance beyond our wildest imagination and the wisest decision we can ever make. Until I actually got to the place of surrender and completely let my desires go, it felt like the hardest decision I ever had to make. I felt like I was letting go of my dreams, but as soon as I did, I saw that there was much more to life than what I knew.

Had it not been for the tough times in my life, I would have never made it to a place of surrender on my knees, offering God all that I had. It was through discipline and darkness that I found true life. Discipline from our earthly father and mother figures isn't always done with the right intent, but the true purpose of discipline is to steer us away from danger. Maybe you didn't have parents that disciplined out of love. Thankfully, I did. I thank the Lord for that. If a parent's discipline is driven by love, the whole point of it is to make sure their kids don't get hurt or take the wrong path.

Let's ponder our eight verses from the psalms today:

73 You made me; you created me.
Now give me the sense to follow your commands.
74 May all who fear you find in me a cause for joy,
for I have put my hope in your word.
75 I know, O Lord, that your regulations are fair;
you disciplined me because I needed it.
76 Now let your unfailing love comfort me,
just as you promised me, your servant.
77 Surround me with your tender mercies so I may live,
for your instructions are my delight.
78 Bring disgrace upon the arrogant people who lied about me; meanwhile, I will concentrate on your commandments.
79 Let me be united with all who fear you,
with those who know your laws.
80 May I be blameless in keeping your decrees;
then I will never be ashamed.
(Psalm 119:73-80)

He made us! He knows us! He disciplines us when He sees us headed for destruction. We can put our hope in His word, and we can ask Him to give us the sense to follow His commands. As we do this, we will desire for others to see a cause for joy within us. Once we find ourselves in a place that we can admit that His discipline is good for us and that we need it, we will want to be *surrounded* by others that love the Lord. As we come to know Jesus, we begin to desire to be blameless in keeping His commands. Our comfort is found in His unfailing love, and it is because of His tender mercies that we live.

I cry to the Lord, *"Surround me. Surround me with people that love you. Surround me with your tangible love. Keep me from walking down the wrong path. You promised that Your unfailing love would comfort me. Surround me in it. Surround me with your tender mercies so that I may live. Surround me, Jesus. Hedge me in so that all I see is You."*

81 I am worn out waiting for your rescue,
but I have put my hope in your word.
82 My eyes are straining to see your promises
come true.
When will you comfort me?
83 I am shriveled like a wineskin in the smoke,
but I have not forgotten to obey your
decrees.
84 How long must I wait?
When will you punish those who persecute me?
85 These arrogant people who hate your
instructions
have dug deep pits to trap me.
86 All your commands are trustworthy.
Protect me from those who hunt me down
without cause.
87 They almost finished me off,
but I refused to abandon your commandments.
88 In your unfailing love, spare my life;
then I can continue to obey your laws.

Psalm 119:81–88

13

How Long Must I Wait

When I am in the middle of a storm, time seems to really drag along. It's hard to see the sunshine when all that is around me are dark, heavy clouds, pouring rain, and thunder, day after day after day.

The psalmist cried out to God, *"How long? Where are you? I'm struggling!"* In his case, he had physical enemies that were after him. He had people that were taunting him and hunting him down. Maybe you have enemies as well that are taunting you and hurting you physically and/or emotionally. Maybe your enemy is your own mind, whether anxiety, fear, lust, pride, or depression. Maybe you realize that Satan is your enemy, and you're tired of getting knocked down by his dirty schemes. After all, Satan is the real enemy we are fighting. *"For we wrestle not against flesh and blood, but against principalities, against powers, against the rulers of the darkness of this world, against spiritual wickedness in high places."* (Ephesians 6:12 KJV)

Regardless of how, who, or what you are struggling with, it may feel as if you are stuck on a boat in the middle of the ocean and there is no place to set your feet on solid ground. The waves are crashing all around you, your boat is rocking, and you feel like you are going to sink right where you are. The ocean seems endless and there is no hope as far as your eyes can see. All you want is to see the shore so you can get out of the storm and move on.

What are we supposed to do when we find ourselves there? *"So God has given both his promise and his oath. These two things are unchangeable because it is impossible for God to lie. Therefore, we who have fled to him for refuge can have great confidence as we hold to the hope that lies before us. This hope is a strong and trustworthy anchor for our souls. It leads us through the curtain into God's inner sanctuary."* (Hebrews 6:18-19)

A ship needs an anchor in order to ride out the storms so that it isn't blown into rocks and reefs that can damage it. The anchor keeps the ship from veering off the path that it is on. It keeps the wind and waves from taking the ship in the wrong direction. Even in the calm, a ship needs an anchor so that it will not drift or hit something and possibly sink.

If we compare our souls to a ship, whether we are in a storm or not, we all need an anchor for our souls to keep us from drifting away, getting lost, hurting ourselves, and to stay afloat. Notice that the anchor doesn't remove us from the storm, instead it keeps us steady and safe in the midst of the storm.

I'll never forget the words that I received at a time when my storm was raging; *"We ask God to change our circumstances, when what He desires is for our circumstances to change us."* Honestly, that is not what I wanted to hear at that time, but for some reason, I couldn't forget those words. God was laying it on my heart heavily. He showed me that I needed to change the way I was looking at my situation. I wasn't trusting Him or allowing Him to use my circumstances to strengthen me, instead I was only looking for and end and a way out. The Lord so kindly reminded me of the importance of learning obedience through suffering and allowing it to strengthen me instead of crush me. Jesus reminded me that no matter how wrong and out of place my life looked to me, that He is sovereign over it all and He had a plan to work it out for good. I had to learn to befriend my problems and get my eyes off the details of my issues and on to the One that could do something about it. Like the psalmist said, *"I am worn out waiting for your rescue, but I have put my hope in your word."* (vs.81) That hope is a strong and trustworthy anchor for our souls.

How are you handling the trials in your life? When things get tough, do you give up and find the easiest escape? Do you find yourself starting over all the time? What if the very struggle in your life was something God could use to make you stronger? What if He wants to get you through it to the other side because there's something on the other end of the struggle that will benefit your life forever? The only way to find out is to surrender, be honest with God, and say, *"I'm done! I'm worn out! I'm tired! But I'm putting my hope in You, so help me, please."*

An anchor has a rope or a chain or something that securely connects it to the boat. Without tying that rope to the boat, the anchor isn't going to have any benefit whatsoever. I like to think of Jesus as the Anchor and the rope as His promises. If Jesus is the Anchor to our souls, then His promises act as the rope that ties our soul to the Anchor. What promises are you holding on to? There are so many promises in His word, and if we give Him time to speak to us, He will give us special promises that speak right to our hearts. We have to grab hold of His promises and tie them to our souls, otherwise, they are just ropes lying useless in our ship that may slip off and sink to the bottom of the ocean. If we don't pick up the rope and secure it, what good is it going to do?

For example, *"If you openly declare that Jesus is Lord and believe in your heart that God raised him from the dead, you will be saved. For it is by believing in your heart that you are made right with God, and it is by openly declaring your faith that you are saved."* (Romans 10:9-10) If I have only read the Scripture, it is like a rope lying in my boat. It's there for me to use, but if I don't take a hold of it and tie it to my anchor, it will not do me any good. Now if I say, *"Yes! I believe in Jesus. I believe He is Lord, and He died for my sins, and God raised Him from the dead,"* and I believe in my heart that those things are true, then that is called faith. Faith allows me to pick up the rope and tie it to the anchor. Because I believe, I have a promise that ties my soul to Jesus, my Anchor, therefore, I am saved! Now I can know that no matter what happens in this life, in this storm, on this ship, Jesus has saved me from sin and death. What a relief! But does that mean the storm stops? Not necessarily. So, in the meantime, what do I do? Find some more rope and use it.

"And this is what he promised us--eternal life." (1 John 2:25) If you have asked and trusted Jesus to be your savior, you have eternal life! That's pretty amazing! Beyond our comprehension. *Eternal* life! What does that even mean? Eternal means: *lasting or existing forever; without end or beginning.* Even if our worn-out body gives up and dies, there's still life! There is no end! There's another rope to tie your soul to your Anchor.

You might be thinking, *"Oh no! There is no end! It just keeps going?"* It's time to find another rope. *"Yet what we suffer now is nothing compared to the glory he will reveal to us later."* (Romans 8:18) Thank you, Jesus. I'll tie that one on!

"For we know that all creation has been groaning as in the pains of childbirth right up to the present time. And we believers also groan, even though we have the Holy Spirit within us as a foretaste of future glory, for we long for our bodies to be released from sin and suffering. We, too, wait with eager hope for the day when God will give us our full rights as his adopted children, including the new bodies he has promised us. We were given this hope when we were saved. (If we already have something, we don't need to hope for it. But if we look forward to something we don't yet have, we must wait patiently and confidently.)" (Romans 8:22-25)

New bodies! It's a promise! I love the end where it says, *"If we already have something, we don't need to hope for it. But if we look forward to something we don't yet have, we must wait patiently and confidently."* The waiting patiently is the part I struggle with, but if I truly believe that those are promises and that God doesn't break promises, then I can wait with *confidence!* Hope fastens us to Jesus and keeps our eyes on Him. It helps us stay on track and persevere to the next step. Hope drives us. It steers us in the direction we want to go and keeps us on the right path.

There is a belief floating around that to have a relationship with Jesus means that life is easy and free of difficulties. That lie gets many of us in trouble. If that belief is embedded in one's heart, then as soon as things begin to get a little rough, the result will be to blame oneself or blame God.

Blaming self invites guilt and shame to take control. Guilt and shame might sound like, *"Something is wrong with me. I have messed up. My faith is not strong enough. I must not be saved because things are going wrong."* Guilt and shame can come crashing in like waves and rock our boat causing our eyes to be on self instead of Jesus. If we are relying on false hope, fear will cripple, and we will find ourselves searching for the easy way out which takes us right back to the very same places again and again.

The other end of the spectrum is blaming God. Some believe that life with Jesus is supposed to result in a pleasant, problem-free life, and when things get crazy, instead of feeling guilt and shame, blame is directed at God. Blaming God might sound like, *"Why in the world would God do that to me? He isn't protecting me. Where is God now? He doesn't even love me. He is cruel to allow unpleasantness to happen. What is the point in believing in God? There is no hope."*

Knowing the truth is so very important. It is vital to our well-being. If we don't know the truth, then the door is wide open for false hope to take hold of our heart. *"This will continue until we all come to such unity in our faith and knowledge of God's Son that we will be mature in the Lord, measuring up to the full and complete standard of Christ. Then we will no longer be immature like children. We won't be tossed and blown about by every wind of new teaching. We will not be influenced when people try to trick us with lies so clever they sound like the truth."* (Ephesians 4:13-14) If we are not mature in the knowledge of Jesus Christ, then our soul will be like that ship, tossed back and forth by the waves, blown here and there by the lies of the enemy. We need the Truth, Jesus. His hope secures us to the Anchor.

"'I have told you all this so that you may have peace in me. Here on earth you will have many trials and sorrows. But take heart, because I have overcome the world.'" (John 16:33) Jesus tells us that we *will* have many trials and sorrows here on earth so that truth exposes the lie that life with

Jesus is easy. He warned us ahead of time that it wouldn't be easy, but He also tells us that we can have peace in Him because He has overcome the world. Without Jesus and His truth, we will be a ship without an anchor wandering aimlessly wherever the wind and the waves take us, or we will not dare get in the ship in fear of what may happen and miss out on all that God has for us. But with Jesus as our Anchor and Truth as our rope to secure us to Him, we can experience peace in the midst of the storms. Peace comes from Him, not the world. We must bind ourselves with Truth so that we can know the One who has already conquered the world. He is the One that has already faced every trial, every temptation, and felt every pain. Ultimately, He has already paid the price for every sin and even tasted death. We can trust in Him. He knows the way through the storms.

Are you begging God to change your circumstances, or will you let your circumstances change you? *"If you need wisdom, ask our generous God, and he will give it to you. He will not rebuke you for asking. But when you ask him, be sure that your faith is in God alone. Do not waver, for a person with divided loyalty is as unsettled as a wave of the sea that is blown and tossed by the wind. Such people should not expect to receive anything from the Lord. Their loyalty is divided between God and the world, and they are unstable in everything they do."* (James 1:5-8)

Find yourself some hope, look for those promises in God's word, and hold on to them. Then when you find yourself worn out and straining to see anything ahead of you, that hope will keep you firmly grounded to the Anchor.

[81] *I am worn out waiting for your rescue,*
but I have put my hope in your word.
[82] *My eyes are straining to see your promises come true.*
When will you comfort me?
[83] *I am shriveled like a wineskin in the smoke,*
***but I have not forgotten to obey your decrees**.*
[84] *How long must I wait?*
When will you punish those who persecute me?
[85] *These arrogant people who hate your instructions*
have dug deep pits to trap me.
[86] ***All your commands are trustworthy.***
Protect me from those who hunt me down without cause.
[87] *They almost finished me off,*
but I refused to abandon your commandments.
[88] *In your unfailing love, spare my life;*
then I can continue to obey your laws.
(Psalm 119:81-88, emphasis added)

Notice the statements in bold letters above. What would it sound like if our faith was not in God alone, but instead divided between God and the world? Perhaps it would sound more like this:

"I have put my hope in your word, but I am worn out waiting for your rescue.

I have not forgotten to obey your decrees, but my eyes are straining to see your promises come true. When will you comfort me? I am shriveled like a wineskin in the smoke.

All your commands are trustworthy. How long must I wait? When will you punish those who persecute me? These arrogant people who hate your instructions have dug deep pits to trap me.

I refused to abandon your commandments, but they almost finished me off."

Do you see the difference? The double-minded version states the truth and shows obedience, but lacks faith. It's backwards. That is what it's like to have our eyes fixed on our circumstances and work out of our own strength to gain good results. The results end up being that we find ourselves exhausted and unable to move forward, leaving us feeling hopeless and lacking faith in His promises.

The example that the psalmist left us, leaves us hopeFULL. *"I am worn out, BUT my hope is in Your word. I am straining to see, BUT I haven't forgotten to obey your decrees. How long must I wait? I KNOW You are trustworthy. They almost finished me off, BUT I refused to abandon You."*

Remember what James 1:5-8 says. If you need wisdom, ask God. Ask Him anything! Ask Him, *"How long must I wait?"* But when you ask Him, be sure that your faith is in God alone so that you won't be unsettled like a wave of the sea, blown and tossed by the wind. Remember His word.

"So God has given both **his promise** *and* **his oath**. *These two things are unchangeable because it is impossible for God to lie. Therefore, we who have fled to him for refuge can have* **great confidence** *as we* **hold to the hope** *that lies before us.* **This hope is a strong and trustworthy anchor for our souls.** *It leads us through the curtain into God's inner sanctuary."* (Hebrews 6:18-19)

89 YOUR ETERNAL WORD, O LORD,
STANDS FIRM IN HEAVEN.
90 YOUR FAITHFULNESS EXTENDS TO EVERY GENERATION,
AS ENDURING AS THE EARTH YOU CREATED.
91 YOUR REGULATIONS REMAIN TRUE TO THIS DAY,
FOR EVERYTHING SERVES YOUR PLANS.
92 IF YOUR INSTRUCTIONS HADN'T SUSTAINED ME WITH JOY,
I WOULD HAVE DIED IN MY MISERY.
93 I WILL NEVER FORGET YOUR COMMANDMENTS,
FOR BY THEM YOU GIVE ME LIFE.
94 I AM YOURS; RESCUE ME!
FOR I HAVE WORKED HARD AT OBEYING YOUR COMMANDMENTS.
95 THOUGH THE WICKED HIDE ALONG THE WAY TO KILL ME,
I WILL QUIETLY KEEP MY MIND ON YOUR LAWS.
96 EVEN PERFECTION HAS ITS LIMITS,
BUT YOUR COMMANDS HAVE NO LIMIT.

PSALM 119:89–96

14

Limitless

God's word is available to everyone. What about the people who don't own a Bible or those that can't have one because it is illegal? *"Even Gentiles, who do not have God's written law, show that they know his law when they instinctively obey it, even without having heard it. They demonstrate that God's law is written in their hearts, for their own conscience and thoughts either accuse them or tell them they are doing right."* (Romans 2:14-15) God has a plan and a way for everything. If someone doesn't have a copy of the Bible, or even further, if they haven't even *heard* it, God writes it in their hearts. Only God can do that. Every other piece of knowledge or history must be learned by reading or hearing it somewhere. It isn't something just written on one's heart or natural instinct. It's learned. *"For the word of God is alive and active."* (Hebrews 4:12a NIV), and if someone doesn't have access to it, God writes it on their heart. That's amazing. It's also comforting to know that no one will be left out no matter what the circumstances. God has a way to reach every single heart.

"They know the truth about God because he has made it obvious to them. For ever since the world was created, people have seen the earth and sky. Through everything God made, they can clearly see his invisible qualities—his eternal power and divine nature. So they have no excuse for not knowing God." (Romans 1:19-20)

"As the rain and the snow come down from heaven and do not return to it without watering the earth and making it bud and flourish, so that it yields seed for the sower and bread for the eater, so is my word that goes out from

my mouth: It will not return to me empty, but will accomplish what I desire and achieve the purpose for which I sent it." (Isaiah 55:10-11 NIV)

No one has an excuse for not knowing God. That doesn't mean we will all know Him fully or understand His word completely, but we have no excuse for not knowing Him. His word tells us that *He, Himself,* has made it obvious! It's not like He's hiding in some hard to find place that only a few ever discover. He is obvious yet mysterious. Only God can weave those two things together. It makes me think of a pregnant woman. It's obvious that there is a baby in there, but so much mystery remains. Jehovah makes His existence obvious. His invisible qualities are clearly seen through everything that He has made, yet there is so much more. The mystery is what continues to draw us to Him. We have no excuse. He will write His word on our hearts, or He will speak to us through nature, through things that we can see. All we have to do is *look.*

It is up to us what we do with the knowledge that we have. Some may think it's foolish to believe in the words recorded in a book. *"Now faith is the substance of things hoped for, the evidence of things not seen."* (Hebrews 11:1 KJV) Notice the definition of faith has two parts. Faith is the substance or reality of things that we *hope* for. First, we have hope, which is the expectation or desire for something to happen or to be true. The second part of faith is the evidence of things *not seen*. When we choose to believe, we receive proof of things not seen. Faith takes hope and heart belief. When we have those two things, then God reveals His invisible qualities through things that we *can* see, which then results in a greater faith within us causing us to continue to seek Him and go to deeper levels of relationship with our Creator.

Believing in the One true God and Jesus Christ takes faith, just like it takes faith to believe in any other piece of history that we learn about. God doesn't leave us with nothing to hold on to, though. He surrounds us with solid proof, substance and evidence that points directly to Him. Without faith, man will always find an explanation other than God to explain the things that we see.

Faith just seems too simple, doesn't it? What about the proof? What about earning something? Have you taken the time to see how important faith is to God and what He says about it in His eternal word? I can't even begin to record all of the verses that the Bible holds about faith and the importance of it, but let's look at a few of them. It's not only a *"New Testament"* thing, either. It began way back in the beginning:

"Through their faith, the people in days of old earned a good reputation. By faith we understand that the entire universe was formed at God's command, that what we now see did not come from anything that can be seen." (Hebrews 11:2-3)

"And Abram believed the Lord, and the Lord counted him as righteous because of his faith." (Genesis 15:6)

"It was by faith that Enoch was taken up to heaven without dying— 'he disappeared, because God took him.' For before he was taken up, he was known as a person who pleased God. And it is impossible to please God without faith. Anyone who wants to come to him must believe that God exlsts and that he rewards those who sincerely seek him.

It was by faith that Noah built a large boat to save his family from the flood. He obeyed God, who warned him about things that had never happened before. By his faith Noah condemned the rest of the world, and he received the righteousness that comes by faith." (Hebrews 11:5-7)

"It was by faith that the people of Israel marched around Jericho for seven days, and the walls came crashing down." (Hebrews 11:30)

"How much more do I need to say? It would take too long to recount the stories of the faith of Gideon, Barak, Samson, Jephthah, David, Samuel, and all the prophets. By faith these people overthrew kingdoms, ruled with justice, and received what God had promised them. They shut the mouths of lions, quenched the flames of fire, and escaped death by the edge of the sword. Their weakness was turned to strength. They became strong in battle and put whole armies to flight. Women received their loved ones back again from death." (Hebrews 11:32-35a)

Did you notice what was said about what faith did for Abram and Noah? *It made them righteous.* It wasn't their works or actions that made them righteous, it was their faith. It was because they expected and believed what God said was true. Because of their hope and belief, God made them righteous.

"But now God has shown us a way to be made right with him without keeping the requirements of the law, as was promised in the writings of Moses and the prophets long ago. We are made right with God by placing our faith in Jesus Christ. And this is true for ***<u>everyone who believes, no matter who we are.</u>***

*For everyone has sinned; we all fall short of God's glorious standard. Yet God, in his grace****, freely makes us right*** *in his sight. He did this through Christ Jesus when he freed us from the penalty for our sins. For God presented Jesus as the sacrifice for sin. People are made right with God when they* ***believe*** *that Jesus sacrificed his life, shedding his blood. This sacrifice shows that God was being fair when he held back and did not punish those who sinned in times past, for he was looking ahead and including them in what he would do in this present time. God did this to demonstrate his righteousness, for he himself is fair and just, and he makes sinners right in his sight when they believe in Jesus."* (Romans 3:21-26, emphasis added)

"Oh, foolish Galatians! Who has cast an evil spell on you? For the meaning of Jesus Christ's death was made as clear to you as if you had seen a picture of his death on the cross. Let me ask you this one question: Did you receive the Holy Spirit by obeying the law of Moses? Of course not! You received the Spirit because you believed the message you heard about Christ. How foolish can you be? After starting your new lives in the Spirit, why are you now trying to become perfect by your own human effort? Have you experienced so much for nothing? Surely it was not in vain, was it?

I ask you again, does God give you the Holy Spirit and work miracles among you because you obey the law? Of course not! It is because you believe the message you heard about Christ.

In the same way, 'Abraham believed God, and God counted him as righteous because of his faith.' The real children of Abraham, then, are those who put their faith in God.

What's more, the Scriptures looked forward to this time when God would make the Gentiles right in his sight because of their faith. God proclaimed this good news to Abraham long ago when he said, 'All nations will be blessed through you.' So all who put their faith in Christ share the same blessing Abraham received because of his faith.

But those who depend on the law to make them right with God are under his curse, for the Scriptures say, 'Cursed is everyone who does not observe and obey all the commands that are written in God's Book of the Law.' So it is clear that no one can be made right with God by trying to keep the law. For the Scriptures say, 'It is through faith that a righteous person has life.' This way of faith is very different from the way of law, which says, 'It is through obeying the law that a person has life.'

But Christ has rescued us from the curse pronounced by the law. When he was hung on the cross, he took upon himself the curse for our wrongdoing. For it is written in the Scriptures, 'Cursed is everyone who is hung on a tree.' Through Christ Jesus, God has blessed the Gentiles with the same blessing he promised to Abraham, so that we who are believers might receive the promised Holy Spirit through faith." (Galatians 3:1-14)

It all goes back to the new law, the new covenant that is talked about in the book of Hebrews. The new law is love. *"So Christ has truly set us free. Now make sure that you stay free, and don't get tied up again in slavery to the law.*

Listen! I, Paul, tell you this: If you are counting on circumcision to make you right with God, then Christ will be of no benefit to you. I'll say it again. If you are trying to find favor with God by being circumcised, you must obey every regulation in the whole law of Moses. For if you are trying to make yourselves right with God by keeping the law, you have been cut off from Christ! You have fallen away from God's grace.

But we who live by the Spirit eagerly wait to receive by faith the righteousness God has promised to us. For when we place our faith in Christ Jesus, there is no benefit in being circumcised or being uncircumcised. What is important is faith expressing itself in love." (Galatians 5:1-6)

"But God is so rich in mercy, and he loved us so much, that even though we were dead because of our sins, he gave us life when he raised Christ from the dead. (It is only by God's grace that you have been saved!)" (Ephesians 2:4-5)

"God saved you by his grace when you **believed**. *And you can't take credit for this; it is a gift from God. Salvation is not a reward for the good things we have done, so none of us can boast about it."* (Ephesians 2:8-9, emphasis added)

"I no longer count on my own righteousness through obeying the law; rather, I become righteous through faith in Christ. For God's way of making us right with himself depends on faith." (Philippians 3:9)

"Yet now he has reconciled you to himself through the death of Christ in his physical body. As a result, he has brought you into his own presence, and you are holy and blameless as you stand before him without a single fault.

But you must continue to believe this truth and stand firmly in it. Don't drift away from the assurance you received when you heard the Good News. The Good News has been preached all over the world, and I, Paul, have been appointed as God's servant to proclaim it." (Colossians 1:22-23)

"But— When God our Savior revealed his kindness and love, he saved us, not because of the righteous things we had done, but because of his mercy. He washed away our sins, giving us a new birth and new life through the Holy Spirit. He generously poured out the Spirit upon us through Jesus Christ our Savior. Because of his grace he made us right in his sight and gave us confidence that we will inherit eternal life." (Titus 3:4-7)

"Everyone who believes that Jesus is the Christ has become a child of God. And everyone who loves the Father loves his children, too. We know we love God's children if we love God and obey his commandments. Loving God means keeping his commandments, and his commandments are not burdensome. For every child of God defeats this evil world, and we achieve this victory through our faith. And who can win this battle against the world? Only those who believe that Jesus is the Son of God." (1 John 5:1-5)

That is only a portion of the faith verses in the Bible. Why do you think it is repeated over and over and over again? I believe that God really wants us to grab hold of this truth and stand firm in it. We are made right with God by faith, and we receive His promises by living and acting out of that faith.

"You will seek Me and find Me when you search for Me with all your heart." (Jeremiah 29:13 NASB) God's word is eternal. His word is faithful to every generation. His word is entirely true.

I agree with the psalmist when he said, *"If your instructions hadn't sustained me with joy, I would've died in my misery."* (vs. 92) I remember that time of depression, a time near hopelessness. He's right, I would have died in my misery. I'm not talking about physically dying, but emotionally, spiritually, and mentally my soul would have died in my misery if it wasn't for the joy in God's word that sustained me. To sustain is to strengthen or support physically or mentally. Here are some synonyms: comfort, help, assist, encourage, support, give strength to, buoy up, carry. That is what God's word does for us. It gives us life!

This chapter is titled *Limitless* because of the words recorded in verse 96. *"Even perfection has its limits, but your commands have no limit."*

What does it mean that His commands have no limit? By now you probably know that I'm going to refer to the new commandments, not the old law that has been cancelled out, but the new one. Do you know what that greatest command is by heart now?

"'Teacher, which is the most important commandment in the law of Moses?'

Jesus replied, 'You must love the Lord your God with all your heart, all your soul, and all your mind.' This is the first and greatest commandment. A second is equally important: 'Love your neighbor as yourself.' The entire law and all the demands of the prophets are based on these two commandments.'" (Matthew 22:36-40)

The first and greatest commandment is to love God. How and why can we love Him with all we have and it be a true genuine love that isn't forced? *"We love him, because he first loved us."* (1 John 4:19 KJV)

The psalmist said that His commands have no limit. The love that we can experience with God is limitless. The love that God has for us is limitless. Boundless. Endless. This means that for our entire lifetime, our relationship with God can continue to grow deeper and deeper. There are no borders. It cannot be measured. It's mysterious. It's infinite. Fathomless. True Love is limitless.

You and I have the ultimate treasure box right under our nose, but until we open it for ourselves and dig through it, we will never know what all it contains. You must look into it on your own to find the personal gifts that belong to you. *"Again, the kingdom of heaven is like treasure hidden in a field, which a man found and hid; and for joy over it he goes and sells all that he has and buys that field."* (Matthew 13:44 NKJV) So often we look at the treasure that someone else has and wonder why we don't have it. The truth is, God has wrapped up gifts with your name written on them, but you have to choose to open them and accept them.

"My child, listen to what I say, and treasure my commands. Tune your ears to wisdom and concentrate on understanding. Cry out for insight and ask for understanding. Search for them as you would for silver; seek them like hidden treasures. Then you will understand what it means to fear the Lord, and you will gain knowledge of God. For the Lord grants wisdom! From his mouth come knowledge and understanding. He grants a treasure of common sense to the honest. He is a shield to those who walk with integrity. He guards the paths of the just and protects those who are faithful to him. Then you will understand what is right, just, and fair, and you will find the right way to go. For wisdom will enter your heart, and knowledge will fill you with joy. Wise choices will watch over you. Understanding will keep you safe." (Proverbs 2:1-11)

Remember God is seeking a *personal* relationship with each of us, and I pray that you are looking for a *personal* relationship with Him. To have a *personal* relationship, means that you will receive *personal* gifts from Him, and those gifts are only found when you *personally* go and look for them.

"'Yes, a person is a fool to store up earthly wealth but not have a rich relationship with God.'

Then, turning to his disciples, Jesus said, 'That is why I tell you not to worry about everyday life—whether you have enough food to eat or enough clothes to wear. For life is more than food, and your body more than clothing. Look at the ravens. They don't plant or harvest or store food in barns, for God feeds them. And you are far more valuable to him than any birds! Can all your worries add a single moment to your life? And if worry can't accomplish a little thing like that, what's the use of worrying over bigger things?

Look at the lilies and how they grow. They don't work or make their clothing, yet Solomon in all his glory was not dressed as beautifully as they are. And if God cares so wonderfully for flowers that are here today and thrown into the fire tomorrow, he will certainly care for you. Why do you have so little faith?

And don't be concerned about what to eat and what to drink. Don't worry about such things. These things dominate the thoughts of unbelievers all over the world, but your Father already knows your needs. Seek the Kingdom of God above all else, and he will give you everything you need.

So don't be afraid, little flock. For it gives your Father great happiness to give you the Kingdom.'" (Luke 12:21-32)

Your Heavenly Father is delighted to give you the Kingdom! Don't you want to know what that means? We have no idea how blessed we truly are! I strongly encourage you to seek for hope on your own. I don't mean that you shouldn't read someone else's opinion or teachings because God speaks through others, and it is wise to surround yourself with godly people and encouragement. What I do mean is when you hear God's word spoken through another, written by another, or expressed in any other way, remember to ask the Lord what He is saying specifically to *you* through that message. Then take it to heart and keep digging because there is *always* more.

I also encourage you to dig into the rough and unfamiliar places. I have heard messages before that I didn't agree with. In the past, I would have avoided the teaching or the portion of Scripture that didn't make sense and tune it out. I learned that instead of shunning the teacher or abandoning God's word altogether, God liked to use the disagreement to draw me into His word to search the Scriptures and find the truth. Not to tell the other person that they were wrong or to try to prove Scripture wrong, but to gain knowledge and wisdom for myself so that I could know the truth and be set free. There have been some things about God's character in the Scriptures that didn't make sense to me that I avoided for a long time. Finally, I asked the Lord to give me understanding of those Scriptures that seemed to contradict the unconditional love that I had heard and read about, and He did. Maybe you can relate to that feeling of confusion about the Scriptures. God's word never contradicts itself, so if you have come across a place that seems contradicting, then there is more to discover, a deeper meaning. I strongly encourage you to ask the Lord to grant you godly wisdom in the areas of questioning and to show you the truth about it. Sometimes it's those very places that the Lord will use to open up a whole new spectrum of His True Love and the ***limitless amount of treasures*** available to us, if only we will look.

"By wisdom a house is built, and through understanding it is established; through knowledge its rooms are filled with ***rare and beautiful treasures.****"* (Proverbs 24:3-4 NIV, emphasis added)

"I want them to be encouraged and knit together by strong ties of love. I want them to have complete confidence that they understand God's mysterious plan, which is Christ himself. In him lie hidden all the ***treasures of wisdom and knowledge.****"* (Colossians 2:2-3, emphasis added)

"Therefore, since God in his mercy has given us this new way, we never give up. We reject all shameful deeds and underhanded methods. We don't try to trick anyone or distort the word of God. We tell the truth before God, and all who are honest know this.

If the Good News we preach is hidden behind a veil, it is hidden only from people who are perishing. Satan, who is the god of this world, has blinded the minds of those who don't believe. They are unable to see the glorious light of the Good News. They don't understand this message about the glory of Christ, who is the exact likeness of God.

You see, we don't go around preaching about ourselves. We preach that Jesus Christ is Lord, and we ourselves are your servants for Jesus' sake. For God, who said, 'Let there be light in the darkness,' has made this light shine in our hearts so we could know the glory of God that is seen in the face of Jesus Christ.

We now have this light shining in our hearts, but we ourselves are like fragile clay jars containing this **great treasure**. *This makes it clear that our great power is from God, not from ourselves.*

We are pressed on every side by troubles, but we are not crushed. We are perplexed, but not driven to despair. We are hunted down, but never abandoned by God. We get knocked down, but we are not destroyed. Through suffering, our bodies continue to share in the death of Jesus so that the life of Jesus may also be seen in our bodies.

Yes, we live under constant danger of death because we serve Jesus, so that the life of Jesus will be evident in our dying bodies. So we live in the face of death, but this has resulted in eternal life for you.

But we continue to preach because we have the same kind of faith the psalmist had when he said, 'I believed in God, so I spoke.' We know that God, who raised the Lord Jesus, will also raise us with Jesus and present us to himself together with you. All of this is for your benefit. And as God's grace reaches more and more people, there will be great thanksgiving, and God will receive more and more glory.

That is why we never give up. Though our bodies are dying, our spirits are being renewed every day. For our present troubles are small and won't last very long. Yet they produce for us a glory that vastly outweighs them and will last forever! So we don't look at the troubles we can see now; rather, we fix our gaze on things that cannot be seen. For the things we see now will soon be gone, but the things we cannot see will last forever." (2 Corinthians 4, emphasis added)

"Teach those who are rich in this world not to be proud and not to trust in their money, which is so unreliable. Their trust should be in God, who richly gives us all we need for our enjoyment. Tell them to use their money to do good. They should be rich in good works and generous to those in need, always being ready to share with others. By doing this they will be **storing up their treasure** *as a good foundation for the future so that they may experience true life."* (1 Timothy 6:17-19, emphasis added)

Limitless treasure is found in His True Love. He is *True Life*. The treasures He has for us, He gives us for our *enjoyment.* His desire is for you to have and live an abundantly joyful life. Isn't that your desire as well? Imagine it.

"Limitless, True Love." Almost sounds too good to be true. Go and find out for yourself!

97 Oh, how I love your instructions!
I think about them all day long.
98 Your commands make me wiser than my enemies,
for they are my constant guide.
99 Yes, I have more insight than my teachers,
for I am always thinking of your laws.
100 I am even wiser than my elders,
for I have kept your commandments.
101 I have refused to walk on any evil path,
so that I may remain obedient to your word.
102 I haven't turned away from your regulations,
for you have taught me well.
103 How sweet your words taste to me;
they are sweeter than honey.
104 Your commandments give me understanding;
no wonder I hate every false way of life.

Psalm 119:97–104

15

You Sanctify Me

Think about the times that you have eaten or taken a drink of something that you have never tried before. Maybe you thought it tasted good, but it was still strange because it wasn't something you were used to. Maybe it tasted awful, but wildly, the more you tried it, the more you began to actually enjoy it. Either way, if you only try it once, you may *never* get to the point of saying, *"I love this!"*

That is how it can be with God's word. If I only digest it once in a while, it may seem strange. I might come across a part that I really like, but if I forget to keep feeding it to myself, then it is still unfamiliar and maybe a bit awkward. Sometimes I might come across a part that I don't like. Then I have to make a choice to either keep trying it because I know that God is all good, and I know that if I keep at it then I will gain understanding. Or I can choose to walk away and not try it again simply because I didn't like it the first time.

Jesus spoke of the nourishment that God's word brings. One time, Jesus was tired and hungry, and the disciples went to get Jesus something to eat. *"Meanwhile, the disciples were urging Jesus, 'Rabbi, eat something.' But Jesus replied, 'I have a kind of food you know nothing about.' 'Did someone bring him food while we were gone?' the disciples asked each other. Then Jesus explained: 'My nourishment comes from doing the will of God, who sent me, and from finishing his work.'"* (John 4:31-34)

"Jesus replied 'Anyone who drinks this water will soon become thirsty again. But those who drink the water I give will never be thirsty again. It becomes a fresh, bubbling spring within them, giving them eternal life.'" (John 4:13-14)

God's word contains nourishment for our bodies. If we aren't drinking or feeding ourselves His word, we may not understand His will for us, and we will become spiritually starving.

How does it strike you when you read the psalmist's words, *"Oh, how I love your instructions! I think about them all day long."* (vs.97) Can you relate, or is that an awkward statement? That is a good question for us to ask ourselves. If that statement doesn't resonate with my heart, maybe it is a sign that I need more of God's word in my diet.

According to the psalmist, why does he love God's instructions so much? They make him wiser, they guide him, they give him insight, they keep him from doing what is evil, they give him pleasure, they give him understanding, and cause him to hate every false way of living.

When we fill our lives with that kind of nourishment, God's word sanctifies us. Do you live the Romans 7 lifestyle? *"So the trouble is not with the law, for it is spiritual and good. The trouble is with me, for I am all too human, a slave to sin. I don't really understand myself, for I want to do what is right, but I don't do it. Instead, I do what I hate. But if I know that what I am doing is wrong, this shows that I agree that the law is good. So I am not the one doing wrong; it is sin living in me that does it. And I know that nothing good lives in me, that is, in my sinful nature. I want to do what is right, but I can't. I want to do what is good, but I don't. I don't want to do what is wrong, but I do it anyway. But if I do what I don't want to do, I am not really the one doing wrong; it is sin living in me that does it I have discovered this principle of life—that when I want to do what is right, I inevitably do what is wrong. I love God's law with all my heart. But there is another power within me that is at war with my mind. This power makes me a slave to the sin that is still within me. Oh, what a miserable person I am! Who will free me from this life that is dominated by sin and death? Thank God! The answer is in Jesus Christ our Lord. So you see how it is: In my mind I really want to obey God's law, but because of my sinful nature I am a slave to sin."* (Romans 7:14-25)

I have felt that struggle! I love God's law with all my heart, but there's just something in me that I am constantly having to war against. I believe this is true for all of us at times, so don't feel like you are alone if that's where you are right now. I think we can fall into that rut several times throughout our lives. Even when we do know His instructions well, we still need reminders. The good news is chapter 8 of Romans gives us instructions on how to get ourselves out of that cycle. Thank you, Jesus, for your instructions!

I would like to dissect Romans 8 so that we can dig up every treasure of freedom found in God's instructions.

"So now there is no condemnation for those who belong to Christ Jesus. And because you belong to him, the power of the life-giving Spirit has freed you from the power of sin that leads to death." (Romans 8:1-2)

Assuming that you have accepted Jesus as your personal Lord and Savior, according to the first two verses of Romans 8, there are three amazing treasures that belong to you! First, no condemnation, which means no punishment, no criticism! It means that God approves of you. Secondly, you have the power of the Holy Spirit. Thirdly, you have freedom from sin and death.

"The law of Moses was unable to save us because of the weakness of our sinful nature. So God did what the law could not do. He sent his own Son in a body like the bodies we sinners have. And in that body God declared an end to sin's control over us by giving his Son as a sacrifice for our sins. He did this so that the just requirement of the law would be fully satisfied for us, who no longer follow our sinful nature but instead follow the Spirit. (Romans 8:3-4)

The law of Moses isn't what saves us. It is the death of Jesus' body, Jesus' blood, that saves us. If you belong to Jesus, you can live free from sin and the death that it leads to. Notice in the end of verse 4 that it says *"He did this... for us, who no longer follow our sinful nature but instead follow the Spirit."* That tells me that we have a choice. Freedom is available to all of God's children, but we each have a choice. We can choose to follow our sinful nature, and that will not disqualify us from being a saved child of God. Remember, no condemnation. But we will not live in freedom. Instead, we will struggle when we choose to follow our own sinful nature. The other option is to choose to follow the life-giving Spirit. The Holy Spirit. God's Spirit. The question is, how do we do that?

"Those who are dominated by the sinful nature think about sinful things, but those who are controlled by the Holy Spirit think about things that please the Spirit. So letting your sinful nature control your mind leads to death. But letting the Spirit control your mind leads to life and peace. For the sinful nature is always hostile to God. It never did obey God's laws, and it never will." (Romans 8:5-7)

How can we determine if we are being led by our sinful nature or by the Spirit? By paying attention to what we are thinking about. Think about what you are thinking about. If we allow the Holy Spirit to control our minds, then we experience life and peace. Yes! That's what we want!

There is an example in the Scriptures on how to do this. *"Don't worry about anything; instead, pray about everything. Tell God what you need and thank him for all he has done. Then you will experience God's peace, which exceeds anything we can understand. His peace will guard your hearts and minds as you live in Christ Jesus."* (Philippians 4:6-7)

First, instead of worrying, give it to God. Then thank Him for what He has already done. Is there something you are worrying about? If you give that worry to God in faith, believing that He can and will handle it, and exchange that worry for thankfulness, Paul says that you will experience God's peace. His peace will guard your heart and mind as you follow the lead of the Spirit. Pay attention to your thoughts and what you dwell on. It can either bring darkness to your life or it can bring light. You have the choice to stay in the dark or turn the light on by trusting God and being thankful. As we focus on what we can be thankful for, everything else fades away. That is the peace that will guard our heart and mind.

"And now, dear brothers and sisters, one final thing. Fix your thoughts on what is true, and honorable, and right, and pure, and lovely, and admirable. Think about things that are excellent and worthy of praise. Keep putting into practice all you learned and received from me—everything you heard from me and saw me doing. Then the God of peace will be with you." (Philippians 4:8-9)

Paul pointed out that the instructions aren't a one-time deal. It is something to keep practicing. Constantly be aware of what you are thinking. Do you call yourself a failure? Is that true? God says there is no condemnation against you. God sees you as righteous, pure. He never gives up on you. He is forever patient. Instead of settling with, *"I'm a failure,"* how about, *"I am learning from my mistakes. I can do all things through Christ who strengthens me. I am a work in progress. I can and will do better. God's love never fails. He never gives up on me."* Try asking God what He thinks about you and what He says about you. Not what another person has said, not what you see, not what the world may see, but what God sees. Don't settle with merely "knowing" what the Bible says, because then it only remains head knowledge. Ask Jesus. Be bold and ask Him what He sees when He sees you. Then expect Him to answer. When He answers you, that head knowledge will become experiential knowledge, and it will allow your heart to believe the truth as well as your head. It will finally feel true when you hear what Jesus has to say about you because He has the whole truth and nothing but the Truth.

Maybe you think you are useless. You have no purpose. Is that true or worthy of praise? Do you think God makes anything that is useless? Try changing that thought to, *"God does not make mistakes. I have life, so I have a purpose. My purpose is to know God and love Him with all I have. God wants my love. My life is precious to God. There is a reason I exist."* Even better than that, ask Jesus to speak the truth over you. Picture Jesus in your mind's eye and ask Him what He thinks about the thought that you are useless.

Questions we can ask ourselves to determine whether we are following our sinful nature or the Spirit are: Is that thought true? Is it honorable? Is it lovely? Is it pure? Is it right? Is it admirable, excellent, worthy of praise? If your answer to any of those questions is no, then stop there and ask the Lord what He has to say about it. If we keep our thoughts lined up with the truth of God's Word, recognize when it doesn't feel true, and ask Jesus to speak the truth over us, then His peace will be with us, and it will be a guard over our minds and protection over our hearts.

"That's why those who are still under the control of their sinful nature can never please God. But you are not controlled by your sinful nature. You are controlled by the Spirit if you have the Spirit of God living in you. (And remember that those who do not have the Spirit of Christ living in them do not belong to him at all.)" (Romans 8:8-9)

Those who are not saved are controlled by their sinful nature. Those who are saved are controlled by the *Spirit of God, who lives in them.* Without God, you have no choice. With God, you get to choose whether you want to take the reins or hand them over to the Spirit of God, who brings life and peace. It all begins with our thoughts.

"And Christ lives within you, so even though your body will die because of sin, the Spirit gives you life because you have been made right with God. The Spirit of God, who raised Jesus from the dead, lives in you. And just as God raised Christ Jesus from the dead, he will give life to your mortal bodies by this same Spirit living within you." (Romans 8:10-11)

Christ lives in you! It's one thing to read or to even say it but think about it. Wow! That is true, honorable, lovely, admirable, pure, right, excellent thinking, and it is definitely worthy of praise! Hallelujah! The Spirit of God, the *same* one that raised Jesus' dead body from the grave, yes that power, lives in you right now! It's a bummer to think that these bodies we have will die, but think about the lovely part of it. The Spirit that lives within you will never die, and as soon as your physical body dies, the Spirit of God will give it life again! Allow that truth to sink in. Use it as one of your ropes. You and I are walking around with the same power that raised Jesus' body from the dead. It's living inside of us. Mind blowing!

"Therefore, dear brothers and sisters, you have no obligation to do what your sinful nature urges you to do. For if you live by its dictates, you will die. But if through the power of the Spirit you put to death the deeds of your sinful nature, you will live. For all who are led by the Spirit of God are children of God. (Romans 8:12-14)

Once again, we have a choice. We are not obligated to do what we don't want to do, but we can if that is what we choose. It isn't always easy. Verse 12 says that your sinful nature urges you. To urge means to force along, to push, or to press. That explains why we end up in the Romans 7 cycle. We do what we don't want to do. When we know what is right, we do what is wrong even though we don't want to. Constantly at war with ourselves. Living that way brings spiritual and emotional death. If we are unhealthy spiritually or emotionally, it can lead to physical problems. Good news is, it isn't our job to strive to put to death the deeds of our sinful nature and have life. According to Scripture, it is done by the power of the Holy Spirit within us! It begins every time with our thought life. What are you thinking about? If it isn't good, find the truth that God has for you and choose life! Now you can ask yourself: *"Is that thought death, or is it life?"* Choose life and the Holy Spirit will put to death your sinful nature that urges you to go its way.

"Don't copy the behavior and customs of this world, but let God transform you into a new person by changing the way you think. Then you will learn to know God's will for you, which is good and pleasing and perfect." (Romans 12:2) Your job is to "notice" what you are thinking about and allow *God* to change the way you think, and *He* will do the transforming in your heart and mind.

"So you have not received a spirit that makes you fearful slaves. Instead, you received God's Spirit when he adopted you as his own children. Now we call him, 'Abba, Father.'" (Romans 8:15)

He adopted me. He adopted us! Think on that for a moment. When someone chooses to adopt, it is because they *want* to out of love. Not because they have to, but because they want to for the child's sake and for the family. God chose to adopt you and I, and He gives us His own Spirit, not a fearful spirit. We can call Him, *"Abba."* That is the more personal way to say *"Father."* It means Daddy or Papa. He is the perfect Father. We cannot compare Him to our earthly examples, although I have a wonderful dad who is a beautiful example of Jesus, I know some of you have not had that experience. So when thinking of God as your Dad, you have to think of Him as that perfect, loving Daddy. One that loves you unconditionally, never gives up on you, and is always proud of you. One that protects, guides, and supports you. One that contains no evil but is only good. You have a perfect Dad, and He is the Creator of the Universe. Wow! You are rich and famous! Did you know that? Take a moment to ponder those good things and allow God to transform you into a new person by changing the way you think. Remember, you are doing the noticing, and He is doing the changing. Your job is to notice your thoughts and ask for His truth. He does the rest.

"For his Spirit joins with our spirit to affirm that we are God's children. And since we are his children, we are his heirs. In fact, together with Christ we are heirs of God's glory. But if we are to share his glory, we must also share his suffering." (Romans 8:16-17)

I told you that you were rich! We are all princes and princesses! Our Daddy is the King of the universe! All that belongs to Him, belongs to us! Those Scriptures are full of wonderful treasures, then we run into the ending that doesn't sound so wonderful. *"...if we are to share his glory, we must also share his suffering."*

Jesus suffered for us while he was completely innocent. Sin has created a darkness that affects us all. Until we reach Heaven, we will have to share Jesus's suffering. When we think upon what Jesus willingly chose to do for us, hopefully we can share His suffering with a good attitude. We can choose to dwell on the suffering in our lives, but is that admirable? I believe it would be better to think on the heavenly things as Paul instructed. *"Yet what we suffer now is nothing compared to the glory he will reveal to us later. For all creation is waiting eagerly for that future day when God will reveal who his children really are. Against its will, all creation was subjected to God's curse. But with eager hope, the creation looks forward to the day when it will join God's children in glorious freedom from death and decay."* (Romans 8:18-21)

How does your heart respond when you read, *"Against its will, all creation was subjected to God's curse."*? There is no evil thing about God, so how can He subject us to a curse? First of all, there had to be discipline for sin.

"And have you forgotten the encouraging words God spoke to you as his children? He said,

'My child, don't make light of the Lord's discipline,
and don't give up when he corrects you.
For the Lord disciplines those he loves,
and he punishes each one he accepts as his child.'

As you endure this divine discipline, remember that God is treating you as his own children. Who ever heard of a child who is never disciplined by its father? If God doesn't discipline you as he does all of his children, it means that you are illegitimate and are not really his children at all. Since we respected our earthly fathers who disciplined us, shouldn't we submit even more to the discipline of the Father of our spirits, and live forever?

For our earthly fathers disciplined us for a few years, doing the best they knew how. <u>But God's discipline is always good for us, so that we might share in his holiness</u>. No discipline is enjoyable while it is happening—it's painful! But afterward there will be a peaceful harvest of right living for those who are trained in this way." (Hebrews 12:5-11, emphasis added)

He did it for our own good. Yes, He could have just cleared all bad away, but then we would have never learned from our mistakes. We wouldn't lean on the Lord, and we wouldn't appreciate Him if all He did was go behind us and clean up our messes, never giving us responsibility or training.

What is the curse? *"Then the Lord God said to the serpent, 'Because you have done this, you are cursed more than all animals, domestic and wild. You will crawl on your belly, groveling in the dust as long as you live. And I will cause hostility between you and the woman, and between your offspring and her offspring. He will strike your head, and you will strike his heel.'*

Then he said to the woman, 'I will sharpen the pain of your pregnancy, and in pain you will give birth. And you will desire to control your husband, but he will rule over you.'

And to the man he said, 'Since you listened to your wife and ate from the tree whose fruit I commanded you not to eat, the ground is cursed because of you. All your life you will struggle to scratch a living from it. It will grow thorns and thistles for you, though you will eat of its grains. By the sweat of your brow will you have food to eat until you return to the ground from which you were made. For you were made from dust, and to dust you will return.'" (Genesis 3:14-19)

Do you know that you don't have to live under that curse? *"But those who depend on the law to make them right with God are under his curse, for the Scriptures say, 'Cursed is everyone who does not observe and obey all the commands that are written in God's Book of the Law.' So it is clear that no one can be made right with God by trying to keep the law. For the Scriptures say,* ***'It is through faith that a righteous person has life.'*** *This way of faith is very different from the way of law, which says, 'It is through obeying the law that a person has life.'*

But Christ has rescued us from the curse pronounced by the law. When he was hung on the cross, he took upon himself the curse for our wrongdoing. For it is written in the Scriptures, 'Cursed is everyone who is hung on a tree.' Through Christ Jesus, God has blessed the Gentiles with the same blessing he promised to Abraham, so that we who are believers might receive the promised Holy Spirit through faith." (Galatians 3:10-14, emphasis added)

"Why, then, was the law given? It was given alongside the promise to show people their sins. But the law was designed to last only until the coming of the child who was promised. God gave his law through angels to Moses, who was the mediator between God and the people. Now a mediator is helpful if more than one party must reach an agreement. But God, who is one, did not use a mediator when he gave his promise to Abraham.

Is there a conflict, then, between God's law and God's promises? Absolutely not! If the law could give us new life, we could be made right with God by obeying it. But the Scriptures declare that we are all prisoners of sin, so we receive God's promise of freedom ***only by believing*** *in Jesus Christ.*

Before the way of faith in Christ was available to us, we were placed under guard by the law. We were kept in protective custody, so to speak, until the way of faith was revealed.

Let me put it another way. The law was our guardian until Christ came; it protected us until we could be made right with God through faith. And now that the way of faith has come, we no longer need the law as our guardian." (Galatians 3:19-25, emphasis added)

When the Scriptures said that all who depend on the law to make them right are under God's curse, He didn't mean that the law was bad. For example, one of the ten commandments is, *"Do not steal."* If you choose to follow that command, is that a bad thing? *No*. The law is good. What the Scripture means is that if one believes that to be accepted by God they must get all of the laws right, then that person will never find rest because they will spend their life trying to live up to standards that are unreachable. The person would be left restless, overwhelmed, discouraged, exhausted, and empty. Trying to earn grace would be a never-ending job.

We are free when we believe in Jesus. Grace isn't anything that we have earned so that no one can boast about it. It is a gift that Jesus paid a *big* price for. When we are led by the Holy Spirit, *He* guides us along paths that *agree* with the law. When we become wrapped up in God's amazing Love, our response is to do what is good and right versus doing what is good and right because we have to. Living by the law is forced love. Living by the Spirit is experiencing True Love.

Following what our sinful nature urges us to do leads to nothing good. Thank you, Jesus, for making it possible for us to contain the Spirit of God so that we no longer have to live under the control of sin and death. We can thank God for disciplining us because it is discipline that teaches us and gives us wisdom. His discipline strengthens us and grows our character. Through discipline we find respect and love. If He didn't care about us, He would let us do whatever we wanted even if what we were doing was hurting us.

We must also understand that suffering doesn't always come because we have disobeyed or done something wrong. First of all, because mankind sinned, the whole world has to suffer the consequences. Suffering doesn't always mean you are on the wrong path. Look at Jesus' life for example. *"While Jesus was here on earth, he offered prayers and pleadings, with a loud cry and tears, to the one who could rescue him from death. And God heard his prayers because of his deep reverence for God. Even though Jesus was God's Son, he learned obedience from the things he suffered.* (Hebrews 5:7-8)

The hardships in life are used as a training ground. Even Jesus had to learn obedience. *Why?* Obedience is not a bad thing. It is for our protection. The word "obey" may come across as strict. When we ask our children to obey, our motive behind it should be for their own good and not merely just to have control over them. I may tell my son that he cannot watch a certain tv show. My reason isn't because *I* just don't want him to watch tv. It isn't because *I* want to watch something different. It isn't because *I* want to have control over him and make him follow my commands. It is because there is content in the show that exposes his little mind to things that the world says is okay, but the reality is that sometimes what is considered "popular" and "cool" leads to trouble.

Any command of God, any instruction, any training that God leads us through is for our best. If we did not have any guidelines to follow, we would end up doing whatever we want, which isn't always good even when we think it is, and we would not need God. God knows that we need Him, therefore He has set some guidelines. He wants us to lean on Him and follow His instructions, not so He can say, *"I am God, and you will do what I say or else..."* Instead, His tone is more like, *"I am your Creator, your Father, and I know what is best for you. I love you, and I only want to protect you and guide you down the best path you can take; a path that leads to life and joy."*

"Dear brothers and sisters, when troubles of any kind come your way, consider it an opportunity for great joy. For you know that when your faith is tested, your endurance has a chance to grow. So let it grow, for when your endurance is fully developed, you will be perfect and complete, needing nothing." (James 1:2-4)

"Not only that, but we rejoice in our sufferings, knowing that suffering produces endurance, and endurance produces character, and character produces hope, and hope does not put us to shame, because God's love has been poured into our hearts through the Holy Spirit who has been given to us." (Romans 5:3-5 ESV)

May God use these truths to transform our hearts and minds as we continue our Romans 8 journey. *"For we know that all creation has been groaning as in the pains of childbirth right up to the present time. And we believers also groan, even though we have the Holy Spirit within us as a foretaste of future glory, for we long for our bodies to be released from sin and suffering. We, too, wait with eager hope for the day when God will give us our full rights as his adopted children, including the new bodies he has promised us. We were given this hope when we were saved. (If we already have something, we don't need to hope for it. But if we look forward to something we don't yet have, we must wait patiently and confidently.)"* (Romans 8:22-25)

As God's children, we have so much to look forward to! Eternal Life. New Bodies. Everlasting Peace. We wait, and the longer we wait, the more exciting it will be when we receive it! We wait patiently and with confidence! While we wait, we get to enjoy a foretaste of future glory.

"And the Holy Spirit helps us in our weakness. For example, we don't know what God wants us to pray for. But the Holy Spirit prays for us with groanings that cannot be expressed in words. And the Father who knows all hearts knows what the Spirit is saying, for the Spirit pleads for us believers in harmony with God's own will." (Romans 8:26-27)

Isn't it comforting to know that when we don't even know what to pray, the Holy Spirit prays for us? That would explain how our heart's desires change to line up with the desires of God. His Spirit dwells in us, and He sanctifies us, cleanses us, and sets us up for freedom.

"And we know that God causes everything to work together for the good of those who love God and are called according to his purpose for them. For God knew his people in advance, and he chose them to become like his Son, so that his Son would be the firstborn among many brothers and sisters. And having chosen them, he called them to come to him. And having called them, he gave them right standing with himself. And having given them right standing, he gave them his glory." (Romans 8:28-30)

God causes *EVERYTHING* to work out for the good of those that love Him. Only God can turn ashes into beauty. Everything that belongs to God, belongs to you as well, including righteousness and His Glory! God is on our side. His plans for us are only good. Do you remember some of those promises that we can use to tie us firmly to the Anchor, Jesus?

"'For I know the plans I have for you,' says the Lord. 'They are plans for good and not for disaster, to give you a future and a hope.'" (Jeremiah 29:11)

"'Come to me, all you who are weary and burdened, and I will give you rest. Take my yoke upon you and learn from me, for I am gentle and humble in heart, and you will find rest for your souls.'" (Matthew 11:28-29)

"'My child, pay attention to what I say. Listen carefully to my words. Don't lose sight of them. Let them penetrate deep into your heart, for they bring life to those who find them, and healing to their whole body.'" (Proverbs 4:20-22)

"What shall we say about such wonderful things as these? If God is for us, who can ever be against us? Since he did not spare even his own Son but gave him up for us all, won't he also give us everything else? Who dares accuse us whom God has chosen for his own? No one—for God himself has

given us right standing with himself. Who then will condemn us? No one—for Christ Jesus died for us and was raised to life for us, and he is sitting in the place of honor at God's right hand, pleading for us.

Can anything ever separate us from Christ's love? Does it mean he no longer loves us if we have trouble or calamity, or are persecuted, or hungry, or destitute, or in danger, or threatened with death? (As the Scriptures say, 'For your sake we are killed every day; we are being slaughtered like sheep.') No, despite all these things, overwhelming victory is ours through Christ, who loved us.

And I am convinced that nothing can ever separate us from God's love. Neither death nor life, neither angels nor demons, neither our fears for today nor our worries about tomorrow—not even the powers of hell can separate us from God's love. No power in the sky above or in the earth below—indeed, nothing in all creation will ever be able to separate us from the love of God that is revealed in Christ Jesus our Lord." (Romans 8:31-39)

Maybe now you can swallow the Scripture at the beginning of this chapter and it actually taste good to your soul.

97 *Oh, how I love your instructions!*
I think about them all day long.
98 *Your commands make me wiser than my enemies,*
for they are my constant guide.
99 *Yes, I have more insight than my teachers,*
for I am always thinking of your laws.
100 *I am even wiser than my elders,*
for I have kept your commandments.
101 *I have refused to walk on any evil path,*
so that I may remain obedient to your word.
102 *I haven't turned away from your regulations,*
for you have taught me well.
103 *How sweet your words taste to me;*
they are sweeter than honey.
104 *Your commandments give me understanding;*
no wonder I hate every false way of life.
(Psalm 119:97-104)

You are transformed by noticing your thoughts and by allowing Jesus to change the way you think. Freedom, life, and peace are present when we allow the Holy Spirit to be our guide. To be led by the Spirit we must think like Jesus. To think like Jesus, we must know Him and know the Truth. I pray that words like obedience, commandments, instructions, and laws have a new meaning to you knowing that God only loves you and wants what is best for you. He sanctifies us, and as we are being transformed, we become more like Him. Finally, we arrive at the place that we can boldly and confidently say, *"Search me, O God, and know my heart; test me and know my anxious thoughts. Point out anything in me that offends you and lead me along the path of everlasting life."* (Psalm 139:23-24)

If you choose to pray that prayer, expect an answer from the Lord. If you journal, I would encourage you to take time now to write that prayer out. If you don't journal and you just want to say it, my encouragement to you is to ask God, and then take some time to be still and listen to what He might say to you. Give God a chance to point something out to you. Will you give Him the permission to examine your heart and lead you along the path that He knows is best for you?

"Oh, how I love your instructions!
I think about them all day long.
How sweet your words taste to me;
they are sweeter than honey."

"Taste and see that the LORD is good. Oh, the joys of those who take refuge in him!" (Psalm 34:8)

105 YOUR WORD IS A LAMP TO GUIDE MY FEET
AND A LIGHT FOR MY PATH.
106 I'VE PROMISED IT ONCE, AND I'LL PROMISE IT AGAIN:
I WILL OBEY YOUR RIGHTEOUS REGULATIONS.
107 I HAVE SUFFERED MUCH, O LORD;
RESTORE MY LIFE AGAIN AS YOU PROMISED.
108 LORD, ACCEPT MY OFFERING OF PRAISE,
AND TEACH ME YOUR REGULATIONS.
109 MY LIFE CONSTANTLY HANGS IN THE BALANCE,
BUT I WILL NOT STOP OBEYING YOUR INSTRUCTIONS.
110 THE WICKED HAVE SET THEIR TRAPS FOR ME,
BUT I WILL NOT TURN FROM YOUR COMMANDMENTS.
111 YOUR LAWS ARE MY TREASURE;
THEY ARE MY HEART'S DELIGHT.
112 I AM DETERMINED TO KEEP YOUR DECREES
TO THE VERY END.

PSALM 119:105–112

16

Hanging in the Balance

Life can throw so many things at us leaving us feeling uncertain, unsettled, or, like he said, "constantly hanging in the balance." People have a huge factor in this. Everyone has their own choices to make and because of that, our lives can be affected by others. That is why it is important to find True Love in Jesus. As long as you have True Love, and I'm talking about Jesus Christ of Nazareth Who came in the flesh, the One and only True Love, He will get you through anything.

At the beginning of the book I shared with you how I felt at a certain point in my life. If I had to use one word to sum it all up, I would use 'Hopeless'. During that hopeless time of my life, I discovered the promise that says, *"Take delight in the Lord and He will give you your heart's desires."* (Psalm 37:4) My heart desired to taste True Love so badly, I was willing to do whatever it took to get it. I was so tired of feeling empty, broken, alone, and miserable that when I heard *"He WILL give me"* that's all it took. The promise required that I take action, *"Take delight in the Lord and..."* so I took action and began to get to know who God was. He showed me that I was looking for True Love in all the wrong places. It took some time, but He was true to His word and He gave me my heart's desire which was *Him.*

I didn't know that it was Him that I was craving, but it makes sense because He is my Creator. He knows me best. He is my True Love, and my prayer is that you experience His Amazing Love along with me and the psalmist. I never knew that the real desire of my heart was Him, but He knew it, and I'm so glad He opened my eyes and allowed me to see His heart.

The psalmist has expressed over and over how he loves God's law. He isn't saying it casually as if it's only words that sound good but mean nothing. He treasures them, and they bring delight to his heart. The writer recorded Psalm 119 before Jesus was physically living on the earth; before He died to put an end to sin and death. His journey was present when the law of Moses was active, before Jesus cancelled it and made it obsolete. Many struggled with the law and became weary and exhausted trying to keep up with it. The law was often rejected because it was nearly impossible to keep it. It must have been frustrating having the demands of the law always hanging over their heads. Why was the psalmist able to genuinely love the laws, commands, statutes, instructions and decrees? What was it that he had that others didn't understand? He found True Love. He got to know His Father's heart and understood that His instructions were for his own good. He discovered that the laws were for his protection, not for chastisement, and he learned that they were training him, not controlling him. He saw that the commands pointed out to him what he needed to work on to better himself and protect his life, not to shame him. The psalmist loved the commands because he knew the One that made the laws truly loved him. He understood that they were the pathway to life. True life.

Today as we read Psalm 119 and allow it to become our journey, I pray you understand that Jesus has made a new commandment, and what He desires most is that we love Him with all our heart, all our soul, all our mind, and all our strength. In the process of getting to know our personal Savior, His Beautiful Love changes us from the inside out. When your True Love is the One whose Spirit lives within you, you can begin to read His word with new eyes and new understanding.

His word is a Lamp to guide our feet, a light for our path. His word is gentle. His instructions aren't demanding, they are simply a lamp, a light to direct our way. Our choice is to decide whether to take the step where the lamp is lit or choose another way.

In order for a lamp's light to be seen, it must be pretty dim or dark around it. What I love about this picture is that it shows us that God makes His way very clear. If everything were bright, it would be hard for us to see the light of the lamp. We would have to do some guessing and hope we end up in the right place. It would be like coming across several paths when you're trying to find a waterfall in the woods. If it's an unfamiliar journey, you hope you took the right trail and keep moving. But the Lord makes His ways clear when we are seeking Him.

Another detail this picture shows me about God's character is patience. Instead of lighting the entire way, showing us every detail of what lies ahead, and giving us a whole list of steps to take, He gives us a few steps at a time, showing us only what we need for now. Sometimes I want to see the whole picture, but He knows that it would be too overwhelming, too much for me to handle, so He gives me what I am ready for. The mystery also keeps the journey exciting and leaves me with something to look forward to!

"'There is so much more I want to tell you, but you can't bear it now.'" (John 16:12) See, He *wants* to tell you, but for your good, He waits.

"Now we see things imperfectly, like puzzling reflections in a mirror, but then we will see everything with perfect clarity. All that I know now is partial and incomplete, but then I will know everything completely, just as God now knows me completely. Three things will last forever—faith, hope, and love—and the greatest of these is love." (1 Corinthians 13:12-13)

Just follow the light. If you get off track, you don't have to wander. The light, *His word and His Spirit*, is always there like a GPS to redirect you. His word is a lamp to guide your feet, a light for your path.

The psalmist knew that the Lord had promised restoration for his life. In the meantime, while he was hanging in the balance, he offered God praise, he dedicated his life to God, and he was determined to follow Him.

105 *Your word is a lamp to guide my feet*
and a light for my path.
106 *I've promised it once, and I'll promise it again:*
I will obey your righteous regulations.
107 *I have suffered much, O Lord;*
restore my life again as you promised.
108 *Lord, accept my offering of praise,*
and teach me your regulations.
109 *My life constantly hangs in the balance,*
but I will not stop obeying your instructions.
110 *The wicked have set their traps for me,*
but I will not turn from your commandments.
111 *Your laws are my treasure;*
they are my heart's delight.
112 *I am determined to keep your decrees*
to the very end.
(Psalm 119:105-112)

He was dedicated in spite of what was going on around him. He said, *"I will obey, I will not stop, I will not turn, I am determined."* He was hanging in there, constantly having to make a choice.

It sounds like faith is an action. We've talked so much about how we aren't bound by the law anymore. The way to be right with God is by faith and believing. When the law and faith are put in comparison, it makes faith sound so easy almost as if faith and belief aren't even actions.

What if I said that faith is an action, or faith requires action? You have to make the choice to have faith in the things that God places in your heart. The first action is choosing to have faith. When you have faith, it means that you believe. Believe is a verb. It's an action. You are accepting something as true.

"If you confess with your mouth, 'Jesus is Lord,' and believe in your heart that God raised Him from the dead, you will be saved. One believes with the heart, resulting in righteousness, and one confesses with the mouth, resulting in salvation." (Romans 10:9-10 HSCB)

Accepting our eternal destiny by faith is an action. We choose to believe and then confess that Jesus is Lord. Action. We speak it out because our heart won't let us hold it in. We will confess because of the faith that God has produced in our heart and because of our choice to accept it. When you feel that feeling of being made right with God, the Spirit moves you to tell someone! Salvation can't be removed from you. It is a free gift to you that is yours to have and to hold forever because it belongs to you and was paid for by the physical blood of Jesus. Therefore, you cannot earn it or un-earn it because you didn't receive it by deserving it or working for it. You received it by believing that Jesus's death on the cross was enough. Nothing you do or don't do can take it away, because Jesus already paid the price for you. It is fully an undeserved privilege that is yours to keep, regardless of how you act or how lawful you are. It doesn't matter what you do, you can't lose it. It's yours. *"Because of our faith, Christ has brought us into this place of undeserved privilege where we now stand, and we confidently and joyfully look forward to sharing God's glory."* (Romans 5:2)

Salvation is a gift that Jesus lived a lifetime to die for. There is no debt to pay. When He died on the cross, He paid for all sins: past, present, and future. You don't have to work to keep it up, your action is to believe and accept the gift. Once you open that gift by choosing to believe, it belongs to you. Even if someone tries to steal it, it still belongs to you. Even if you try to hide it, it still belongs to you. No one or no thing can take that gift from you. It forever belongs to you.

We have another choice. We can stop in our Christian lives right there and choose to be content with knowing our eternal destination is Heaven, or we can pursue a relationship with the One who paid our debts with His life. Sure, we will still go to Heaven either way, but we will miss out on so many other blessings and gifts that God wants us to receive here on this earth if we settle at salvation. He has more! He has endless treasures with your name on them. To receive those promises, faith requires action. You don't have to follow a bunch of rules and regulations to receive the gift. Your action is to believe, and then live like you believe!

"It was by faith that Noah built a large boat to save his family from the flood. He obeyed God, who warned him about things that had never happened before." (Hebrews 11:7a)

Noah believed what God had told him was true even though he had never even seen rain. What do you think would have happened if Noah didn't build the boat? He probably would have died along with all his family in the flood that God warned him about. Believing alone is not what saved his earthly body and his family. If Noah wanted to receive the blessings and benefits on this earth, he had to take action. He had to build a boat. The physical rescue in Noah's case, required belief followed by action. He lived like he believed, regardless if people thought he was crazy. Noah believed and did something about it.

"It was by faith that even Sarah was able to have a child, though she was barren and was too old. She believed that God would keep his promise. And so a whole nation came from this one man who was as good as dead—a nation with so many people that, like the stars in the sky and the sand on the seashore, there is no way to count them." (Hebrews 11:11-12)

I found the faith of Abraham and Sarah very encouraging after going back and reading their story from the beginning.

"Some time later, the Lord spoke to Abram in a vision and said to him, 'Do not be afraid, Abram, for I will protect you, and your reward will be great.'

But Abram replied, 'O Sovereign Lord, what good are all your blessings when I don't even have a son? Since you've given me no children, Eliezer of Damascus, a servant in my household, will inherit all my wealth. You have given me no descendants of my own, so one of my servants will be my heir.'

Then the Lord said to him, 'No, your servant will not be your heir, for you will have a son of your own who will be your heir.' Then the Lord took Abram outside and said to him, 'Look up into the sky and count the stars if you can. That's how many descendants you will have!'

And Abram believed the Lord, and the Lord counted him as righteous because of his faith." (Genesis 15:1-6)

Abraham was about seventy-five years old when he brought that complaint to the Lord. God told him that he would have a son of his own and that his descendants would be a very great number. At seventy-five years old, when God first spoke to Abraham about the promise, he believed God.

"Now Sarai, Abram's wife, had not been able to bear children for him. But she had an Egyptian servant named Hagar. So Sarai said to Abram, 'The Lord has prevented me from having children. Go and sleep with my servant. Perhaps I can have children through her.' And Abram agreed with Sarai's proposal. So Sarai, Abram's wife, took Hagar the Egyptian servant and gave

her to Abram as a wife. (This happened ten years after Abram had settled in the land of Canaan.)" (Genesis 16:1-3)

Ten years had gone by and still no children. Abraham and Sarah decided to take matters into their own hands and come up with a way that they could have children. It sounds like their faith was being challenged. They were starting to wonder if there was a way.

"Then God said to Abraham, 'Regarding Sarai, your wife—her name will no longer be Sarai. From now on her name will be Sarah. And I will bless her and give you a son from her! Yes, I will bless her richly, and she will become the mother of many nations. Kings of nations will be among her descendants.'

Then Abraham bowed down to the ground, but he laughed to himself in disbelief. 'How could I become a father at the age of 100?' he thought. 'And how can Sarah have a baby when she is ninety years old?' So Abraham said to God, 'May Ishmael live under your special blessing!'

But God replied, 'No—Sarah, your wife, will give birth to a son for you. You will name him Isaac, and I will confirm my covenant with him and his descendants as an everlasting covenant.'" (Genesis 17:15-19)

Oops! Looks like their plan with the servant, Hagar, wasn't what God had in mind. He meant that Sarah would be the mother. At that point, Abraham was ninety-nine years old. Almost twenty-five years had gone by since God took him out and told him, *"You will have a son. Count the stars. That's how many descendants you will have."* Twenty-five years! And Abraham laughed in disbelief that he and Sarah could still have a son! He even offered God the option of allowing Ishmael, his son from Hagar, to live under the blessing. His faith seemed to be running thin! But then, after God left, Abraham chose to believe what he was told.

Now let's examine Sarah's faith.

"'Where is Sarah, your wife?' the visitors asked. 'She's inside the tent,' Abraham replied.

Then one of them said, 'I will return to you about this time next year, and your wife, Sarah, will have a son!'

Sarah was listening to this conversation from the tent. Abraham and Sarah were both very old by this time, and Sarah was long past the age of having children. So she laughed silently to herself and said, 'How could a worn-out woman like me enjoy such pleasure, especially when my master—my husband—is also so old?'

Then the Lord said to Abraham, 'Why did Sarah laugh? Why did she say, "Can an old woman like me have a baby?" Is anything too hard for the Lord? I will return about this time next year, and Sarah will have a son.'

Sarah was afraid, so she denied it, saying, 'I didn't laugh.'

But the Lord said, 'No, you did laugh.'" (Genesis 18:9-15)

It cracks me up that Sarah lied to the Lord, and God said, *"No, you did laugh."* He called her out. I'm laughing now!

We're looking at a man and a woman who both believed in God's promise. After some time went by, they made their own plans to make the promise come true instead of waiting for God's will to be done, and they both laughed in disbelief of the promise being possible through their own blood. Yet, in spite of their impatient ways and regardless of their moments of disbelief, look at how Abraham and Sarah are described in God's word.

"Clearly, God's promise to give the whole earth to Abraham and his descendants was based not on his obedience to God's law, but on a right relationship with God that comes by faith. If God's promise is only for those who obey the law, then faith is not necessary and the promise is pointless. For the law always brings punishment on those who try to obey it. (The only way to avoid breaking the law is to have no law to break!)

So the promise is received by faith. It is given as a free gift. And we are all certain to receive it, whether or not we live according to the law of Moses, ***if we have faith like Abraham's. For Abraham is the father of all who believe.*** *That is what the Scriptures mean when God told him, 'I have made you the father of many nations.' This happened* ***because Abraham believed*** *in the God who brings the dead back to life and who creates new things out of nothing.*

Even when there was no reason for hope, ***Abraham kept hoping—believing that he would become the father of many nations.*** *For God had said to him, 'That's how many descendants you will have!' And* ***Abraham's faith did not weaken, even though, at about 100 years of age, he figured his body was as good as dead—and so was Sarah's womb.***

Abraham never wavered in believing God's promise. *In fact,* ***his faith grew stronger****, and in this he brought glory to God.* ***He was fully convinced that God is able to do whatever he promises. And because of Abraham's faith, God counted him as righteous.*** *And when God counted him as righteous, it wasn't just for Abraham's benefit.* ***It was recorded for our benefit, too****, assuring us that God will also count us as righteous if we believe in him, the one who raised Jesus our Lord from the dead. He was handed over to die because of our sins, and he was raised to life to make us right with God."* (Romans 4:13-25, emphasis added)

*"****It was by faith that even Sarah was able to have a child****, though she was barren and was too old.* ***She believed that God would keep his promise.*** *And so a whole nation came from this one man who was as good as dead—a nation with so many people that, like the stars in the sky and the sand on*

the seashore, there is no way to count them." (Hebrews 11:11-12, emphasis added)

It encourages me to read their story because even though Abraham and Sarah went through times of disobedience, they chose their own will over God's will, and they had moments of laughing in disbelief, their faith was still seen as *strong and unwavering.* Abraham was said to be *fully convinced.* Sarah was viewed as a *woman of faith* believing that God would keep His promise. God did not hold those moments against them. He didn't punish them for it, and He didn't take the promise away from them. He still blessed them. He *still* counted them as righteous. God saw them as a man and woman of strong faith, and He blessed them in a way that is impossible for us to understand. I believe He purposely waited to give them a son when He did so that the world could see the power and the glory and the faithfulness of God. I'm sure Abraham and Sarah had a closer relationship with God and an even stronger, bolder faith than before, after having their miraculous promise fulfilled.

Without the details of Abraham and Sarah's faith, I might have compared my life to theirs and felt disqualified. They questioned things just like I do! God didn't condemn them for it. He still sent the blessing!

That is only one story among many in the Bible that describe times of disbelief and disobedience. My faith is strengthened by knowing that Abraham, the father of all who believe, was not perfect. He was an ordinary man who had seasons of disbelief, but he dared to dream. He dared to believe when there was no reason for hope. Faith was in his heart even though he had no idea how it would be possible. He just knew that God could, so he kept believing. Even when it didn't make sense to his head, his heart believed. That story alone, shows me how God sees our faith. Let's read what Jesus said about faith.

"'You don't have enough faith,' Jesus told them. 'I tell you the truth, if you had faith even as small as a mustard seed, you could say to this mountain, "Move from here to there," and it would move. Nothing would be impossible.'" (Matthew 17:20)

A mustard seed is tiny! They are about one to two millimeters in diameter. Tiny! Jesus said even if you had faith as small as a mustard seed, it would be enough to move mountains! What?! He said nothing would be impossible. Nothing! Nothing impossible, with faith as small as a mustard seed. Wow. Now that is mind-blowing!

Sarah was barren and too old to have a child, but nothing was impossible for her and she had a child. Why? Because she had faith. Even if that faith was as small as a mustard seed, it was *great faith* in God's eyes. It was enough faith to unlock the impossible.

I pray that this encourages you like it has me. I have more faith now, knowing that my faith doesn't have to be perfect, and that I don't have to be perfect. Even if I mess up, I won't miss out. I can believe God will keep His promises in my heart even when my head tells me to laugh in disbelief. God loves to do the *"impossible"* so that He can be revealed by leaving no other explanation except, "GOD." He loves to do the impossible so that you will draw even nearer to Him. He wants your heart to have eyes for Him.

Keeping balance in our lives will always be a skill we practice, but even as we are hanging in the balance, there is one thing that is always for sure. That is the faithfulness and the never-ending Love of the God that created you and me. Stick to His word, hang on to His promises, and keep believing even when it feels like it is impossible. Give God a chance to blow your mind.

113 I hate those with divided loyalties,
but I love your instructions.
114 You are my refuge and my shield;
your word is my source of hope.
115 Get out of my life, you evil-minded people,
for I intend to obey the commands of my God.
116 Lord, sustain me as you promised, that I may live!
Do not let my hope be crushed.
117 Sustain me, and I will be rescued;
then I will meditate continually on your decrees.
118 But you have rejected all who stray from your decrees.
They are only fooling themselves.
119 You skim off the wicked of the earth like scum;
no wonder I love to obey your laws!
120 I tremble in fear of you;
I stand in awe of your regulations.

Psalm 119:113–120

17

My Refuge and Shield

Knowing Jesus, truly knowing Him, changes who we are. I look back at some of the choices and decisions I made, and I wonder why in the world did I think that it was good, fun, cool, or okay to do some of the things I did. During a time of my life, I just did what my sinful nature urged me to do in the moment. Later, when the moment was over, I was ashamed. But, for some reason, it wouldn't be long until I did it again.

The reason is that I knew about my Savior Jesus Christ because of what I had heard people say and because of the little amount of time that I had read His word. I did not know Him personally or deeply. I did not know Him well enough to allow the Holy Spirit to be my guide. Instead, the things that I knew I should or shouldn't do were only rules to me, and they were so easy to break! When I began to discover the compassionate love that Jesus has for me, He became my refuge and my hiding place. Then I understood why the rules existed. It was all for my protection.

When you choose to seek Him wholeheartedly, you find Him. When you find Him, He becomes your refuge and your shield. Then your perspective of things change. Instead of seeing things as blended and grey, things become black or white. The Holy Spirit within you begins to turn you away from evil-minded people. Your heart loses the desire for any wicked way, and Jesus living within you becomes a shield around your heart and mind protecting you from the destructive ways of the world.

"He has enabled us to be ministers of his new covenant. This is a covenant not of written laws, but of the Spirit. The old written covenant ends in death; but under the new covenant, the Spirit gives life.

The old way, with laws etched in stone, led to death, though it began with such glory that the people of Israel could not bear to look at Moses' face. For his face shone with the glory of God, even though the brightness was already fading away. Shouldn't we expect far greater glory under the new way, now that the Holy Spirit is giving life? If the old way, which brings condemnation, was glorious, how much more glorious is the new way, which makes us right with God! In fact, that first glory was not glorious at all compared with the overwhelming glory of the new way. So if the old way, which has been replaced, was glorious, how much more glorious is the new, which remains forever!

Since this new way gives us such confidence, we can be very bold. We are not like Moses, who put a veil over his face so the people of Israel would not see the glory, even though it was destined to fade away. But the people's minds were hardened, and to this day whenever the old covenant is being read, the same veil covers their minds so they cannot understand the truth. And this veil can be removed only by believing in Christ. Yes, even today when they read Moses' writings, their hearts are covered with that veil, and they do not understand.

But whenever someone turns to the Lord, the veil is taken away. For the Lord is the Spirit, and wherever the Spirit of the Lord is, there is freedom. So all of us who have had that veil removed can see and reflect the glory of the Lord. And the Lord—who is the Spirit—makes us more and more like him as we are changed into his glorious image." (2 Corinthians 3:6-18)

It is the Spirit of Lord who changes us. It isn't us striving to change. We don't have to wear ourselves out trying to be different. We just simply get to know Jesus, and then His Spirit does the work within us. Effortless.

Paul left us a letter in the Scriptures that describe what it looks like to lived changed by the Spirit. *"For we know that when this earthly tent we live in is taken down (that is, when we die and leave this earthly body), we will have a house in heaven, an eternal body made for us by God himself and not by human hands. We grow weary in our present bodies, and we long to put on our heavenly bodies like new clothing. For we will put on heavenly bodies; we will not be spirits without bodies. While we live in these earthly bodies, we groan and sigh, but it's not that we want to die and get rid of these bodies that clothe us. Rather, we want to put on our new bodies so that these dying bodies will be swallowed up by life. God himself has prepared us for this, and as a guarantee he has given us his Holy Spirit.*

So we are always confident, even though we know that as long as we live in these bodies we are not at home with the Lord. For we live by believing and not by seeing. Yes, we are fully confident, and we would rather be away from these earthly bodies, for then we will be at home with the Lord. So whether we are here in this body or away from this body, our goal is to please him. For we must all stand before Christ to be judged. We will each receive whatever we deserve for the good or evil we have done in this earthly body.

Because we understand our fearful responsibility to the Lord, we work hard to persuade others. God knows we are sincere, and I hope you know this, too. Are we commending ourselves to you again? No, we are giving you a reason to be proud of us, so you can answer those who brag about having a spectacular ministry rather than having a sincere heart. If it seems we are crazy, it is to bring glory to God. And if we are in our right minds, it is for your benefit. Either way, ***Christ's love controls us.*** *Since we believe that Christ died for all, we also believe that we have all died to our old life. He died for everyone so that those who receive his new life will no longer live for themselves. Instead, they will live for Christ, who died and was raised for them.*

So we have stopped evaluating others from a human point of view. At one time we thought of Christ merely from a human point of view. How differently we know him now! This means that anyone who belongs to Christ has become a new person. The old life is gone; a new life has begun!

And all of this is a gift from God, who brought us back to himself through Christ. And God has given us this task of reconciling people to him. For God was in Christ, reconciling the world to himself, no longer counting people's sins against them. And he gave us this wonderful message of reconciliation. So we are Christ's ambassadors; God is making his appeal through us. We speak for Christ when we plead, 'Come back to God!' For God made Christ, who never sinned, to be the offering for our sin, so that we could be made right with God through Christ." (2 Corinthians 5, emphasis added)

Pleasing the Lord doesn't mean getting everything right and getting our acts together. It isn't about merely being a good person and making good decisions. Pleasing Him is doing what He asked. Doing the thing that He said was most important. That is *Loving Him*. When we focus on loving Him and letting Him love us back, then His love can control us, and we can allow our new lives in Him to flow freely.

"As God's partners, we beg you not to accept this marvelous gift of God's kindness and then ignore it. For God says, 'At just the right time, I heard you. On the day of salvation, I helped you.' Indeed, the 'right time' is now. Today is the day of salvation.

We live in such a way that no one will stumble because of us, and no one will find fault with our ministry. In everything we do, we show that we are true ministers of God. We patiently endure troubles and hardships and calamities of every kind. We have been beaten, been put in prison, faced angry mobs, worked to exhaustion, endured sleepless nights, and gone without food. We prove ourselves by our purity, our understanding, our patience, our kindness, by the Holy Spirit within us, and by our sincere love. We faithfully preach the truth. God's power is working in us. We use the weapons of righteousness in the right hand for attack and the left hand for defense. We serve God whether people honor us or despise us, whether they slander us or praise us. We are honest, but they call us impostors. We are ignored, even though we are well known. We live close to death, but we are still alive. We have been beaten, but we have not been killed. Our hearts ache, but we always have joy. We are poor, but we give spiritual riches to others. We own nothing, and yet we have everything." (2 Corinthians 6:1-10)

Coming from a man whose new life had truly begun, Paul shows us what the fruits of a life lived by the control of God's love are. He had been around people with divided loyalties. He dealt with the evil-minded and was rejected just like the psalmist wrote about. Paul was beaten, accused, ignored, poor, hungry, heartbroken, exhausted, endured sleepless nights, he was slandered, and he lived close to death. Paul's response to life is almost opposite of what I would expect to hear. *"We live close to death, but we are still alive! We have been beaten, but we have not been killed! Our hearts ache, but we always have joy! We are poor, but we give spiritual riches to others! We own nothing, and YET WE HAVE EVERYTHING!"*

Why were Paul and those with him able to be so positive in those circumstances? It was God's power working in them. It wasn't their own strength. The Holy Spirit produced in them purity, understanding, patience, kindness, sincere love, faith, and strength. Did those things come by following laws? No. They were a work of the Holy Spirit within them produced by experiencing the True Love of God. Righteousness became their weapons. Their natural act of righteousness produced by the work of the Holy Spirit protected them. Even though people were still slandering, ignoring, and attacking them, no one truly had anything they could say or do against them. They were confident in the One who Loves them. The Holy Spirit kept their minds sound, and they were satisfied to have nothing. Literally nothing.

If an innocent person behind bars can be content, be beaten nearly to death and simply praise God that they still have breath, be hated and ridiculed and still have joy, then I want what that person has. Don't you? *"I have nothing, yet I have everything."* What does that mean? That means that True Love is truly all we need. God's Love is *THAT* good!

Paul also advises us to be aware of who we partner up with in life. The last thing Satan wants is for anyone to experience the True Love of God because he knows once we taste it, we won't turn back. If we team up with evil-minded people, it will be really hard to stay living led by the Holy Spirit. Paul says, *"Don't team up with those who are unbelievers. How can righteousness be a partner with wickedness? How can light live with darkness? What harmony can there be between Christ and the devil? How can a believer be a partner with an unbeliever? And what union can there be between God's temple and idols? For we are the temple of the living God. As God said: 'I will live in them and walk among them. I will be their God, and they will be my people. Therefore, come out from among unbelievers, and separate yourselves from them, says the Lord. Don't touch their filthy things, and I will welcome you. And I will be your Father, and you will be my sons and daughters,' says the Lord Almighty."* (2 Corinthians 6:14-18)

"Because we have these promises, dear friends, let us cleanse ourselves from everything that can defile our body or spirit. And let us work toward complete holiness because we fear God." (2 Corinthians 7:1)

"For the kind of sorrow God wants us to experience leads us away from sin and results in salvation. There's no regret for that kind of sorrow. But worldly sorrow, which lacks repentance, results in spiritual death." (2 Corinthians 7:10)

The psalmist was experiencing the cleansing work of God in his life: *"I hate those with divided loyalties, but I love your instructions. You are my refuge and my shield; your word is my source of hope. Get out of my life, you evil-minded people, for I intend to obey the commands of my God. Lord, sustain me as you promised, that I may live! Do not let my hope be crushed. Sustain me, and I will be rescued; then I will meditate continually on your decrees. But you have rejected all who stray from your decrees. They are only fooling themselves. You skim off the wicked of the earth like scum; no wonder I love to obey your laws! I tremble in fear of you. I stand in awe of your regulations."* (Psalm 119:113-120)

I believe the wicked and evil-minded people that these verses are referring to, are those who have intentionally rejected God and His ways. Therefore, they are basically serving Satan. That is why one of the verses above asked, *"What harmony can there be between Christ and the devil?"* Again, this advice is for our protection. God isn't asking us to be hateful or judgmental. He knows it isn't wise to partner up with evil so He cautions us to stay away. We have the Holy Spirit to caution our own spirit when someone isn't safe to be around so we don't have to rely fully on our own understanding.

Dear friend, keep seeking the definition of God's Love and His characteristics. Like His word tells us, Moses's face shone so brightly because of the Glory of God that the people couldn't even stand to look at his face. That Glory is even more glorious now that we have this new way. The new way is the work of the Holy Spirit. Not our own works! Praise the Lord! The ways of the Holy Spirit are overwhelmingly glorious!

Stand in awe of the regulations of the Lord, and keep searching for *Who He Is.* Let His work in you be your strength and your shield. *"You are my refuge and my shield; your word is my source of hope."* (vs.114) Stay ever so close to Him and allow His Word to be your guide.

121 Don't leave me to the mercy of my enemies,
for I have done what is just and right.
122 Please guarantee a blessing for me.
Don't let the arrogant oppress me!
123 My eyes strain to see your rescue,
to see the truth of your promise fulfilled.
124 I am your servant; deal with me in unfailing love,
and teach me your decrees.
125 Give discernment to me, your servant;
then I will understand your laws.
126 Lord, it is time for you to act,
for these evil people have violated your instructions.
127 Truly, I love your commands
more than gold, even the finest gold.
128 Each of your commandments is right.
That is why I hate every false way.

Psalm 119:121–128

18

Eye of the Storm

Do your eyes still strain to see His rescue? Are you just waiting for Him to act? Notice how the psalmist wants God to handle his situation. *"Deal with me in unfailing Love."* It never fails. We always go back to True Love. Do you believe that Jesus truly loves you with a love greater than you ever knew? Do you know that He cares for you? Do you know that He prays for you? Yes, He prays for you.

"'Now I am coming to you. I told them many things while I was with them in this world so they would be filled with my joy. I have given them your word. And the world hates them because they do not belong to the world, just as I do not belong to the world. I'm not asking you to take them out of the world, but to keep them safe from the evil one. They do not belong to this world any more than I do. Make them holy by your truth; teach them your word, which is truth. Just as you sent me into the world, I am sending them into the world. And I give myself as a holy sacrifice for them so they can be made holy by your truth.

I am praying not only for these disciples but also for all who will ever believe in me through their message. I pray that they will all be one, just as you and I are one—as you are in me, Father, and I am in you. And may they be in us so that the world will believe you sent me. I have given them the glory you gave me, so they may be one as we are one. I am in them and you are in me. May they experience such perfect unity that the world will know that you sent me and that you love them as much as you love me. Father, I want these whom you have given me to be with me where I am. Then they can see all the glory you gave me because you loved me even before the world began! O righteous Father, the world doesn't know you, but I do; and these disciples know you sent me. I have revealed you to them, and I will continue to do so. Then your love for me will be in them, and I will be in them.'" (John 17:13-26)

Jesus said, *"I am in them, and You are in Me."* He has given us His Glory and made us one with Him. Jesus wants us to experience the perfect unity with Himself and with the Father so that we can know how much God loves us. Jesus said those things just prior to His death on the cross, and He expressed how His prayer was not only for those who were living there with Him at that moment, but also for us. He said that He came and revealed God to them and that He would continue to reveal the Father to us. His purpose was so that God's love would be in us.

As long as we live in this world, we will have issues. This world is not where we belong, but for now, we are living here among people who are evil-minded and among those who will cause trouble. Really, the one behind all the trouble is Satan himself. He is the one we are fighting.

Though pain, suffering, and trouble are inevitable, we can have joy, peace, and hope because of the way we are loved. We are guaranteed blessings and we are given a love that never dies out, never gives up, and never reaches its highest point. He always has more to give.

When you feel like the psalmist did, like God has left you to the mercy of your enemies, whether that enemy is a person, a disease, or a disaster, know that He is right there. When you feel like it is time for Him to do something, know that He remains in control.

"As evening came, Jesus said to his disciples, 'Let's cross to the other side of the lake.' So they took Jesus in the boat and started out, leaving the crowds behind (although other boats followed). But soon a fierce storm came up. High waves were breaking into the boat, and it began to fill with water.

Jesus was sleeping at the back of the boat with his head on a cushion. The disciples woke him up, shouting, 'Teacher, don't you care that we're going to drown?'

When Jesus woke up, he rebuked the wind and said to the waves, 'Silence! Be still!' Suddenly the wind stopped, and there was a great calm. Then he asked them, 'Why are you afraid? Do you still have no faith?'

The disciples were absolutely terrified. 'Who is this man?' they asked each other. 'Even the wind and waves obey him!'" (Mark 4:34-41)

The disciples were still learning who the man named Jesus was. They spent a lot of time with Jesus and listened to His teachings. Just before their journey across the lake, they witnessed some miraculous healings, but they didn't yet understand how deep the depths of His power and love could go. They were terrified when He spoke to the wind and the waves and nature obeyed Him! They had never seen anything like that! Even the wind and waves obey Him!

"Lord, save us! We're going to drown!" They were shouting out to the Lord to wake up and save them, yet at the same time they were confessing that they were going to die. In their minds, they knew that He could help them because of what they had witnessed Him do for others, but in their hearts, they believed they were as good as dead. Have you ever experienced that? Your mind believed one thing maybe because you had read it or known someone else that had experienced something, but your heart didn't really feel like it was true for you or that it was even possible. That is called double-minded.

"If any of you lacks wisdom, let him ask of God, who gives to all liberally and without reproach, and it will be given to him. But let him ask in faith, with no doubting, for he who doubts is like a wave of the sea driven and tossed by the wind. For let not that man suppose that he will receive anything from the Lord; he is a double-minded man, unstable in all his ways." (James 1:5-8 NKJV)

Being double-minded is an unhealthy state to be in, but we all struggle with the issue. Many of us contain knowledge in our minds which we know to be true, but our hearts can't grab hold of the truth and trust in it. How do we get out of a double-minded state of being? One of the major basic steps is to get to know Jesus. Knowing His character puts our hearts in a position that allows the Holy Spirit to convince us of the truth. If we don't ask Him for the truth, then our hearts may remain unbelieving.

Getting to know His character is as simple as meditating over Scripture. In the story we just read, did the disciples unbelief keep Jesus from saving them? No. Jesus silenced the wind and calmed the waves. He did exactly what they asked for, and then He talked with them. What does that say about the character of God to you?

This is a good journal question. You might even ask Jesus, *"What do you want to say to me about your character in this story?"* Then you could read it again and put yourself in the story and watch and see what Jesus says to you.

The story shows me that He cares about our well-being. He is patient with our growth. He wants us to be able to trust Him. He is comfortable being with us, and He doesn't disown us when we don't get it right. He asks us questions that cause us to examine our own hearts because He wants us to know and accept the Truth. He desires to see us bold in faith and fearless with Him by our side.

One time, Jesus had just fed five-thousand plus people with five loaves of bread and two fish and they ended up with left overs! What a miracle! Then He insisted that the disciples get back in the boat and cross to the other side of the lake. He sent the rest of the people home, and Jesus went up into the hills by Himself to pray. Night fell. The guys on the boat were in trouble. They were fighting very strong winds and heavy waves again. Then came Jesus walking on water.

Do you think that Jesus just decided that He would take a short cut and walk across the water so He could catch up with the guys? I don't believe Jesus took short cuts for His benefit. I believe Jesus did it to teach the disciples a very specific lesson.

"When the disciples saw him walking on the water, they were terrified. In their fear, they cried out, 'It's a ghost!'

But Jesus spoke to them at once. 'Don't be afraid,' he said. 'Take courage. I am here!'

Then Peter called to him, 'Lord, if it's really you, tell me to come to you, walking on the water.'

'Yes, come,' Jesus said.

So Peter went over the side of the boat and walked on the water toward Jesus. But when he saw the strong wind and the waves, he was terrified and began to sink. 'Save me, Lord!' he shouted.

Jesus immediately reached out and grabbed him. 'You have so little faith,' Jesus said. 'Why did you doubt me?'

When they climbed back into the boat, the wind stopped. Then the disciples worshiped him. 'You really are the Son of God!' they exclaimed." (Matthew 14:26-33)

Jesus told Peter to come to Him, and Peter walked on the water! For that moment, however long it was, Peter locked eyes with Jesus, and he experienced what it meant to be totally engaged in Jesus. He saw what faith could do. When we lock eyes with Jesus, especially in the eye of a storm, He can get us through the impossible.

When Peter took his eyes off Jesus and focused on the wind and the waves, he became terrified, lost his confidence, lost faith, and started to sink. That is what happens when we look around at the storm. When we start focusing on all the trouble that we find ourselves in, we can easily begin to sink in fear, doubt, pain, discouragement, and hopelessness. That's how we drown spiritually. Sorrows and struggles will suffocate us and cut off our oxygen supply if we allow them to be our focus.

We all find ourselves sinking at times, but the good news is we can always refocus. Peter lost track of Jesus and began to sink, but he realized it, turned his focus back to Jesus, and called out for help. Did Jesus leave Peter to sink because he didn't keep his eyes on Him? No. The Scriptures tell us that Jesus *immediately* reached out and saved him. Not only did He save Peter, but He also stopped the wind.

Do you see how Jesus allowed that storm to happen so that Peter and all the disciples who were with him could learn a lesson that would strengthen their faith? Maybe Jesus is asking you that very same question, *"Why do you doubt me?"*

Jesus came to reveal God to us. The story of Peter walking on water shows us more about the depth of God's Love. It shows us how much He cares about our heart. He took the time to show them what faith in Him will do. His purpose is so that we don't have to fear. He doesn't want to see us scared and trembling in fear of life's storms. Instead, He wants us to thrive and be triumphant in the storms. It also reveals that He is gentle and not demanding us to follow Him and look at Him. He gives us the free will to choose Him. Not so that He can say *"I told you so,"* but only because He cares deeply and wants what is best for us.

The story captures the patience of God. He allows us to choose. Then He is patient with our decisions. He doesn't act out in rage and yell at us saying, *"When will you ever learn?!!"* then jerk us out of the water and set us on our feet. What He does do is show us what He has in store for us and when we get off track and ask for help, He gently grabs us and pulls us into His arms, carries us back to a safe place, sets our feet on solid ground, and calmly asks us why we have little faith. The questions He asks aren't intended for condemnation. Remember there is no condemnation for those who belong to Jesus (Romans 8:1). His intention is that we would examine our hearts to discover what belief is causing us to have little faith. He desires that we refocus, fix our gaze on Him, and trust Him so that He can guide us along the path of everlasting life and abundant joy.

I also see a picture of God's Grace. Even when we do lose our way and begin to sink, He saves us. He never gives up. Not only does He pull us out of the water, but He calms the wind even though He knows we still have a long way to go and a lot to learn.

When you find yourself going through a storm, don't let the chaos drown you. Let it be an opportunity for you to experience things that you didn't even know you could do, like walking on water. Let the waves crash while you look for Jesus, and when you see Him, step out and walk to Him. Keep your eyes fixed on Him by remembering who He is. He formed the world with you in mind. He gave you life so that He could love you and you could love Him. He is Almighty God who became a baby for you. He is the One and only Holy and Pure who chose to become sin so that you could be righteous. He endured the greatest amount of pain and suffering that a person could ever face because you were on His mind, and He loves you more than His own life. He chose death so that you could have life. He provides all that you need even when you can't see it, but the proof of His love surrounds you. If you will take the time to lock eyes with Jesus and rest in His True Love, He will take you on adventures that will blow your mind.

Let the truths of His word be what secures you to Him. Fill your boat, your heart, with His treasures which are finer than the finest gold. Ask for discernment. Ask for wisdom. Expect an answer. Keep looking for opportunities to uncover the heart of God, and don't be intimidated to tell Him that your faith is weak. Ask Him to help. He's longing to be gracious to you.

"Yet the LORD longs to be gracious to you; therefore he will rise up to show you compassion. For the LORD is a God of justice. Blessed are all who wait for him!" (Isaiah 30:18 NIV)

129 Your laws are wonderful.
No wonder I obey them!
130 The teaching of your word gives light,
so even the simple can understand.
131 I pant with expectation,
longing for your commands.
132 Come and show me your mercy,
as you do for all who love your name.
133 Guide my steps by your word,
so I will not be overcome by evil.
134 Ransom me from the oppression of evil people;
then I can obey your commandments.
135 Look upon me with love;
teach me your decrees.
136 Rivers of tears gush from my eyes
because people disobey your instructions.

Psalm 119:129–136

19

True Love

The psalmist continued to have an overwhelming passion and desire for God's word, yet he longed for more. If you remember in the beginning of Psalm 119, he was desperate. He was torn and lying in dust. He wanted God to teach him His decrees and help him to understand. Now the psalmist knows the benefits of the truth and has a compassion for the Lord and His word that he didn't know before. True Love burned in the psalmist's heart causing him to draw nearer to the Lord and His word. Because he had experienced True Love, his heart broke to see people who disobeyed the Lord. He knew that God's instructions brought freedom, life, and a love for himself that was unexplainable. It hurt him to see the way people were treating God and cheating themselves out of freedom and peace.

God is Love. There is a difference in "God *IS* Love" and "God *has* Love." Scriptures tell us that He *IS* Love which means that Love is what He is made of. Since He is Love, then all the love in the world has to come *from* Him because He is the never-ending source of Love. He doesn't run out. Love is what drives Him. Understanding the depths of His True Love, allows us to read the Scriptures with fresh eyes and new understanding. That is the reason why this entire book focuses on the Love of God. True Love is what transforms your entire life.

There is a man in the Scriptures by the name of Saul. He was very evil-minded. Saul was a persecutor of believers in Jesus Christ. *"As for Saul, he made havoc of the church, entering every house, and dragging off men and women, committing them to prison."* (Acts 8:3 NKJV) I imagine it was people like Saul that were after our psalmist. They were the ones causing rivers of tears to gush from the psalmist's eyes because he couldn't stand the way they disregarded the instructions of the Lord.

Saul was a wicked man, and God had a plan for his life. One day, he had an encounter with Jesus. Once Jesus got a hold of Saul and revealed Himself to him, he decided to change his ways. He discovered True Love. Saul had two names. His other name was Paul. *"Then Saul, who also is called Paul, filled with the Holy Spirit, looked intently at him"* (Acts 13:9 NKJV) In the Bible from that point on, he is referred to as Paul. Here is a letter from the changed man named Paul. *"I thank Christ Jesus our Lord, who has given me strength to do his work. He considered me trustworthy and appointed me to serve him, even though I used to blaspheme the name of Christ. In my insolence, I persecuted his people. But God had mercy on me because I did it in ignorance and unbelief. Oh, how generous and gracious our Lord was! He filled me with the faith and love that come from Christ Jesus.*

This is a trustworthy saying, and everyone should accept it: 'Christ Jesus came into the world to save sinners'—and I am the worst of them all. But God had mercy on me so that Christ Jesus could use me as a prime example of his great patience with even the worst sinners. Then others will realize that they, too, can believe in him and receive eternal life. All honor and glory to God forever and ever! He is the eternal King, the unseen one who never dies; he alone is God. Amen." (1 Timothy 1:12-17)

God got a hold of Paul and filled him with faith and love, transforming his evil mind to a Christ-like mind and his wicked heart of stone to a tender, compassionate heart of love. True Love radically changed Paul. It impacted him so greatly that we now have a New Testament that was mostly written by Saul also known as Paul. Isn't it amazing how seeing things through eyes of Love changes things?

Paul preached about the amazing love of Christ and the importance of it. We can trust his teaching because, *"All Scripture is inspired by God and is useful to <u>teach us what is true</u> and to <u>make us realize what is wrong</u> in our lives. It corrects us when we are wrong and teaches us to do what is right.* (2 Timothy 3:16, emphasis added)

Paul said, *"The purpose of my instruction is that all believers would be filled with love that comes from a pure heart, a clear conscience, and genuine faith. But some people have missed this whole point. They have turned away from these things and spend their time in meaningless discussions. They want to be known as teachers of the law of Moses, but they don't know what they are talking about, even though they speak so confidently."* (1 Timothy 1:5-7)

Paul's words were given out of love, and the purpose of his instructions were so that we would be filled with love. If all love comes from God, then we can conclude that all of God's commands, instructions, discipline, laws, regulations, and statutes are birthed from True Love with the ultimate intention that we would be filled by HIM.

"When I think of all this, I fall to my knees and pray to the Father, the Creator of everything in heaven and on earth. I pray that from his glorious, unlimited resources he will empower you with inner strength through his Spirit. Then Christ will make his home in your hearts as you trust in him. Your roots will grow down into God's love and keep you strong. And may you have the power to understand, as all God's people should, how wide, how long, how high, and how deep his love is. May you experience the love of Christ, though it is too great to understand fully. Then you will be made complete with all the fullness of life and power that comes from God.

Now all glory to God, who is able, through his mighty power at work within us, to accomplish infinitely more than we might ask or think. Glory to him in the church and in Christ Jesus through all generations forever and ever! Amen." (Ephesians 3:14-21) *-Paul*

According to Paul, what keeps us strong? *God's Love!* What does Paul desire that we have the power to understand? *The widths, the lengths, the heights, and the great depths of God's Love.* What makes us complete? *The experience of the Love of Christ.*

Why then, would I start anywhere other than getting to know my Savior personally? If I started with examining laws before knowing True Love, I would not have been able to see the Love in the laws and commands. We must experience True Love before we can understand that all the commandments are given from a heart of Love.

As we trust Him, He makes His home in our hearts. His Love makes us strong and complete, giving us all the fullness of life and power. Our number one priority should be seeking His love. Ask Him questions. *"Do you love me?"* Go a step further and write your question down, then sit in silence to see what He might say. Write down what you believe He might be saying back to you. Ask Him why He loves you. Seek Him, ask questions, and listen for His answers. He may answer you through a spontaneous thought, through another person, through music, or nature. There is no limit to the ways that God can speak to you. Ask and then, with faith, expect an answer like the psalmist. "*I pant with expectation."* (vs. 131)

"Ever since I first heard of your strong faith in the Lord Jesus and your love for God's people everywhere, I have not stopped thanking God for you. I pray for you constantly, asking God, the glorious Father of our Lord Jesus Christ, to give you spiritual wisdom and insight so that you might grow in your knowledge of God. I pray that your hearts will be flooded with light so that

you can understand the confident hope he has given to those he called—his holy people who are his rich and glorious inheritance.

I also pray that you will understand the incredible greatness of God's power for us who believe him. This is the same mighty power that raised Christ from the dead and seated him in the place of honor at God's right hand in the heavenly realms. Now he is far above any ruler or authority or power or leader or anything else—not only in this world but also in the world to come. God has put all things under the authority of Christ and has made him head over all things for the benefit of the church. And the church is his body; it is made full and complete by Christ, who fills all things everywhere with ***himself****."* (Ephesians 1:15-23, emphasis added) *-Paul*

When you seek knowledge of God, you put your heart in a position to receive confident hope. *You* are His rich and glorious inheritance. The value that you have in God's eyes is priceless. If you can see yourself the way God sees you, your life will be transformed and your love for the Lord will catch fire. Paul expressed the importance of knowing God not only to know who He is, but also to understand what He has given us. It is ridiculous how much He loves us.

"I pray that your love will overflow more and more, and that you will keep on growing in knowledge and understanding. For I want you to understand what really matters, so that you may live pure and blameless lives until the day of Christ's return. May you always be filled with the fruit of your salvation—the righteous character produced in your life by Jesus Christ—for this will bring much glory and praise to God." (Philippians 1:9-11)

Paul wanted us to understand what *really* matters, and knowing Jesus is what matters most. *"Yes, everything else is worthless when compared with the infinite value of knowing Christ Jesus my Lord. For his sake I have discarded everything else, counting it all as garbage, so that I could gain Christ and become one with him. I no longer count on my own righteousness through obeying the law; rather, I become righteous through faith in Christ. For God's way of making us right with himself depends on faith. I want to know Christ and experience the mighty power that raised him from the dead. I want to suffer with him, sharing in his death, so that one way or another I will experience the resurrection from the dead!"* (Philippians 3:8-11, emphasis added)

Infinite. A concept describing something without any bounds. Infinite Value. Knowing Christ has infinite value. Knowing Him. Experiencing Him. Finding True Love in Him. That is all that *REALLY* matters.

137 O Lord, you are righteous,
and your regulations are fair.
138 Your laws are perfect
and completely trustworthy.
139 I am overwhelmed with indignation,
for my enemies have disregarded your words.
140 Your promises have been thoroughly tested;
that is why I love them so much.
141 I am insignificant and despised,
but I don't forget your commandments.
142 Your justice is eternal,
and your instructions are perfectly true.
143 As pressure and stress bear down on me,
I find joy in your commands.
144 Your laws are always right;
help me to understand them so I may live.

Psalm 119:137–144

20

JOY IN SUFFERING

Children of God are able to find joy in suffering. *"As pressure and stress bear down on me, I find joy in your commands."* (vs. 143) Whether the suffering is caused by our own choices, caused by others, or by something that has happened with no real apparent reason why, we *can* find joy.

"'Now listen to the explanation of the parable about the farmer planting seeds: The seed that fell on the footpath represents those who hear the message about the Kingdom and don't understand it. Then the evil one comes and snatches away the seed that was planted in their hearts. The seed on the rocky soil represents those who hear the message and immediately receive it with joy. But since they don't have deep roots, they don't last long. They fall away as soon as they have problems or are persecuted for believing God's word. The seed that fell among the thorns represents those who hear God's word, but all too quickly the message is crowded out by the worries of this life and the lure of wealth, so no fruit is produced. The seed that fell on good soil represents those who truly hear and understand God's word and produce a harvest of thirty, sixty, or even a hundred times as much as had been planted!'" (Matthew 13:18-23)

The person that has the good soil can find joy in suffering. I want to be one who hears and understands, but a lot of the time I don't understand. The psalmist has taught us that it is okay if we don't understand. In one way or another, within each section of Psalm 119 that we are reading, he says, *"Give me understanding."* The important part is that I *want* to understand and that I keep asking and seeking Him. If we are yearning for wisdom and seeking Him, then He becomes the good soil.

Paul taught us where to find good soil. *"Your roots will grow down into God's love and keep you strong."* (Ephesians 3:17b) The good soil is God's Love. Wow! All this time that we have been learning about God, who He is, and of His unfailing Love, we have been filling our hearts with heaps of good soil. Each seed of truth can grow and root deeply, our faith can become strong and immovable, good fruit can be produced, and the harvest can be plentiful! When we are deeply rooted in His Love, we can find joy even in suffering.

"So be truly glad. There is wonderful joy ahead, even though you must endure many trials for a little while. These trials will show that your faith is genuine. It is being tested as fire tests and purifies gold—though your faith is far more precious than mere gold. So when your faith remains strong through many trials, it will bring you much praise and glory and honor on the day when Jesus Christ is revealed to the whole world. You love him even though you have never seen him. Though you do not see him now, you trust him; and you rejoice with a glorious, inexpressible joy. The reward for trusting him will be the salvation of your souls." (1 Peter 1:6-9)

Have you ever thought of the endurance of trials being like fire that purifies gold? The purpose of putting a flame to the gold is to get out anything that is not pure. God cherishes us so much that he takes the time to purify us. When the heat is turned up in your life it doesn't feel good, but the joy you can find is in knowing that you are precious to God and when the process is over, you will be more Christ-like than before. *"He will sit like a refiner of silver, burning away the dross."* (Malachi 3:3a)

"The Old Refiner"

He sat by a fire of seven-fold heat,
As He watched by the precious ore,
And closer He bent with a searching gaze
As He heated it more and more.
He knew He had ore that could stand the test,
And He wanted the finest gold
To mould as a crown for the King to wear,
Set with gems with a price untold.
So He laid our gold in the burning fire,
Tho' we fain would have said Him 'Nay,'
And He watched the dross that we had not seen,
And it melted and passed away.
And the gold grew brighter and yet more bright,
But our eyes were so dim with tears,
We saw but the fire–not the Master's hand,

And questioned with anxious fears.
Yet our gold shone out with a richer glow,
As it mirrored a Form above,
That bent o'er the fire, tho' unseen by us,
With a look of ineffable love.
Can we think that it pleases His loving heart
To cause us a moment's pain?
Ah, no! but He saw through the present cross
The bliss of eternal gain.
So He waited there with a watchful eye,
With a love that is strong and sure,
And His gold did not suffer a bit more heat,
Than was needed to make it pure.
(*Streams in the Desert* by L. B. Cowman 407)

> *"Our Father, who seeks to perfect His saints in holiness, knows the value of the refiner's fire. It is with the most precious metals that the assayer takes the most pains, and subjects them to the hot fire, because such fires melt the metal, and only the molten mass releases its alloy or takes perfectly its new form in the mould. The old refiner never leaves his crucible, but sits down by it, lest there should be one excessive degree of heat to mar the metal. But as soon as he skims from the surface the last of the dross, and sees his own face reflected, he puts out the fire."* (Arthur T. Pierson)

"Not only that, but we rejoice in our sufferings, knowing that suffering produces endurance, and endurance produces character, and character produces hope, and hope does not put us to shame, because God's love has been poured into our hearts through the Holy Spirit who has been given to us." (Romans 5:3-5 ESV)

I can handle suffering one of two ways. I can kick and scream and squirm my way out, running away from the problem the best I know how. I can avoid every issue by trying to fix things on my own, hoping I don't run into the same problem later. Or I can look into the Eye of my Father and ask Him if He is allowing the heat for my good. If He is, then I can ask Him to show me His Hand at work so I can cooperate with the refining process that He wants to accomplish.

Suffering can be compared to surgery. A surgery might be necessary to remove an unwanted mass affecting one's body. Surgery doesn't feel good. In fact, it can leave pain, but the removal of the infection is for one's good. Suffering produces endurance and patience. We need strength and patience to live in this corrupted world. If we never had anything to worry about and God just handed everything over to us, we would never learn patience, we wouldn't get any stronger, and we wouldn't know how to help those in need because we would never have to experience it. Learning patience and endurance produces character.

Your character is your mental and moral qualities that make you distinctive. Have you ever been around a person that complains about everything? It's like the end of the world when any little thing goes wrong or doesn't go their way. That type of person is probably negative about most things except for when they have what they want and even then, are quick to find something wrong. Having little patience and not much endurance results in irritation and negativity.

I am prone to be impatient and negative at times, as I'm sure we all are, but if my roots are growing deep into God's love, it is easier to recognize that bad fruit and allow God to uproot those weeds instead of letting them to continue to grow. If God's love isn't the soil that my roots are growing into, then I will end up living the miserable life like Paul described in Romans 7 always doing what I know isn't right, knowing what I should do, but then inevitably do what I shouldn't.

"When you follow the desires of your sinful nature, the results are very clear: sexual immorality, impurity, lustful pleasures, idolatry, sorcery, hostility, quarreling, jealousy, outbursts of anger, selfish ambition, dissension, division, envy, drunkenness, wild parties, and other sins like these." (Galatians 5:19-21a)

"But the Holy Spirit produces this kind of fruit in our lives: love, joy, peace, patience, kindness, goodness, faithfulness, gentleness, and self-control. There is no law against these things!" (Galatians 5:22-23)

If you notice any of those fruits that are a result of desires of a sinful nature growing in your life, take it to the Lord. Ask Him to show you what your heart's intentions are. Allow Him to reveal to you what drives you to participate in anything led by a sinful nature. Just as God is a Master Refiner, He is also a Master Gardener. Will you allow Him to be the Gardener of your heart? He can pluck the bad fruits and pull up the weeds, so the good fruit has more room to grow freely.

"The temptations in your life are no different from what others experience. And God is faithful. He will not allow the temptation to be more than you can stand. When you are tempted, he will show you a way out so that you can endure." (1 Corinthians 10:13)

"And remember, when you are being tempted, do not say, 'God is tempting me.' God is never tempted to do wrong, and he never tempts anyone else." (James 1:13) If God doesn't tempt us then it must be Satan

doing the tempting. God will allow it to happen, but not more than we can bear, and He always gives us an escape route. Satan tempts us, and God allows us to take the test. Satan's intention is that we miserably fail the test and get held back, bogged down, rebellious, and hopeless. God's intention is that we examine ourselves, look for answers, learn from our mistakes, become wiser, pass the test, grow, move forward, and, ultimately, lean on Him.

The fruits of the Spirit have an opposer. The opposer would be the sinful nature. Love vs. Hate. Joy vs. Misery. Peace vs. Turmoil. Patience vs. Intolerance. Kindness vs. Cold-heartedness. Goodness vs. Wickedness. Faithfulness vs. Untrustworthiness. Gentleness vs. Harshness. Self-Control vs. Rashness. A temptation doesn't always come from a physical outside source, like someone trying to talk me into doing something I know I shouldn't do. Sometimes the temptation is between me and myself. For example, I can be tempted to hate, whether it be myself or someone else. I can be tempted to allow misery to rob my joy or cause turmoil resulting in robbing someone else's joy. I can be tempted to be cold-hearted or harsh. I can be tempted to make rash decisions that I will regret later. The war isn't always visible. We can wage war against ourselves, fighting the sinful nature.

If we know what kinds of fruits God's Spirit produces, it helps us to see where we have bad fruits, weeds, thorns, rocks, and hard soil in our lives. Then we can take those things that we struggle with and ask the Lord, our Gardener and Refiner, what He wants to teach us. He will show us through His eyes of Love.

"Since you have heard about Jesus and have learned the truth that comes from him, throw off your old sinful nature and your former way of life, which is corrupted by lust and deception. Instead, let the Spirit renew your thoughts and attitudes. Put on your new nature, created to be like God—truly righteous and holy." (Ephesians 4:21-24)

Think of a tree that has dead branches or rotten fruit. The dead parts need to be removed so that the tree won't be hindered from growing to its fullest and producing the fruit that it was made to produce. When we have things in our lives that need to be cut away, it can be painful, but it is necessary so we can become the person that God created us to be and produce the fruit that He created us to produce. When our soil is rich with His Love, we can produce a harvest of thirty, sixty, or even a hundred times more than was planted.

"Dear brothers and sisters, when troubles of any kind come your way, consider it an opportunity for great joy. For you know that when your faith is tested, your endurance has a chance to grow. So let it grow, for when your endurance is fully developed, you will be perfect and complete, needing nothing." (James 1:2-4)

"So humble yourselves under the mighty power of God, and at the right time he will lift you up in honor. Give all your worries and cares to God, for he cares about you.

Stay alert! Watch out for your great enemy, the devil. He prowls around like a roaring lion, looking for someone to devour. Stand firm against him, and be strong in your faith. Remember that your family of believers all over the world is going through the same kind of suffering you are.

In his kindness God called you to share in his eternal glory by means of Christ Jesus. So after you have suffered a little while, he will restore, support, and strengthen you, and he will place you on a firm foundation. All power to him forever! Amen." (1 Peter 5:6-11)

Every one of us have a little or lot of dross in our lives. Dross is rubbish, junk, debris. It is foreign matter, waste, scum on the surface of molten metal. We are like molten metal because He can shape us and mold us into a new creation. He can put a little warmth to us, and we can shine with a brilliant glow. Sometimes in order to see that radiant glow in us, He must melt away the dross by allowing heat in our lives to rise, but never more than we can handle. He knows how much we can really handle. The tough part is, it's often more than we think we can handle. We have to trust the Old Refiner.

I personalized "The Old Refiner" poem as if He were speaking directly to me. I will share it with you in hopes that it will bless you too.

"I sit by a fire of seven-fold heat,
As I watch you, My precious ore,
And closer I bend with a searching gaze
As I allow you to heat up more.
I know I have ore that can stand the test,
And I want the finest gold
To mold as a crown for King Jesus to wear,
Set with gems of a price untold.
So I lay you in the burning fire,
You would gladly say "Not today"
And I watch the dross that you have not seen,
As it melts and passes away.
You grow brighter and yet more bright,
But your eyes are so dim with tears,
You saw the fire–not My Hand,
And questioned with anxious fears.
Yet you shine out with a richer glow,
As you mirror a Form above,
That bent over the fire, though unseen by you,

With a look of ineffable love.
Can you think that it pleases My loving heart
To cause you a moment's pain?
Ah, no! but I see through the present cross
The bliss of eternal gain.
So I wait here with a watchful Eye,
With a Love that is strong and sure,
And you will not suffer a bit more heat,
Than is needed to make you pure."

"The Old Refiner" portrays such a beautiful picture of how specific and personal God is. We are like fine gold or precious stone, but we are worth much more than gold to our Father. In His eyes, we are worth the blood of Jesus. Let that sink in for a moment. YOU are worth the *blood of Jesus!* His Love is the Truest.

"When you pass through the waters, I will be with you; And through the rivers, they shall not overflow you. When you walk through the fire, you shall not be burned, Nor shall the flame scorch you." (Isaiah 43:2 NKJV)

145 I pray with all my heart; answer me, Lord!
I will obey your decrees.
146 I cry out to you; rescue me,
that I may obey your laws.
147 I rise early, before the sun is up;
I cry out for help and put my hope in your words.
148 I stay awake through the night,
thinking about your promise.
149 In your faithful love, O Lord, hear my cry;
let me be revived by following your regulations.
150 Lawless people are coming to attack me;
they live far from your instructions.
151 But you are near, O Lord,
and all your commands are true.
152 I have known from my earliest days
that your laws will last forever.

Psalm 119:145–152

21

Answer Me

It might feel as if the Lord is being silent during the times that the heat is turned up to a degree that we aren't quite sure we can handle. We long for His rescue wondering how much longer we can hold up. The psalmist was at a place of great heat in his life. He was doing all that he could to stay strong. He knew that he must stay close to Lord or he might give into temptation. He knew that his help came from the Lord, so he chose to get up before the sun came up to cry out to the Lord and hang on His words throughout the day. At night he would lie awake thinking about the promises of God. His strength was only in the truth of God's word.

The Lord knows we are stronger than we think we are. He knows our breaking point, and He knows exactly what we need to accomplish a good work within our lives. More than likely, we will want to give up before it's time. During those moments, we have to trust completely in His perception.

Sometimes we hit rock bottom before we look to Him. While God has multiple plans and purposes to use our suffering for our good, I believe there is always one important goal that He wants to achieve, and that is to get us to look to Him.

Have you ever thought of suffering as a privilege? Odd question, huh? *"For you have been given not only the privilege of trusting in Christ but also the privilege of suffering for him."* (Philippians 1:29) That might sound morbid but think of it this way; Jesus came and suffered in order to gain a relationship with you and to pay for righteousness for you. He considered it a privilege to die, so that you could live. His suffering came with the benefit of eternal life for you. The world and sin are the cause of His suffering, not God.

But God allowed Jesus to go through the trials because He trusted that Jesus was strong enough to handle the oppression, knowing that not only would He come out better in the end, but many would be saved because of what Jesus went through.

God didn't find it enjoyable to watch His son struggle. His eyes were tender to His wounds, but He knew the great benefit that would come to the world by allowing the sufferings to take place. What if that is how God sees you? You are His precious child, and it breaks His heart to see you hurting. He also sees you as strong. He sees the healed you, the confident you, the transformed you. He sees the benefits that your circumstances can bring about in your life. He chooses you. He chooses your life to be a testimony. He knows that the trial can sharpen you and strengthen you, and when you are ready to come out of the fire, you will be unstoppable. He knows that when people see what you have gone through and witness the way that your life turns out, they will want what you have. Your life can benefit not only yourself, but many, many others who are struggling like you are. You can be a bright light to those in bitter darkness. You can be hope to the hopeless. What if your suffering is what brings lives to Jesus Christ? Your suffering might save someone from the eternal pits of Hell. Consider it a privilege and an honor to suffer for the sake of Jesus, because He chooses you, your very life, circumstances and all, to be a beacon of light to a dying world.

What if Jesus said to you, *"Son, Daughter, I know this is tough, and it grieves my heart to watch you go through this, but the ending is so great, too great for you to fully understand. I see a masterpiece, the beauty in the brokenness. I see the new things that will come from this. Will you do this for Me? If you will do this for Me, I promise to be with you every step of the way, and I promise to bless you and those around you in ways that are beyond your imagination."*

If you had a choice, what would your answer be? If someone asked me, *"Would you suffer for me?"* I would have a hard time quickly jumping in to say, *"YES!"* But having known that the One who was asking me, literally gave His all to have me, I might not be so quick to say no either. Suffering: "a privilege." What a deep thought to ponder. Imagine how your life might change if you consider that the hard times you go through are for a purpose beyond your control that reaps benefits far beyond your imagination.

Paul chose to view his sufferings as a privilege. *"Not that I was ever in need, for I have learned how to be content with whatever I have. I know how to live on almost nothing or with everything. I have learned the secret of living in every situation, whether it is with a full stomach or empty, with plenty or little. For I can do everything through Christ, who gives me strength.* (Philippians 4:11-13)

Prior to those verses, Paul described the secret to living with contentment. The secret is turning worries into prayers, trusting God with those petitions, and practicing thinking about things that are worthy of praise, honorable, right, lovely, pure, and excellent. Remember now? It starts by changing the way you think. Think about what you are thinking about. That is what the psalmist was doing. He knew the secret. He turned his worries into prayers, and then he fixed his thoughts on God's word and His promises. His hope came from the Lord.

I pray that the benefits of suffering are becoming clearer. Suffering makes us stronger. It builds our endurance and patience. When the heat is turned up, some of the dirt and grime melts away allowing our true character to shine through. With every degree our hope becomes greater. *"We were given this hope when we were saved. (If we already have something, we don't need to hope for it. But if we look forward to something we don't yet have, we must wait patiently and confidently.)"* (Romans 8:24-25)

The waiting process can increase faith and hope, but it is way easier said than done. That is why it is so important to have God's word and promises engraved in our hearts and minds. Paul understood this all too well. Scriptures tell us that he was given a thorn in his flesh to keep him from becoming conceited. Paul begged the Lord three different times to remove it from him. *"But he said to me, 'My grace is sufficient for you, for my power is made perfect in weakness.' Therefore I will boast all the more gladly of my weaknesses, so that the power of Christ may rest upon me. For the sake of Christ, then, I am content with weaknesses, insults, hardships, persecutions, and calamities. For when I am weak, then I am strong."* (2 Corinthians 12:9-10 ESV) The psalmist was begging the Lord for change, too. Breaking down and crying out to the Lord does not represent failure. It is in those weak moments that we turn fully to Jesus, the One who understands everything we are facing. Once we turn to him in weakness, He makes us strong and turns our sorrows into joy. The author of Psalm 119 shows us clearly that ups and downs are natural and perfectly okay. It gives us good practice to look to the One that our help comes from.

To examine our hearts, we can ask ourselves, *"Do I trust God in the trials? Do I trust that He will bring good out of disaster? Do I have hope that better things are yet to come?"* Spend some time with Jehovah and ask Him those questions:

"Do I trust you?"

"Will You bring good out of bad?"

"What do I have to hope for?"

He answered Paul, and He will answer you. Take some time to hear and see what God would tell you about your situation. He may have a very specific answer for you as He did for Paul.

If you are not going through a difficult time right now, look back at a time that you were struggling, pick out all the good things that came from it, and thank the Lord for what He did. After you have looked back, ponder the thought that you can look forward to the next time you feel the heat coming on, knowing that you are in the hands of the "Old Refiner", and He knows exactly how much heat is needed to make you shine brighter. For when you are weak, then you are strong!

"I look up to the mountains—
does my help come from there?
My help comes from the Lord,
who made heaven and earth!
He will not let you stumble;
the one who watches over you will not slumber.
Indeed, he who watches over Israel
never slumbers or sleeps.
The Lord himself watches over you!
The Lord stands beside you as your protective shade.
The sun will not harm you by day,
nor the moon at night.
The Lord keeps you from all harm
and watches over your life.
The Lord keeps watch over you as you come and go,
both now and forever." (Psalm 121:1-8)

He is True Love.

153 Look upon my suffering and rescue me,
for I have not forgotten your instructions.
154 Argue my case; take my side!
Protect my life as you promised.
155 The wicked are far from rescue,
for they do not bother with your decrees.
156 Lord, how great is your mercy;
let me be revived by following your regulations.
157 Many persecute and trouble me,
yet I have not swerved from your laws.
158 Seeing these traitors makes me sick at heart,
because they care nothing for your word.
159 See how I love your commandments, Lord.
Give back my life because of your unfailing love.
160 The very essence of your words is truth;
all your just regulations will stand forever.

Psalm 119:153–160

22

TRUTH WINS OUT

While we are waiting as patiently as we know how for our rescue, we must occupy our time and our mind with truth. Staying in the truth, especially during a troubling time, will keep us from wallowing in fear and doubt. Truth will put a good distance from us and the danger of slipping into the pit of self-pity. Truth will keep us hopeful, and it will protect our sanity!

The life of the psalmist was like a roller coaster. Up one minute and down the next. I can relate to that, can you? Life is like a roller coaster. To some, roller coasters are scary and not enjoyable at all. They wouldn't dare get on one willingly, and if for some reason they got talked into it, the whole ride would be a miserable, tense, mess! To others, roller coasters are a thrill, and the best part is anticipating the next drop, turn, or flip. Either way, once you get on a roller coaster, you have no choice but to ride it until it's over. That's life. We have no choice but to ride it out, but we *can* choose how we ride it out. Attempting to take control, we can grab hold tightly until our knuckles are white, grit our teeth, and kick our feet only to realize that our attempt gets us nowhere. Fear can be crippling if we dread every time life takes us down. We can be miserable when life takes an unexpected turn or lose it when things flip upside down. Fear can lead to a place of absolute misery, hatred, depression, or anxiety.

Our other option is to view life as an adventure and look forward to where it will take us next. When we are way up high and suddenly begin to drop, as long as True Love is sitting right next to us, we can throw our hands up and say, *"I'm ready!"* and look forward to what it will teach us. When we take an unexpected turn, we can know that True Love has good plans. Even though the turn wasn't expected, we can know that it will work out for our good. When we go through loop after loop after loop and feel like we are going backwards just as much as we are moving forward not seeming to make any progress, we can look at it as training. We are getting stronger, learning more, becoming more patient, building character, and gaining hope. Eventually True Love will have your heart so captured that you can throw your hands up in the air and enjoy life even in the rough places. The low places will be easier to handle even if they are tough, because you know Who is in control. You have faith, hope, and love, and the greatest is True Love.

Truth, God's word, is what gives us hope. Truth reveals God's love. Truth is the belt that holds everything together. We must know and have the truth. The psalmist understood the benefits of not only knowing the word of the Lord, but also the importance of allowing it to be part of his everyday life. God's instructions were written on his heart and engraved in his soul. They were part of his inner core. The psalmist didn't even have the New Testament, and he knew how good the instructions were for him because he had an unshakeable relationship with God.

Perhaps the psalmist was familiar with the words the Lord gave to Joshua. *"'Study this Book of Instruction continually. Meditate on it day and night so you will be sure to obey everything written in it. Only then will you prosper and succeed in all you do. This is my command—be strong and courageous! Do not be afraid or discouraged. For the Lord your God is with you wherever you go.'"* (Joshua 1:8-9)

When I first read that Scripture, it never left my mind. It was like my conscience kept pulling the verses back up because I was not doing what it said. I thought God was commanding that I read and study the Bible day and night and it was quite intimidating. Immediately, I felt like a failure because I knew I wouldn't be able to keep that command. Studying the Bible day and night would require a lot of my time and dedication. As much as I wanted to be *that* dedicated, it was too overwhelming. I became discouraged and thought, *"Well, I guess I will never truly be successful or prosperous until I get my act together."* Maybe that is why God kept placing that Scripture in particular on my heart; so that I would keep looking and understand.

I remember the day like it was yesterday. With those verses on my mind, I was feeling like I needed to get my four-year old son, Kemper, started early learning the Scriptures. As he sat in the bathtub playing with his toys, I went and grabbed my Bible, plopped down on the bathroom floor next to the tub, and opened it up to Joshua 1:8-9 and said, *"Son listen to what this says."* I read it aloud to him, and as I read it, I had a whole new understanding of it! *"Study this Book of Instruction continually..."* Suddenly, I noticed it didn't say study it day and night. It said *continually.* Continually means to make it an ongoing thing, not just once here and there, but continue to study the Bible. *"Well I can do that!"* I thought to myself. *"Meditate on it day and night so you will be sure to obey everything written in it."* Ah ha! I'm supposed to *meditate* on it day and night. To meditate means to think about, to ponder, to consider in my mind. God wasn't asking me to sit and study His word day and night. He was just asking me to think about it day and night.

To "study" day and night sounds impossible to me. Especially to those who have a full-time job, a family to tend to, and hobbies to enjoy. It would be difficult to do even if we wanted to. I believe God desires that reading our Bible becomes a passion instead of an obligation. Meditating on God's word is something that anyone can do day and night! We all think anyway, so we just need to practice thinking on God's instructions.

"This is my command-" When I first read over those verses, I thought God was commanding that I study the Bible day and night. The day that I read it to Kemper, I saw it differently. *"Be strong and courageous! Do not be afraid or discouraged."* His command was to be strong, not afraid; to be courageous, not discouraged. Then He gave an excellent reason why I could do what He was commanding. *"For the Lord your God is with you wherever you go."* Wow! Those two verses formed a whole new meaning to me. There is nothing about them that makes me feel defeated any longer. Instead, they give me hope!

God was trying to tell me, *"If you will continue to get to know Me by finding out about Me in the Bible and think about the things you learn throughout the day and night, then you will find Me and know Me personally. You won't have to be afraid because you will realize that I am for you and with you. Then you will prosper and succeed in all you do because you won't be doing anything alone. I will be your helper, and I will be your guide. You can do anything with Me. You just have to choose to let Me be with you. Continue to wrap Truth around you and trust Me."*

God's commands are never harsh or rash. They are always for our protection. His commands are always out of love and never to make us feel guilty and defeated. I am so thankful that Jehovah didn't allow those Scriptures to leave my mind until I understood His purpose. I am also grateful that He revealed the meaning to me as I was teaching Kemper so that I didn't misdirect him! God is the greatest Teacher!

I know I have repeated my words many times throughout this book. I was concerned about that until I realized that is what Psalm 119 is all about. God repeats His words over and over from the beginning of creation to Revelation so that we will be sure to understand. Remember Jesus' prayer for us, *"Sanctify them by the truth; your word is truth."* (John 17:17 NIV) We need truth to protect our hearts and our minds.

Having a close relationship with God and gaining wisdom and knowledge about Him doesn't mean that we will have an uninterrupted life with peace and no troubles on this earth. Jesus' words were, *"I'm not asking you to take them out of the world, but to keep them safe from the evil one."* Jesus, who was God himself, had a very interrupted life and endured every kind of pain. Why should I have a perfect life?

"Behold, I send you out as sheep in the midst of wolves. Therefore be wise as serpents and harmless as doves." (Matthew 10:16 NKJV)

When Jesus prayed for us to our Heavenly Father, one thing He said was, *"Just as you sent me into the world, I am sending them into the world."* (John17:18) *He* sends us out. That means we have a mission to carry out. We have a purpose to fulfill. Life is an adventure. Adventures are exciting and usually involve danger at some point, but it is worth it because of where it leads us and what we get to see and learn along the way. Life is awesome! God the Creator of the universe chose you, made you, and set you out on a mission. You have an important role to play in an adventure chosen by God. Every one of God's children will end up in the same place in the end of this world only to begin forever in another world. I can't wait until the day that I get to meet you and hear about what you had to go through before you arrived in Heaven. I can't wait to hear how you fought off the wolves and conquered the waves. The way that life affects us depends on how we see it. We can change the way we think by lining it up with the truth so that the truth will always win out. My prayer is that your experience will bring you to a place that you can say, *"It's all worth it."*

If Jesus is the one that compares us to sheep and sends us out among the wolves, then He must be confident that we can survive. He says, *"'I am the good shepherd. The good shepherd sacrifices his life for the sheep. A hired hand will run when he sees a wolf coming. He will abandon the sheep because they don't belong to him and he isn't their shepherd. And so the wolf attacks them and scatters the flock. The hired hand runs away because he's working only for the money and doesn't really care about the sheep.*

I am the good shepherd; I know my own sheep, and they know me, just as my Father knows me and I know the Father. So I sacrifice my life for the sheep. I have other sheep, too, that are not in this sheepfold. I must bring them also. They will listen to my voice, and there will be one flock with one shepherd.'" (John 10:11-16)

Twice He says, *"I am the good Shepherd."* Not only does He send us out, but He keeps a close watch on us because He cares.

"The Lord says, 'I will rescue those who love me.
I will protect those who trust in my name.
When they call on me, I will answer;

I will be with them in trouble.
I will rescue and honor them.
I will reward them with a long life
and give them my salvation.'" (Psalm 91:14-16)

"What, then, shall we say in response to these things? If God is for us, who can be against us? He who did not spare his own Son, but gave him up for us all—how will he not also, along with him, graciously give us all things? Who will bring any charge against those whom God has chosen? It is God who justifies. Who then is the one who condemns? No one. Christ Jesus who died—more than that, who was raised to life—is at the right hand of God and is also interceding for us. Who shall separate us from the love of Christ? Shall trouble or hardship or persecution or famine or nakedness or danger or sword? As it is written:

'For your sake we face death all day long;
we are considered as sheep to be slaughtered.'

No, in all these things we are more than conquerors through him who loved us. For I am convinced that neither death nor life, neither angels nor demons, neither the present nor the future, nor any powers, neither height nor depth, nor anything else in all creation, will be able to separate us from the love of God that is in Christ Jesus our Lord." (Romans 8:31-39 NIV)

Study God's instruction continually. Meditate on it day and night. Then you will be prosperous and successful. Remember God's command to be strong, not afraid. Be courageous, not discouraged because HE is with YOU *WHEREVER* you go, and if HE is for YOU, then who could be against you? He doesn't expect you to be a vicious lion, seeking to protect yourself and take control. He calls you to be harmless sheep because He is your protector, who has already overcome the world. He is the God of Angel Armies, and the angels are your guard dogs. He is by YOUR side. You have every reason to be strong and courageous no matter where life takes you next. Throw your hands up! True Love is by your side.

161 POWERFUL PEOPLE HARASS ME WITHOUT CAUSE,
BUT MY HEART TREMBLES ONLY AT YOUR WORD.
162 I REJOICE IN YOUR WORD
LIKE ONE WHO DISCOVERS A GREAT TREASURE.
163 I HATE AND ABHOR ALL FALSEHOOD,
BUT I LOVE YOUR INSTRUCTIONS.
164 I WILL PRAISE YOU SEVEN TIMES A DAY
BECAUSE ALL YOUR REGULATIONS ARE JUST.
165 THOSE WHO LOVE YOUR INSTRUCTIONS HAVE GREAT PEACE
AND DO NOT STUMBLE.
166 I LONG FOR YOUR RESCUE, LORD,
SO I HAVE OBEYED YOUR COMMANDS.
167 I HAVE OBEYED YOUR LAWS,
FOR I LOVE THEM VERY MUCH.
168 YES, I OBEY YOUR COMMANDMENTS AND LAWS
BECAUSE YOU KNOW EVERYTHING I DO.

PSALM 119:161–168

23

Great Peace

"But you must remain faithful to the things you have been taught. You know they are true, for you know you can trust those who taught you. You have been taught the holy Scriptures from childhood, and they have given you the wisdom to receive the salvation that comes by trusting in Christ Jesus. All Scripture is inspired by God and is useful to teach us what is true and to make us realize what is wrong in our lives. It corrects us when we are wrong and teaches us to do what is right. God uses it to prepare and equip his people to do every good work." (2 Timothy 3:14-17)

The words recorded in the Bible are inspired by God. He chose every thought, every story, every word that was written. Just because God was speaking to a specific person in the Bible, does not mean that it isn't for you. All Scripture is useful for teaching, and God uses it all to prepare and equip us. For instance, we read about the promises that God gave to Abraham for his faith. *"And now that you belong to Christ, you are the true children of Abraham. You are his heirs, and God's promise to Abraham belongs to you."* (Galatians 3:29) When Jesus spoke to the disciples, the words to them are for you as well. *"Jesus said to the people who believed in him, 'You are truly my disciples if you remain faithful to my teachings. And you will know the truth, and the truth will set you free.'"* (John 8:31-32) You are a disciple. Jesus says you are the salt of the earth and the light of the world. God didn't choose to record the stories that we find in the Bible so that one day we would have a good history book to read. It is alive and active. It's the instruction manual to life. Everlasting life. True peace. True Love. He wrote it for you. Jesus has so much to say to us if we just give Him the chance to talk. The remainder of this chapter will be Jesus' words found in the Scriptures written to *you.*

"'Do not let your hearts be troubled. You believe in God; believe also in me. My Father's house has many rooms; if that were not so, would I have told you that I am going there to prepare a place for you? And if I go and prepare a place for you, I will come back and take you to be with me that you also may be where I am. You know the way to the place where I am going.'" (John 14:1-4 NIV) *"'**I am the way and the truth and the life**. No one comes to the Father except through me. If you really know me, you will know my Father as well. From now on, you do know him and have seen him.'"* (John 14: 6-7 NIV) *"'If you love me, keep my commands. And I will ask the Father, and he will give you another advocate to help you and be with you forever— the Spirit of truth. The world cannot accept him, because it neither sees him nor knows him. But you know him, for he lives with you and will be in you. I will not leave you as orphans; I will come to you. Before long, the world will not see me anymore, but you will see me. Because I live, you also will live. On that day you will realize that I am in my Father, and you are in me, and I am in you. Whoever has my commands and keeps them is the one who loves me. The one who loves me will be loved by my Father, and I too will love them and show myself to them.'"* (John 14:15-21 NIV, emphasis added) *"'Anyone who loves me will obey my teaching. My Father will love them, and we will come to them and make our home with them. Anyone who does not love me will not obey my teaching. These words you hear are not my own; they belong to the Father who sent me. All this I have spoken while still with you. But the Advocate, the Holy Spirit, whom the Father will send in my name, will teach you all things and will remind you of everything I have said to you. Peace I leave with you; my peace I give you. I do not give to you as the world gives. Do not let your hearts be troubled and do not be afraid.'"* (John 14:23-27 NIV)

"'I am the true grapevine, and my Father is the gardener. He cuts off every branch of mine that doesn't produce fruit, and he prunes the branches that do bear fruit so they will produce even more. You have already been pruned and purified by the message I have given you. Remain in me, and I will remain in you. For a branch cannot produce fruit if it is severed from the vine, and you cannot be fruitful unless you remain in me.

Yes, I am the vine; you are the branches. Those who remain in me, and I in them, will produce much fruit. For apart from me you can do nothing. Anyone who does not remain in me is thrown away like a useless branch and withers. Such branches are gathered into a pile to be burned. But if you remain in me and my words remain in you, you may ask for anything you want, and it will be granted! When you produce much fruit, you are my true disciples. This brings great glory to my Father.

I have loved you even as the Father has loved me. Remain in my love. When you obey my commandments, you remain in my love, just as I obey my Father's commandments and remain in his love. I have told you these things so that you will be filled with my joy. Yes, your joy will overflow! This is my commandment: Love each other in the same way I have loved you. There is no greater love than to lay down one's life for one's friends. You are my friends if you do what I command. I no longer call you slaves, because a master doesn't confide in his slaves. Now you are my friends, since I have told you everything the Father told me. You didn't choose me. I chose you. I appointed you to go and produce lasting fruit, so that the Father will give you whatever you ask for, using my name. This is my command: Love each other.

If the world hates you, remember that it hated me first. The world would love you as one of its own if you belonged to it, but you are no longer part of the world. I chose you to come out of the world, so it hates you. Do you remember what I told you? "A slave is not greater than the master." Since they persecuted me, naturally they will persecute you. And if they had listened to me, they would listen to you. They will do all this to you because of me, for they have rejected the one who sent me. They would not be guilty if I had not come and spoken to them. But now they have no excuse for their sin. Anyone who hates me also hates my Father. If I hadn't done such miraculous signs among them that no one else could do, they would not be guilty. But as it is, they have seen everything I did, yet they still hate me and my Father. This fulfills what is written in their Scriptures: "They hated me without cause."

But I will send you the Advocate—the Spirit of truth. He will come to you from the Father and will testify all about me. And you must also testify about me because you have been with me from the beginning of my ministry.'" (John 15)

"'I have told you all this so that you may have peace in me. Here on earth you will have many trials and sorrows. But take heart, because I have overcome the world.'" (John 16:33)

While reading through His words again, I caught something with a new understanding that I didn't see before. That's the way His word is. Alive. Active. Always. John 14:15 is a verse I have avoided digging into because my human understanding couldn't make sense of it. Jesus said, *"If you love me, obey my commandments."* I used to feel guilty when I read that because I didn't think I did a very good job at obeying His commandments, but I do love Him. Also, it sounded demanding. It's kind of like reading a text message. Sometimes we just don't understand the tone of voice used because we can't actually here the person's voice. We have to be careful with that. I heard a different tone of voice when I read that Scripture that didn't line up with the character of God. *"If you love me. Do what I say!"*

Knowing what I know now, it makes sense. His commandments are to Love. First Him, then others as yourself. So *"if I love Him"* then I am already obeying His command to love Him, and because of that, I can love others. If we obey His commandments, then we love Him. If we love Him, then we will listen to His teachings. Loving Him results in obedience to everything else.

"When you obey my commandments, you remain in my love, just as I obey my Father's commandments and remain in his love. This is my command- Love one another." He is the Creator of the entire Universe and all He asks of you and me is *love.* Love must be one powerful force. Thank you, Jesus, for your truth.

The psalmist said, *"I will praise you seven times a day..."* (vs. 164) Let us respond back to Jesus with praises.

'Tis so sweet to trust in Jesus,
Just to take Him at His word;
Just to rest upon His promise,
And to know, "Thus saith the Lord!"

Jesus, Jesus, how I trust Him!
How I've proved Him o'er and o'er;
Jesus, Jesus, precious Jesus!
Oh, for grace to trust Him more!

Oh, how sweet to trust in Jesus,
Just to trust His cleansing blood;
And in simple faith to plunge me
'Neath the healing, cleansing flood!

Yes, 'tis sweet to trust in Jesus,
Just from sin and self to cease;
Just from Jesus simply taking
Life and rest, and joy and peace.

I'm so glad I learned to trust Thee,
Precious Jesus, Savior, Friend;
And I know that Thou art with me,
Wilt be with me to the end.

("Tis' So Sweet to Trust in Jesus" by Louisa M. R. Stead)

With our hearts, minds, and souls fixed on Him, we can have internal peace.

"Powerful people harass me without cause,
but my heart trembles only at your word.
I rejoice in your word
like one who discovers a great treasure.
I hate and abhor all falsehood,
but I love your instructions.
I will praise you seven times a day
because all your regulations are just.
Those who love your instructions have **great peace** *and do not stumble.*
I long for your rescue, Lord,
so I have obeyed your commands.
I have obeyed your laws,
for I love them very much.
Yes, I obey your commandments and laws
because you know everything I do." (Psalm 119:161-168, emphasis added)

I am so thankful that it is possible to experience Great Peace even while we are still longing for the Lord to rescue us. It seems as if those two things shouldn't even be said in the same sentence. But God, only God, can manifest true peace during a season of longing. Even if you haven't experienced that peace, there's evidence that it exists. We have found that evidence by following one psalmist's life experiences. I'm sure there are many others that can testify as well. Ask God to send you people that have experienced this great peace; people that can walk alongside you and encourage you as you wait and seek Him. *"And let us not neglect our meeting together, as some people do, but encourage one another, especially now that the day of his return is drawing near."* (Hebrews 10:25)

169 O Lord, listen to my cry;

give me the discerning mind you promised.

170 Listen to my prayer;

rescue me as you promised.

171 Let praise flow from my lips,

for you have taught me your decrees.

172 Let my tongue sing about your word,

for all your commands are right.

173 Give me a helping hand,

for I have chosen to follow your

commandments.

174 O Lord, I have longed for your rescue,

and your instructions are my delight.

175 Let me live so I can praise you,

and may your regulations help me.

176 I have wandered away like a lost sheep;

come and find me,

for I have not forgotten your commands.

Psalm 119:169–176

24

Come Find Me

I am remembering the beginning of my Psalm 119 journey. I would go to my bedroom every chance I could get away and fall to my knees at my bedside crying for help just like the psalmist did. I would tell the Lord, *"I know that You love me, and I know You have answers, but I am so miserable! Why do I have to go through this? What am I supposed to do? You know my hearts desires, and I'm trying so hard to do what is right! I am seeking You and Your word. What have I done to deserve this?"*

It seemed like every time I began to throw a pity party for myself, I would think of Jesus on the cross. *"But many were amazed when they saw him. His face was so disfigured he seemed hardly human, and from his appearance, one would scarcely know he was a man."* (Isaiah 52:14) My problem seemed almost microscopic at the thought of Jesus being beaten so severely that one could hardly tell He was even a man, and to top it off, He could've put a stop to it at any point.

"'Or do you think that I cannot now pray to My Father, and He will provide Me with more than twelve legions of angels?'" (Matthew 26:53 NKJV) Jesus endured all of sorrow and pain willingly so that I could have life eternally, and not only so I could have life, but because He loves me that much. He loves *us* that much. Who would willingly put their self through torture and gruesome death if there was no love behind it? It was a strong desire for True Love that drove Jesus to the cross, a love like fire that cannot be quenched.

"My servant [Jesus] grew up in the Lord's presence like a tender green shoot, like a root in dry ground. There was nothing beautiful or majestic

about his appearance, nothing to attract us to him. He was ***despised*** *and* ***rejected****—a* ***man of sorrows****, acquainted with* ***deepest grief****. We turned our backs on him and looked the other way. He was despised, and we did not care. Yet it was* ***our weaknesses he carried;*** *it was* ***our sorrows that weighed him down****. And we thought his troubles were a punishment from God, a punishment for his own sins! But he was* ***pierced*** *for our rebellion,* ***crushed*** *for our sins. He was* ***beaten*** *so we could be whole. He was* ***whipped*** *so we could be healed.*

All of us, like sheep, have strayed away. We have left God's paths to follow our own. Yet the Lord ***laid on him the sins of us all****. He was* ***oppressed*** *and* ***treated harshly****, yet he never said a word. He was led like a lamb to the* ***slaughter****. And as a sheep is silent before the shearers, he did not open his mouth.* ***Unjustly condemned****, he was led away. No one cared that he died without descendants, that* ***his life was cut short*** *in midstream. But he was* ***struck down*** *for the rebellion of my people. He had done no wrong and had never deceived anyone. But he was* ***buried like a criminal;*** *he was put in a rich man's grave. But it was the Lord's good plan to* ***crush*** *him and cause him* ***grief****.*

Yet when his life is made an offering for sin, he will have many descendants. He will enjoy a long life, and the Lord's good plan will prosper in his hands. When he sees all that is accomplished by his ***anguish****, he will be satisfied. And because of his experience, my righteous servant will make it possible for many to be counted righteous, for he will* ***bear all their sins****.*

I will give him the honors of a victorious soldier, because he ***exposed*** *himself to death. He was* ***counted among the rebels****. He* ***bore the sins of many*** *and interceded for rebels."* (Isaiah 53:2-12, emphasis added)

I can read about His suffering and try to imagine it, and I will never truly understand the severity of it, but He most certainly understands mine. My point is not to make you feel bad for complaining about your situation that you are in, but instead to help you understand that you have a Savior, a Friend, and Heavenly Father that deeply loves you and understands what you are going through because He has felt it all. There is no situation too big for Him. When we can focus on Him and relate our life to his, we can be closer to Him and understand His perfect love that He has for us. Just as the song says, *"Turn your eyes upon Jesus. Look full in His wonderful face, and the things of the earth will grow strangely dim in the light of His glory and grace."*

We can weep with sorrow and cry out to the Lord for help because He cares, and He understands. Jesus cried out to His Father to take away the suffering, but He was willing to surrender to it if it was God's will.

I needed to be revived and encouraged, and Psalm 119 told me that it was Yahweh's word that would lead me to what I needed most. *"The LORD is near to the brokenhearted and saves those who are crushed in spirit."* (Psalm 34:18 NASB) *"He heals the brokenhearted and binds up their wounds."* (Psalm 147:3 NIV) *"And we know that God causes everything to work together for the good of those who love God and are called according to his purpose for them."* (Romans 8:28) I grabbed hold of those verses and held on to them like my life depended on it. It encouraged me to know that the Lord was near to me, and He would save me from my broken and crushed spirit. I was revived because His word said that He would heal me and bind up my wounds. I was hopeful because, even though I couldn't understand the reason for the pain and suffering, God was going to work it out for my good. I relied on His word.

"'My thoughts are nothing like your thoughts,' says the Lord. 'And my ways are far beyond anything you could imagine. For just as the heavens are higher than the earth, so my ways are higher than your ways and my thoughts higher than your thoughts. The rain and snow come down from the heavens and stay on the ground to water the earth. They cause the grain to grow, producing seed for the farmer and bread for the hungry. It is the same with my word. I send it out, and it always produces fruit. It will accomplish all I want it to, and it will prosper everywhere I send it. You will live in joy and peace. The mountains and hills will burst into song, and the trees of the field will clap their hands! Where once there were thorns, cypress trees will grow. Where nettles grew, myrtles will sprout up. These events will bring great honor to the Lord's name; they will be an everlasting sign of his power and love.'" (Isaiah 55:8-13)

Trusting in His word brought me comfort.

Do you feel as if you have wandered away like a lost sheep, and you're wondering if your Shepherd will ever come find you? Do you think that maybe He is too busy to come looking for you? Do you feel like He has other things that are much more important than finding you? Do you think that you aren't worth finding because He has many other sheep, and you aren't worth leaving them behind to tend to you? Let Jesus tell you what He thinks about that.

"'If a man has a hundred sheep and one of them gets lost, what will he do? Won't he leave the ninety-nine others in the wilderness and go to search for the one that is lost until he finds it? And when he has found it, he will joyfully carry it home on his shoulders. When he arrives, he will call together his friends and neighbors, saying, "Rejoice with me because I have found my lost sheep." In the same way, there is more joy in heaven over one lost sinner who repents and returns to God than over ninety-nine others who are righteous and haven't strayed away!'" (Luke 15: 4-7)

"'You are my flock, the sheep of my pasture. You are my people, and I am your God. I, the Sovereign Lord, have spoken!'" (Ezekiel 34:31)

"For this is what the Sovereign Lord says: 'I myself will search and find my sheep. I will be like a shepherd looking for his scattered flock. I will find my sheep and rescue them from all the places where they were scattered on that dark and cloudy day.'" (Ezekiel 34:11-12) *"'I myself will tend my sheep and give them a place to lie down in peace,' says the Sovereign Lord. 'I will search for my lost ones who strayed away, and I will bring them safely home again. I will bandage the injured and strengthen the weak.'"* (Ezekiel 34:15-16a)

"'I tell you the truth, anyone who sneaks over the wall of a sheepfold, rather than going through the gate, must surely be a thief and a robber! But the one who enters through the gate is the shepherd of the sheep. The gatekeeper opens the gate for him, and the sheep recognize his voice and come to him. He calls his own sheep by name and leads them out. After he has gathered his own flock, he walks ahead of them, and they follow him because they know his voice. They won't follow a stranger; they will run from him because they don't know his voice.' Those who heard Jesus use this illustration didn't understand what he meant, so he explained it to them: 'I tell you the truth, I am the gate for the sheep. All who came before me were thieves and robbers. But the true sheep did not listen to them. Yes, I am the gate. Those who come in through me will be saved. They will come and go freely and will find good pastures. The thief's purpose is to steal and kill and destroy. My purpose is to give them a rich and satisfying life.

I am the good shepherd. The good shepherd sacrifices his life for the sheep. A hired hand will run when he sees a wolf coming. He will abandon the sheep because they don't belong to him and he isn't their shepherd. And so the wolf attacks them and scatters the flock. The hired hand runs away because he's working only for the money and doesn't really care about the sheep.

I am the good shepherd; I know my own sheep, and they know me, just as my Father knows me and I know the Father. So I sacrifice my life for the sheep. I have other sheep, too, that are not in this sheepfold. I must bring them also. They will listen to my voice, and there will be one flock with one shepherd.'" (John 10:1-16)

"'Fear not, little flock; for it is your Father's good pleasure to give you the kingdom.'" (Luke 12:32 KJV)

Wonder no more! Jesus will come after you! He loves you so dearly that even though He has thousands of other sheep, He will leave them to come find you! He is the Good Shepherd.

"He will feed his flock like a shepherd. He will carry the lambs in his arms, holding them close to his heart. He will gently lead the mother sheep with their young." (Isaiah 40:11)

It warms my heart to picture Jesus holding me close to His heart as He would a little lamb. We have nothing to fear. Our Jesus is the best Shepherd. We are a blessed flock to be under His care.

"God showed how much he loved us by sending his one and only Son into the world so that we might have eternal life through him. This is ***real love****—not that we loved God, but that he loved us and sent his Son as a sacrifice to take away our sins.*

Dear friends, since God loved us that much, we surely ought to love each other. No one has ever seen God. But if we love each other, God lives in us, and his love is brought to full expression in us.

And God has given us his Spirit as ***proof*** *that we live in him and he in us. Furthermore, we have seen with our own eyes and now testify that the Father sent his Son to be the Savior of the world. All who declare that Jesus is the Son of God have God living in them, and they live in God. We know how much God loves us, and we have put our trust in his love.*

God is love, and all who live in love live in God, and God lives in them. And as we live in God, our love grows more perfect. So we will not be afraid on the day of judgment, but we can face him with confidence because we live like Jesus here in this world." (1 John 4:9-17)

Like our 119 psalmist, we are only foreigners in this land. There is much more to this life than just getting by. Our lives are beyond our earthly possessions and our worldly successes. Life is much more than our jobs and homes, even more than marriage and family. Those things can be good things, but not first things. You see, when seeking God comes first in your life, He *gives* you the rest! All those things I mentioned above and then some, they are extensions to our lives, perks that our Good Father wants to bless us with. Seek Him, and He will line you up for the right job. Seek Him, and He will guide you in your marriage or, if you are single, lead you to the one to marry. Seek Him, and He will show you which house to buy. *"'But seek first the kingdom of God and his righteousness, and all these things will be added to you.'"* (Matthew 6:33 ESV)

If you chose this book because of the title, my guess is you would like to find True Love, true satisfaction, the desires of your heart. Things of this world can make us happy, but only temporarily. There is so much depression, anxiety, anger, fear, and hopelessness lurking around because many don't understand that lasting peace can't be found in this world. God is True Love, and He blesses us with the gifts of others to share our lives with and things to have and look forward to. *"'I am leaving you with a gift--peace of mind and heart. And the peace I give is a gift the world cannot give. So don't be troubled or afraid.'"* (John 14:27)

The Bible defines Love for us in 1 Corinthians chapter 13. We have learned from God's word that He is Love. Since God *is* Love, then it would be safe to put God's name in the place of love to define God.

God is patient and kind. God is not jealous or boastful or proud or rude. God does not demand His own way. God is not irritable, and He keeps no record of being wronged. God does not rejoice about injustice but rejoices whenever the truth wins out. God never gives up, never loses faith, is always hopeful, and endures through every circumstance. Three things will last forever—faith, hope, and God—and the greatest of these is God.

I believe Jehovah desires for us to know Him that way. He is True Love. He *is* that perfect love every human seeks. *"Such love has no fear, because perfect love expels all fear. If we are afraid, it is for fear of punishment, and this shows that we have not fully experienced his perfect love. We love each other because he loved us first."* (1 John 4:18-19)

"Even before he made the world, God loved us and chose us in Christ to be holy and without fault in his eyes. God decided in advance to adopt us into his own family by bringing us to himself through Jesus Christ. This is what he wanted to do, and it gave him great pleasure." (Ephesians 1:4-5)

BEFORE HE MADE THE WORLD, *He loved you!*

BEFORE HE MADE THE WORLD, *He chose you!*

IN HIS EYES, *you are faultless and holy!*

IN ADVANCE, *He adopted you!*

THIS IS WHAT HE ***WANTED*** *TO DO AND IT GAVE HIM* ***GREAT PLEASURE!!!***

I had no idea the Bible talked so much about love. Until Jesus showed me that it was Him that I was searching for, I would have never known that He was looking for another love story to write. Are you willing to give Him a chance at being the love of your life? If so, call out to Him, *"Come find me!"* and brace yourself for the best love story ever. Yours.

"You'll never know how much you're worth, until you know the One who loves you most."

Jesus. ***True Love.*** A love like fire that cannot be quenched. I pray He becomes a wildfire in your soul.

Appendix

33:3 ASK ME by Lacey Nichole Godfrey

Understanding the character of God is a huge key in developing a close relationship with Him. It is very tricky to "teach" someone relationship because it is by experience that two people become closely acquainted. It is my desire that everyone know Jesus deeply and closely. I desperately want everyone to experience His True Love because of the way that it changed my life for the better forever. All I can do is share my own experience and trust that God will use it however He desires to bless the one who hears it. *True Love: Like Fire that Cannot be Quenched* is a Biblical road map that God used to teach me about Himself, but what I did with the knowledge He gave me was up to me. As a reader, gaining knowledge is one thing, but actually living in a close relationship with Him is another. Through my Psalm 119 journey, Jesus taught me how to have conversations with Him. Conversations between two best friends can be quite personal, but I believe Jesus wants me to share our conversations with anyone who desires to have a model of what it could look like to live in sync with God. *33:3 Ask Me* is a book of my own personal journal entries with Jesus. My purpose in sharing is not to entertain the reader with a personal story, but instead, to reveal what having a relationship with Jesus looks like in a more personal and tangible way. I heard so many times that the key to life was to have a relationship with Jesus, but I had no idea how to start a relationship with someone I could not see. *33:3 Ask Me* was written so that you can see how easy it is to hear God's voice speaking personally to you. He is very talkative and so incredibly creative in the ways that He speaks. You can hear God's voice daily! I invite you to peek into my world so you can see just how simple it really is.

Works Cited

Cowman, L.B. *Streams in the Desert.* Zonderman, 1997.

"I Want You to Want Me (Early Studio Version)" *YouTube*, uploaded by Cheap Trick, 25 January 2017, https://youtu.be/6VCmNu5qXI8

Lemmel, Helen Howarth. "Turn Your Eyes Upon Jesus." *Glad Songs*, 1922.

Morris, Robert. *Frequency.* Thomas Nelson, 2016.

Stead, Louisa M.R. "Tis So Sweet to Trust in Jesus." Melody by William J. Kirkpatrick, 1882.

The Silversmith's Reflection. *"When He Can See His Own Image." https://www.earnestlycontending.com/KT/Stories/ST/silversmith .html*

Virkler, Mark & Patti. *4 Keys to Hearing God's Voice.* Destiny Image, 2010.

About the Author

Tucked away in the Ozark Mountains lives an author who loves Jesus with all her heart, soul, mind, and strength. Lacey Nichole Godfrey is a homeschooling mother of two boys, a Bible-study facilitator, and an active reader of God's word. She has discovered the vital importance of hearing God's voice and desires to walk with God as Enoch did. Lacey is also the author of *33:3 Ask Me*. The title is based on Jeremiah 33:3, "Ask me and I will tell you remarkable secrets you do not know about things to come." Her purpose in writing is stirred by a passion for others to know Jesus intimately so that they can live in the peace that Jesus offers. Aside from writing and sharing the love of Jesus, Lacey loves spending time with her family and taking time to marvel at God's creation.

Printed in Great Britain
by Amazon

83564384R00127